Pottery & Porcelain Tablewares

Pottery &
Porcelain Tablewares

John P Cushion

William Morrow & Company, Inc.
New York

To the memory of James Cross
Chairman of the Morley College Ceramic Circle
and a grand collector.

Library of Congress Catalog Card Number 75-45518

ISBN 0-688-03055-6

Produced by Walter Parrish International Limited, London
Designed by Judy A. Tuke

Set in Bembo 270 11 on 12pt

Printed and bound in Spain by
Novograph S.A., Madrid

D.L.M 26857/1976

Half-title: BOWL, *standing on a foot, tin-glazed earthenware decorated in high-temperature blue and metallic lustres. The side lobes illustrate the 'Tree of Life' design. Spanish (Manises, Valencia), early 15th c.; dia. 45.7 cm/18 in.*

Frontispiece: *Italian porcelain, including a tin-glazed hard-paste porcelain* PLATE *produced at Doccia, c.1775; a* CUP *and* SAUCER *also of Doccia porcelain, c.1795; a* SUGAR-BASIN *and* COVER *of soft-paste porcelain made at Capodimonte, between 1745 and 1750; and a hard-paste porcelain* TEAPOT *made at Cozzi's factory in Venice, c.1770.*

Author's Acknowledgements

The author would like to express his sincere thanks to the many friends who have so generously helped in the preparation of the material for this volume. Curators of many museums, both in this country and abroad, and many of London's major antique dealers and private collectors have been especially kind in permitting photographers to have access to their pottery and porcelain, enabling many examples to be illustrated for the first time.

This is my first publication since retiring from the Victoria and Albert Museum, and I should like to express my thanks to all my colleagues in the Department of Ceramics, both past and present, with whom I enjoyed working for so many years.

Finally I wish to extend my gratitude to the personnel of Walter Parrish International for the co-operation and patience shown in the preparation of this book and to Christopher Evans for his excellent illustrations.

Contents

Author's Preface

Almost all of us have at some time bought a cup or a plate for our own use and in so doing have participated in an area of collecting alongside the dedicated collector with specialised and expert knowledge. In antique shops, and jumble sales, odd teacups and saucers from Aunt Mollie's attic sit together with a Staffordshire teapot and a lustre-glazed platter. And the surprise is that they may all be from the same factory! That simple fact is the basic reason for this book—for many years, it has been my ambition to help those interested in identifying ceramic wares by showing in a totally new way how form and design play a fundamental role in pottery and porcelain tableware. Basic similarities often obscure individual detail which makes it possible to pinpoint the region, the period, the factory, and very occasionally, the modeller or decorator. The fine or heavy modelling of a rim, the angle of a spout, the curve of a handle, and the way it's attached —all the tiny points which make up the answer to the question 'where does this come from, and where was it made?' Sometimes this can be the most difficult to answer. Often, the products that were produced in the greatest quantity and sent around the world were made in English factories and, perhaps deliberately, left unmarked. This is also true of some American pottery, although American porcelain generally does have some indication of its source.

Marks help, of course, and by the end of the 19th century, almost all factories had a reliable and easily verified mark or symbol. Obviously, unless the mark is faked, identification is then a fairly straightforward matter, so I have concentrated here on unmarked pieces covering the main categories of earthenware, stoneware and porcelain tableware, made in Europe and America during the 18th and 19th centuries.

To have covered the entire production of every known factory would have taken a very long time and 20 volumes of text. In order to make this a really practical guide, the emphasis is on those pieces most likely to be seen by the average collector and dealer, and also on those which are so similar that

confusion is likely to occur, even in the expert mind. PART ONE is a general history of tablewares made by the major factories, and gives a necessarily brief account of the techniques, craftsmen, patterns and materials. Anyone seriously interested in the work of a particular factory or area should look in the bibliography for individual studies. The same is true of factory and decorator marks. Painters who worked on tablewares have traditionally been rather nomadic, and in the course of a lifetime often worked at several different potteries. In addition, a popular motif which sold well was soon imitated by competitors; and just to complicate matters, there was always a percentage which sold 'in the white', i.e. undecorated, and then ornamented in artists' workshops, by professionals working at home, or even by amateur designers who wanted to have their own individual teapot or sugar bowl.

For all these reasons, I have in general disregarded surface decoration such as enamel painting or copperplate engravings. Instead, I hope the reader, whether the owner of a single cup or a professional dealer, will learn through PART TWO, the Identification Guide, to recognize examples by observation and comparison of shape and form. There are around 1,000 drawings showing the features of rims, moulding, handles etc., which were produced with moulds. Despite the high rate of plagiarism, one factory never used the exact mould of another, unless it was bought out, and these rare occasions are fairly well documented. Certainly there were fashions and trends, so a feel for the period can help in establishing dates, but exactly duplicated shapes are almost unknown.

The drawings are arranged by type, so that the owner of a new tea-cup who knows only that it was used for drinking tea, will be able to look through that section and find a cup or a handle which will give the right clue. Underneath each drawing is a brief caption giving factory, country and estimated date. There is some text on most pages giving helpful details about what to look for in that particular section. Always learn to handle body and glazes so you get to know the authentic touch in your fingertips.

Introduction

Pottery was of little use for the table (or floor!) until a lead-glaze to seal the otherwise porous low-fired clay was used, such as that produced by the Near Eastern potters from the early years of the second millennium B.C. Such glazes consisted of a lead compound which fused to the surface of a pot at the comparatively low temperature of about 800°C. Furthermore a variation of colours was obtainable by using various metallic oxides such as copper, which produced a leaf-green, or iron to give variations of yellow or brown. Further variations in colour were later introduced by the Roman potters at the time of the birth of Christ, by the application of contrasting coloured clay slips (watered-down clay). Knowledge of these early glazing techniques soon spread throughout Europe, to Italy, Gaul, the Rhineland and even to Great Britain where such glazes were being used in Denbighshire by the start of the 3rd century A.D. Another effective type of brilliant glaze was produced by the Egyptian potter with the use of natron, a readily fusible compound of natural soda found in Egypt. This was a glaze which, when used with copper, resulted in a glass-like turquoise blue and it could be decorated with designs incised into the clay prior to firing.

Even in the early centres of Rome and Constantinople the potter was catering basically for the more humble folk and the kitchen, the wealthy preferring to eat from wares of the more precious materials, at least until the 8th or 9th centuries when their living standards declined.

During the early Middle Ages the Italian potter was producing not only wares for the storage of food and drink but also finer objects of elegant classical shapes for use at the table and in the pharmacy. By about A.D. 1000 the strongly coloured lead-glazes were being replaced by less colourful applications, which showed to advantage either painted decoration, or *sgraffiato* (decoration incised through a contrasting coloured clay slip).

It was about this time that the European potter began to make use of an earlier Islamic technique whereby his transparent glazes were rendered white and opaque by means of tin oxide being added to the glaze. With this process the Italian potter later produced his famous *maiolica*.

From the end of the Roman period, the French potter abandoned the consistent use of a lead-glaze and it was only in the 14th century that the technique was again adopted for both tablewares and tiles.

A similar situation arose in England, and with the departure of the Romans in the early 5th century there was a return to the cruder type of pottery associated with the earlier Iron Age, sometimes with stamped decoration, but more usually left plain. From the 7th century trade with north-west Europe introduced the English potter to the more refined wares of the Rhineland, bringing about by the early 10th century, the manufacture of many English tablewares, which were lead-glazed in a variety of colours but limited of course, to the available metallic oxides. Even so pottery manufacture in England was to remain a comparatively crude craft until at least the 12th century, when faster-turning potters' wheels were used to produce better shapes like jugs, for instance, which have survived more than any other type of vessel.

It was not until the early 16th century that improved potting techniques and control of kiln temperatures resulted in a large variety of vessels being produced in the familiar red-clay body, covered with a rich brown glaze. A somewhat similar class of ware produced during the 17th century is today referred to as Cistercian wares, owing to its association with monks of the Cistercian order. Such vessels, including the multi-handled drinking cups termed 'tygs', have an almost black glaze, sometimes decorated with an applied white clay slip. It should be noted that manufacture of similar types continued long after the dissolution of the monasteries in 1539.

During the 17th century the English potter developed the art of slip-decoration, applied under a rich lead-glaze, which completely transformed the otherwise dull clay body. Apart from the everyday necessities, the potter was capable of producing highly decorative wares, usually for commemorative events. Outstanding areas for this type of manufacture were Wrotham, in Kent, the Harlow area of Essex which, according to archaeological discoveries, supplied the majority of so-called 'Metropolitan wares' for London, and the whole area of North Staffordshire where the potter's name of Toft has for many years been generally associated with a large number of slip-decorated chargers, often portraying Royal 'portraits' or other well-known subjects, such as the mermaid with a comb and a brush in her hand, or the Pelican in Piety—all outstanding examples of the craft of the English potter. Research over more recent years has revealed the whereabouts and productions of other important English pottery centres, including Tickenhall (Derbyshire), Wiltshire, Buckinghamshire, Essex, North Devon, Somerset and Hampshire.

The greatest early contribution made by the German potter to the history of the art was the introduction of the process of glazing high-fired stonewares by throwing common salt into the kiln at the peak firing temperature. Glaze of this type was used from the end of the 14th century in Siegburg and other German centres. Stoneware consists of a clay rich in silicic acid, enabling the ware to be fired at such a high temperature that the material vitrifies, so producing an entirely non-porous body of a rather unpleasant texture. This was remedied by the economic method of applying a tight-fitting 'salt-glaze'. This same technique is still used in parts of Germany today to produce the popular grey-and-blue drinking tankards thus satisfying the needs of natives and tourists alike.

It was the English potter John Dwight who was granted a patent in 1672 to produce a ware similar to that made in Germany (vulgarly called Cologne Ware) at his Fulham pottery. It was obviously the intention of John Dwight to try and discover how to produce a Chinese-type porcelain but, to the best of our knowledge, he only managed to make a fine-grained, near-white stoneware, which when extremely thin did in fact become partially translucent. Recent excavations on the site of John Dwight's factory have provided certain evidence which may yet prove that he partly succeeded in his aim to produce a hard, white porcelain. The wares of Dwight,

which may well have also included the high-fired red stoneware, like that being produced at the time in Yi-hsing, China, were soon to be imitated by numerous other potters, some of whom Dwight was to take legal action against in order to try and protect his patent. They included John and David Elers, James Morley of Nottingham and members of the Wedgwood family of Burslem, Staffordshire.

The introduction of tin-glazing was to prove very popular, resulting in a whole range of wares from the 9th century to the present. The first highly decorative wares were those produced in the southern regions of Spain during the Moorish occupation—the so-called 'Hispano-Moresque' wares, dating from at least the 13th century, when Malaga became the centre of manufacture of the 'golden pottery of Aragon' (wares decorated with metallic lustre produced from oxides of copper or silver, fired in a reduction kiln).

The tin-glazed earthenwares of the Italian potter were possibly slightly earlier than those produced in Spain, but were decorated in a fairly simple fashion until the 15th century, when great advances were made in both forms and styles of decoration. The colours used were once again limited to the sparse range of metallic oxides, which were painted on to the white powder-like glaze, and then fired to-

Opposite: CUP *and* SAUCER *of hard-paste porcelain, decorated 'with figure subjects in low relief' in enamel colours. Italian (Doccia), third quarter of the 18th century; dia. (saucer) 13.6 cm/5½ in.*

Overleaf: *A group of stoneware drinking vessels. A rare* TANKARD *of salt-glazed stoneware, the armorial panel with crowned double eagle is dated 1583. German (Raeren, workshop of Baldens Mennicken).* TANKARD *of salt-glazed stoneware with pewter mountings including lid with cypher and date 1708. German (Altenberg).* PUZZLE JUG *of salt-glazed stoneware with bright blue glaze and contemporary pewter lid. German (Westerwald), early 17th century.* SCHNELLE *of salt-glazed stoneware by the* Formschneider *Hans Hilgers. German (Siegburg), 1570, pewter mount 18th century.* TANKARD *of salt-glazed stoneware with relief decorations in enamel colours. German (Kreussen), c.1660. Baluster* JUG *(Trichterkrug) decorated with portrait medallions. German (Siegburg) decorated with portrait medallions. German (Siegburg), c.1560.* MUG *of salt-glazed stoneware with high-temperature blue decoration. German (Grenzhausen), 18th century; ht. (puzzle jug) 20 cm/8 in.*

Overleaf: TANKARD, *tin-glazed earthenware (fayence) decorated with enamel colours and signed 'WR', the initials of the painter Wolf Rössler. German (Nuremberg), c.1685; ht. 22 cm/9 in.*

Opposite: TEA-SERVICE *of hard-paste porcelain, moulded with the osier pattern on borders and painted in enamel colours, marked with the crossed-swords in blue. German (Meissen), c.1745.*

gether with the glaze, a process which, in its difficulty, can well be compared to applying brushwork to a piece of chalk. The major Italian centre for *maiolica* became Faenza, which was to result in the wares produced in France by the Italian migrant potters being referred to as 'faience'.

The early tin-glazed earthenwares of both France and the Netherlands are at times very difficult to distinguish from those made in Italy and certainly do not justify the terms 'faience' or 'Delft'. Although the majority of tin used in both Italy and the Netherlands came from the Cornish tin mines in south-west England, it was not until 1567 that Flemish potters started to manufacture tin-glazed earthenware, first in Norwich, East Anglia, and later in London itself. It is noticeable that in England the manufacture remained restricted to such areas as London, Bristol, Liverpool, and in Scotland and Ireland also to places within easy reach of sea-routes for the transporting of the tin from Cornwall. To the best of our knowledge no tin-glazed wares were ever produced in the Staffordshire area.

From the early 18th century there was a marked improvement in the quality of Staffordshire earthenwares and stonewares. The centre was ideally situated: there were readily available supplies of the necessary clays, coal and water. The only disadvantage was the difficulty of the transportation of the finished wares to the eastern and western ports, but this was remedied during the 18th century by the building of the canals. Apart from some refined lead-glazed wares, such as those associated with the names of Astbury and Whieldon, Elers-type red-stonewares were still produced throughout Staffordshire, especially in connection with the preparation and drinking of tea. Similar wares were also being produced in the various early potteries of Yorkshire.

Similar refinement was also to be seen on the salt-glazed stonewares which by the 18th century were generally not only whiter, but more finely potted than the majority of the 17th century examples. This improvement was aided by the introduction in about 1720 of clays from Devon – which were sometimes merely used as a top-dressing – and calcined flints, enabling a lighter and tougher ware to be made. These cheaply produced stonewares remained popular until the 1760s. In about 1745 the English potter began to use moulds of plaster of Paris, enabling him to produce a large range of highly decorative relief wares, in a comparatively easy manner, by the slip-casting process. The technique, which was also used at the Chelsea porcelain and other English and French factories, called first for an original model, such as a teapot in the form of a house, or monkey, to be carved from a material such as alabaster or wax. Clay intaglio moulds were then produced, which were in turn used to produce a master block-mould of fired and glazed clay. This fired block was then used to produce plaster of Paris moulds in sections which could be assembled to receive the slip, or watered-down clay. The plaster immediately started to absorb the water from the slip and in so doing built up a thin layer of clay on the inside wall of the mould, after which the surplus slip was poured off; in a short time the mould could be opened to reveal the hollow reproduction of the original model. Any additional claywork, such as spouts or handles, would then be applied before any drying, and consequent shrinkage, took place. Such wares were later decorated in the porcelain fashion by the applying and firing of enamel colours.

Probably the greatest contribution made by the English potter to the history of ceramic materials was the introduction of cream-coloured earthenware. Basically, creamware was composed of the same body as salt-glazed stoneware, but fired at a lower temperature, which resulted in a porous earthenware and called for the application of a refined lead glaze by dipping into a liquid solution prior to firing in the 'glost' kiln.

The best-known English potter, Josiah Wedgwood, first became a master-potter in 1759 and whilst he cannot be credited with having invented creamware, credit must be given him for perfecting the material to a degree that it was acceptable to all levels of society and ideal for producing wares in the popular classical styles. A further material refined by Wedgwood was black 'basaltes', which was once again an ideal body for the reproduction of early Grecian vases, at that time being excavated in Herculaneum and Naples and resulting in the popularity of the neo-classical style.

By 1789 both Josiah Wedgwood and many of his contemporaries were producing an earthenware called 'pearlware', a near-white body with a distinctly blued glaze, which helped to give the impression of a white ware, the forerunner of today's domestic earthenware made throughout Europe and the United States of America.

The Chinese potter was producing a hard-paste porcelain from about the middle of the 9th century, but similar material was not to be made in Europe until about 1718; in the meantime experiments were to take place resulting in an artificial, or soft-paste porcelain. The first porcelain of this type was made in Florence between 1575 and 1587, produced at the instigation of the Grand Duke Francesco I de' Medici; this rare porcelain is referred to today as Medici porcelain. No further experiments are known to have been made until the last quarter of the 17th century, when a glassy imitation porcelain was made by Louis Poterat at Rouen, but knowledge of this manufacture is very scanty. This is not the case with the later concern belonging to the family of the faience potter at Saint Cloud, Pierre Chicaneau, who, it seems, passed on sufficient knowledge of his experiments to enable his descendants to establish a very successful manufacture, which continued until 1766. The later soft-paste concerns of Chantilly and Mennecy were to be overshadowed by the introduction of a hard-paste porcelain at Meissen, at the Royal Saxon Porcelain Manufactory, established in 1710.

Prior to producing a white porcelain at Meissen, Böttger and Count von Tschirnhaus had succeeded in developing a fine hard red stoneware which could be polished in the manner of a precious stone; but with the introduction of white porcelain Böttger endeavoured to cater for the demands of Augustus II by producing wares fashioned after oriental originals and tablewares formed in the styles of contemporary gold, silver or pewter. These early wares were decorated in a very sparse manner until the arrival at Meissen of Johann Gregor Höroldt who came to Saxony from the factory of Du Paquier at Vienna. Here he had perfected many fine enamel colours which he was to employ at Meissen in his unique *chinoiseries*—a fairyland fantasy based on the Far East, but pleasing to the European.

Meissen was to become the fashion-setter in the world of European porcelain until the time the factory was occupied by the troops of Frederick the Great of Prussia, during the Seven Years War (1756-63). This period coincides with the change of styles from the baroque to the rococo.

By the end of the war the unique position of Meissen had been taken over by the comparatively new French porcelain factory which had started at Vincennes as early as 1738, moving to Sèvres in 1756. With the exception of Vienna and the short-lived Vezzi factory in Venice (1720-27), Meissen had little competition from any rival concerns until the middle of the century, when many other factories were started in various German states, mostly aided by such renegade workers as Ringler, from Vienna, who helped to establish at least eight porcelain undertakings, all of whom were producing a hard-paste porcelain.

The beauty of the early Vincennes and Sèvres porcelain is due to the fact that their graceful rococo shapes were all produced in a beautiful soft-paste porcelain and it was not until 1772 that a hard-paste porcelain was also used at the factory to any great extent. As the Seven Years War brought an end to the dominance of Meissen, so the French Revolution brought about changes in the wares produced at Sèvres and very little porcelain of any importance was made from the time when the factory was taken over by the French Republic in 1793, to the time when the factory was again restored to prosperity during the Consulate and Empire periods. In 1768 with the discovery at Saint Yrieix of the materials essential to the production of true porcelain—china-clay and china-stone—Limoges became the centre of a new hard-paste porcelain industry, as well as supplying the necessary raw materials for many new factories in both Paris and elsewhere in France.

When considering the porcelain factories of England, it is essential to remember that they did not enjoy the same princely patronage that the majority of the concerns elsewhere in Europe did, and were compelled to survive on their sales and profits, rather than the State purse.

To the best of our knowledge the Chelsea factory of Nicholas Sprimont was the first English factory to become a successful enterprise, surviving independently in the period 1745–70, and then continuing under William Duesbury, the proprietor of the Derby factory, until 1784. Chelsea wares were of a fine soft-paste porcelain, but showed very little in the way of original styles of decoration or form, the makers preferring to base their earlier styles on the popular baroque fashions of Meissen and then looking towards Sèvres for interpretations of the spirit of rococo.

The other major English factories were also influenced, to a somewhat lesser degree, by the Continental factories and tended in some instances also to compete with the porcelains being imported by the East India Companies from China, and to a lesser degree, Japan—especially those decorated in underglaze-blue, and the palettes of the *famille verte* and *famille rose*. The factory of Bow, which was producing wares in commercial quantities by about 1747, was the first factory, to our knowledge, to make use of calcined animal bone (bone-ash) which helped to give a tough and stable body. The small factory at Lowestoft, in Suffolk (1757–c.99) produced a similar body and made wares which at times are difficult to distinguish from those of the Bow factory.

In 1748 Lund and Miller produced a porcelain at their Bristol factory which had almost all the advantages of true porcelain—it withstood sudden changes in temperature, the glaze only rarely crazed and consequently discoloration of the body under the glaze was also very rare. This new type of porcelain included a high proportion of soapstone (steatite). It seems likely that in order either to obtain this formula or to prevent competition, Dr Wall and his partners took over the Bristol concern in 1752. It is difficult at times to distinguish the wares of the short-lived Bristol concern from those made in the early years of the Worcester factory.

Worcester was the first English porcelain factory to decorate its wares by 'transfer-printing'. This process was probably first used in England as early as 1751 to decorate the attractive enamel 'toys' of Birmingham. The technique called for a flat copper-plate, which was line-engraved with the pattern to the scale required to fit the ware to be decorated. Liquid enamel was then rubbed into the engraving, after which the surplus enamel was removed with the aid of a palette knife. The enamel was then transferred to the glaze of the ware by means of a paper tissue which was first laid down in close contact with the copper-plate, so that when removed it 'lifted' the enamel colour from the engraved lines; the tissue was then accurately placed on the glaze of the ware and again firmly 'rubbed-down'. The paper was then soaked off, leaving the engraved design ready for firing in a muffle kiln, at a temperature which would rarely exceed 800°C. This same process could likewise by used with underglaze-blue (cobalt), but in this case the transfer was applied on to the once-fired body (the biscuit), lightly fired to fix, and then glazed and fired to the full temperature. During the early years of the 19th century the use of chrome enabled further underglaze colours, such as pinks and greens, also to be transfer-printed as underglaze colours. The advantages of soapstone porcelain were soon realised and further English factories, including Caughley (1772–99) and some of the Liverpool factories produced a similar body to that of Bristol and Worcester.

It is somewhat surprising that the numerous potters of Staffordshire were not more interested in the manufacture of porcelain at an earlier date, and the only major mid-18th century enterprise to survive for a few years was that at Longton Hall (1749–60). The Staffordshire potters who were so conversant with earthenwares and stonewares appeared to have found it difficult to apply their skills to the more sophisticated material of porcelain and in most cases the results might well be considered rather crude, their forms and decoration having much more in common with earlier pottery styles.

The major Derby porcelain factory started in 1756, although there was a limited production from about 1750 associated with Andrew Planché, consisting mainly of figures. There is little doubt that it was during the so-called 'Chelsea-Derby' period (1770–84), that some of the most practical and tastefully decorated tablewares were produced, mostly in the styles popularised by Sèvres.

It was 1768 before William Cookworthy, the Plymouth chemist, was to produce a hard-paste porcelain in England. This undertaking was moved from Plymouth to Bristol in 1770, where it remained in production until 1781, when the remaining period of the patent was sold to a group of Staffordshire potters who formed the New Hall company. It was Champion who claimed for his wares the hardness of Dresden (Meissen) and the elegance of Sèvres.

Josiah Spode introduced the standard English bone-china soon after 1796, when the New Hall patent had expired, and any other manufacturers were free to use the materials of china-clay and china-stone in the manufacture of translucent bodies. The beauty and practicability of this new material was greatly appreciated and by about 1850 at least twenty factories were producing tablewares of bone-china (it is the wares of many of these factories we will be endeavouring to identify by shapes, rather than decoration). Bone-china consists roughly of 25% each of china-clay and china-stone, together with 50% calcined animal bone.

During the early decades of the 19th century the pottery and porcelain industry of England, and elsewhere, manufactured many wares decorated with transfer-prints. The earlier prints, which initially were used as illustrations in topographical publications, were by far the most interesting; the later, duller prints were mostly designed specifically for use on pottery and porcelain wares and included such subjects as rural scenes, fantasies inspired by *chinoiseries* (in the style of the so-called 'Willow' pattern) and flowers and foliage. Designs inspired by the Classics also proved popular. These cheaply produced wares were very popular in England and were exported in great quantities to both Europe and the United States, thereby prompting the potters in the majority of these countries to produce similarly decorated wares for themselves.

During the 1840s a new decorative form became popular on many tablewares, 'Gothic', a style seen most frequently on the somewhat impractical relief-decorated stoneware jugs. This fashion was quickly followed by the vogue for naturalism, and jugs were covered with high relief flowers and foliage, a forerunner of the more elegant Art Nouveau.

By the middle of the 19th century many pottery and porcelain factories in the United States were producing similar relief-decorated tablewares, usually in 'parian' ware (the ivory tinted form of a hard-paste porcelain introduced by Copelands in about 1842) and the heavier and crudely moulded earthenwares, which were sometimes decorated with the rich 'treacle-brown' glaze, today still associated with the name of 'Rockingham'.

In the second decade of the 19th century the majority of potters engaged in the manufacture of bone-china or hard-paste porcelain were producing at least some wares in the 'revived rococo' style, a fashion that for some unaccountable reason has for many years been wrongly associated solely with the short-lived porcelain production of the Rockingham factory, where bone-china was only made between 1826 and 1842.

The hard-paste porcelain made in the United States from the 1820s onwards was influenced by the imports of various European wares, in particular French wares. The much sought-after Tucker-ware made at Philadelphia is at times very difficult to distinguish from the contemporary wares of France.

From the time of the International Exhibition, held in London in 1862, the western world became exposed to the wares of Japan, which had for so many years been unavailable to the European. Designers and manufacturers of pottery and porcelain became increasingly influenced by this new Oriental taste which was to survive into the 1900s, when it became embodied in Art Nouveau, a style adopted in varying degrees by almost all manufacturers.

Opposite: PLATE *of soft-paste porcelain, painted in under-glazed-blue, and marked with the dome of Florence Cathedral over 'F' in blue. Italian (Medici), 1575–87; dia. 21.5 cm/ 8½ in.*

Part 1
Major Factories

SPAIN
Faience

Hispano-Moresque Ware

Prior to the Arab conquest of Spain in the early 8th century, the pottery of Europe was of a practical, but dull ware, more fitting for the kitchen than the dining-table. But the new knowledge of the technique of tin-glazing, as practised by the Near Eastern potters, meant that a much more colourful and decorative type of ware could be produced. From the early 13th century cobalt blue was being used either upon, or under, a soft white glaze, sometimes with added rich lustre painting derived from metallic oxides; silver resulted in shades of yellow and brown, whilst copper produced rich shades of reds and gold. These lustre colours were achieved by painting the metallic oxides on to the previously fired glaze and then re-firing in a kiln to which the supply of air was restricted (a reduction kiln).

The main centre of manufacture was in the southeast and included Malaga, Murcia, Almeria and possibly Granada, but the early wares of these areas are difficult to identify with any degree of accuracy—a task made even more hazardous by prolific export to both European and Near Eastern ports.

The early wares of Malaga tend to show a higher standard of potting than those attributed to Valencia, but the shapes in both instances show great similarities, large conical-shaped bowls, cups and spouted vessels following metal forms, and two-handled jars.

Tin-glazed wares with lustre decoration were made in Spain in quantity in the traditional manner until the late 18th century, since which time a small production has continued until the present day; but these wares are very inferior in every way and are produced primarily for the tourist.

From the early 16th century the influence of Italian tin-glazed wares, *maiolica,* is to be seen in Spain in the pottery made in Seville and Talavera. Seville is best known for its fine pottery tiles of the 13th century, many of which were later produced by the *cuerda seca* (dry-cord) technique, which consisted of using a finely applied line of grease and manganese to keep the opaque tin-glaze colours from intermingling. The same device was used during the 15th century to produce boldly decorated plates, depicting grotesque animal and foliage forms, reminiscent of the animals seen on some of the lustre wares of Valencia. The Louvre possesses a rare *aquamanile* (water-ewer) in the form of a ram in this style of decoration.

The pottery of Talavera again clearly shows the influence of the Italian craftsmen, and by the mid-16th century a large export trade had been established. The best wares were produced towards the end of the 17th century, when large basins, dishes, ewers, and broad, flat-bottomed jugs were made, painted in strong high-temperature greens, orange-yellows and purples, depicting hunting-scenes, birds and animals with backgrounds of trees and buildings. Pottery manufacture has continued in Talavera to the present day, but later Talavera reproductions of Wedgwood-type wares were of a very poor quality.

During the second quarter of the 18th century the faience of Alcora, near Valencia, reached an extremely high standard and, owing to the employment there of faience decorators formerly employed at the French factory of Moustiers, there is a great similarity in the wares of both factories.

During its best period, the factory undertook the change from heavy baroque-styled table centre-pieces to basins, plates and dishes modelled in the new rococo fashions—a style which the Spanish potters interpreted in an even more fantastical manner than the French.

Opposite: EWER *of earthenware, decorated with coloured glazes. French (Saintes, Bernard Palissy or followers), 2nd half of 16th c.; ht. 27 cm/10¾ in.*

ITALY
Maiolica

The beauty of the early Italian tin-glazed earthenware is in the painting rather than the form, and many shapes were employed in the same manner as an artist uses a canvas. The early functional wares were made primarily for the apothecary rather than for table use, and it is thought that even the beautifully decorated 16th-century dishes, sometimes of metalwork forms, were intended for ornament rather than for use.

During the second half of the 16th century, when the earthenware potters were better acquainted with Chinese porcelain, ewers and dishes, sometimes in the form of openwork baskets, became more common. At this same time the Fontana workshop, and others in Urbino, achieved fame for their large salvers and wine-coolers, painted in the *istoriato* manner, with scenes illustrating mythological, biblical or historical events. Another style of decoration on Urbino wares, which became very popular towards the end of the 16th century, consisted of graceful arabesques on a white ground, reminiscent of the paintings by Raphael in the Loggie of the Vatican, which were of course in turn inspired by the work of the ancient Romans.

During the early 17th century the area of Florence once again became a well-known pottery centre owing to the importance of the *maiolica* production at Montelupo. These early wares often depicted crudely painted figures of soldiers in contemporary uniforms, but towards the end of the century the leaf and fruit decoration on their tablewares had much in common with the early tin-glazed wares of Holland and England.

It was the Ligurian potteries in such cities as Genoa, Savona and Turin which first endeavoured to reproduce the hard-paste porcelains of China in their own, more robust materials. It is very difficult to distinguish the 17th- and 18th-century wares of these two Italian centres and it is probable that they could equally well have both been influenced by the contemporary Delftware, rather than the original Chinese wares. Apart from the large baroque-styled vases and drug-pots, many plates and dishes were produced, often with edges moulded after gadrooned metalwork, or with *putti* in relief. They even endeavoured to produce wares of a fine enough quality to grace the 18th-century tea-table, often decorated solely in blue on a white ground.

The best wares of the 18th-century Turin factory have much in common with the faience of France, and often used the same formal foliage, *lambrequins*, masks and grotesques, as seen on the wares of Rouen or Moustiers.

In 1693 Count Annibale Carlo Ferniani acquired a *maiolica* factory in Faenza, a concern which remained in his family until 1900. In consequence wares which can be attributed to this factory are by no means uncommon and they are difficult to date accurately as from the second half of the 18th century since the factory produced wares not only in the limited range of high-temperature colours, but also in the whole palette offered by the lower-fired enamel colours, often preferring the stylised flower painting of Japan or China.

The 18th-century pottery techniques permitted a greater manufacture of refined earthenware suitable for tablewares; greater use was made of casting, pressing or moulding methods, enabling identical shapes to be produced in large quantities. One Italian factory which used the new and popular enamel colours to advantage was that of Casali and Caligari at Pesaro, where jugs and dishes were produced in imitation of Chinese porcelain and the popular neo-classical styles.

Opposite: CENTRE-PIECE *of hard-paste porcelain decorated in enamel colours, and marked with the crossed-swords in underglaze-blue. German (Meissen), 1750–55; ht. 47 cm/ 16¾ in.*

Overleaf: PLATE *of hard-paste porcelain decorated with enamel colours, and marked with the impressed Bavarian shield-of-arms. German (Nymphenburg), c.1760; dia. 47 cm/ 16¾ in.*

Porcelain

Medici & Vezzi

Overleaf: COFFEE-SERVICE *of hard-paste porcelain in neo-classical form decorated with enamel colours, and marked with the Vienna shield in underglaze-blue and the impressed year-mark '800' (1800). Austrian (Vienna), 1800.*

Opposite: TUREEN *and* STAND *of tin-glazed earthenware (Delftware), painted in high-temperature blue and yellow, and marked with a hatchet in blue. Dutch (Delft, De Porce-leyne Byl [Porcelain Hatchet] factory, Justus Brouwer period), c.1755; lgth. (stand) 34 cm/13½ in.*

The Italians were almost certainly the first Europeans to become familiar with Chinese hard-paste porce-lain; even Marco Polo is said to have returned from his travels in the Far East with precious examples and an intimate knowledge of this new and exciting ware. It is therefore not surprising to learn that almost certainly the first porcelain to be produced in Europe was the work of an Italian craftsman. The first experiments were apparently sponsored by the Grand Duke Francesci I de' Medici and carried out by Buontalenti, painter, sculptor and architect, between about 1575 and 1587.

Medici porcelain, of which there are only about sixty examples known to exist, is of an artificial, or soft-paste porcelain composed basically of 80% white-firing clay and 20% frit, a form of powdered glass. Because of the nature of the material, the wares were inclined to sag or warp, despite the fact that they were heavily potted.

The pieces were generally small, most were intended to serve as tablewares and included basins, jugs, ewers, wine-vessels and oil-and-vinegar bottles; nearly all followed either Chinese porcelain forms, or contemporary earthenware forms, like those being made in Italy by the *maiolica* potters. The decoration in high-temperature blue (cobalt), sometimes out-lined with purple (manganese), was more in the European taste and included armorials and grotesques or leaf-and-flower patterns somewhat akin to those seen on the Turkish Isnik pottery. During the early part of the 17th century, experiments at Padua and Pisa resulted in some further rare examples of soft-paste porcelains for the table.

No further reproductions of porcelain of any kind are recorded in Italy until the first quarter of the 18th century, when Francesco Vezzi founded a factory in Venice for the production of a hard-paste porcelain, which survived from 1720 to 1727. The quality of Vezzi's porcelain equalled that of the early Meissen factory, which is not surprising as it was the Meissen renegade C. K. Hunger who assisted in the establish-ment of the concern and also brought about its closure when he returned to Meissen in 1727 and revealed to the authorities that Vezzi was relying upon clays from Saxony for his manufacture.

Vezzi was primarily concerned with tewares, which followed the contemporary baroque silver fashions, his best-known style being an octagonal teapot with angular handle and relief decoration in the form of acanthus leaves or swags.

EWER *of soft-paste porcelain, painted in underglaze-blue, marked with dome of Florence cathedral over 'F' in blue. Italian (Medici), 1575-87; ht. 14 cm/5⅝ in.*

Doccia

One of the most prolific Italian porcelain factories was established in 1735 at Doccia, near Florence, by the Marchese Carlo Ginori, but it was eleven years before the productions were offered for public sale. Its early wares were of a very poor quality material, grey in tone, with an ill-fitting smeary glaze, resulting in what is best described as a hybrid hard-paste porcelain.

Apart from many interesting figures, the early wares included many tablewares inspired by the Chinese exports, some of which were of the double-wall variety, the outer wall being pierced with a design to reveal the inner, i.e. reticulated. This same form of decoration can be seen on Chinese porcelain of the late Ming dynasty (1368-1644), when it was referred to as *Ling-lung* ware, or 'devil's work', due to the extreme skill demanded of the potter.

The teapots and coffee-pots made from this early hybrid material were certainly based upon those the Chinese had produced for the European market during the previous century, with long snake-like spouts terminating in the modelled head of the creature and strengthened with a short connecting scroll to the body of the vessel. It has recently been discovered that the underglaze-blue decoration on some of these early wares was applied by a form of transfer-printing, probably from an engraved wood block; further decoration was applied by stencilling. Between 1770 and 1790, owing to the poor colour of the porcelain, use was made of a white opaque tin-glaze, such as that used on *maiolica* or Delftware, which proved very beneficial for well-decorated tablewares. Plates and dishes made at Doccia during this period were usually produced with thickly moulded wavy-edges—far too clumsy to be termed 'rococo', a style which the Doccia modellers never successfully managed to achieve.

A form of decoration like that seen on Doccia wares, which has been subject to many misnomers since it was first introduced in the mid-18th century, is relief moulding depicting mythological or hunting-scenes, usually with swags of flowers or foliage. The quality of the porcelain suggests that the majority of these wares were produced towards the end of the 18th century, when the use of imported china-clay *(kaolin)* enabled a much whiter ware to be made. These relief-decorated wares have for many years been wrongly attributed to Capodimonte—a factory which produced only a beautiful soft-paste porcelain. The majority of Doccia-type wares of this kind were, in fact, made in some of the many German factories of Thuringia, by such potters as Ernst Bohne of Rudolstadt. They are usually marked with an 'N' under a crown in underglaze-blue, a mark which originated at the Royal Naples factory in 1771.

The Doccia factory was run by descendants of the family until 1896, and still continues to this day producing useful wares.

(For colour illustration, see pp. 2 and 11)

SUGAR BOWL *with* COVER, *soft-paste porcelain enamelled in colour, marked 'FRF' monogram under a crown in blue enamel. Italian (Naples) c.1775; ht. 11 cm/4⅝ ins.* PLATE *of hard-paste porcelain in enamel colours. Italian (Venice (Cozzi)) c.1765; dia. 20 cm/8 in.* TEAPOT *of hard-paste porcelain in enamel colours. Italian (Doccia) c.1860-70; ht. 12 cm/4¾ in.*

Venice & Le Nove

One of the most important Italian porcelain factories was established in Venice in 1764, continuing until 1812, during which time large quantities of hard-paste porcelain were produced, both for the home market and for export all over Europe. The founder of this Venetian factory was Geminiano Cozzi, who succeeded in producing a comparatively low-fired, grey-bodied ware from clays located at Tretto, on the Venetian mainland. Owing to the interest shown in the concern by the Senate, many documents and catalogues have been preserved which throw much light on its everyday wares and its special orders.

It was the aim of Cozzi to compete with the pieces produced by the Meissen factory which, owing to the Seven Years War, was by this time in a state of decline. Cozzi produced many tablewares: some had very distinctive features, such as coffee-pots with a rather unusual pouring spout, moulded with leaf decoration. The spout was unusual because it was inserted into a hole made in the side of the vessel rather than being in line with the rim, as in the normal pouring lip. The handles were rather poorly shaped, with moulded acanthus-leaf decoration and rather impractical knobs in the shape of fruit. The decoration is likewise rather distinctive, often favouring figures from the Italian Comedy, in typical Italian garden settings, all painted in a very distinctive palette, including a rich red, emerald green and violet, sometimes coupled with a good quality, soft gilding.

A short-lived porcelain factory was set up in Venice by two refugees from Saxony, N. F. Hewelke and his wife; they moved to Venice from Udine in 1757, and their factory was in operation only until 1763, even though they had been granted a twenty-year privilege. Their wares, which were marked with a 'V' in red enamel, or incised, were of a grey paste and are extremely rare today.

A much more successful porcelain manufactory was established at Le Nove, near Bassano by Paquale Antonibon. Antonibon's father had been engaged in the production of tin-glazed wares since 1728, and from the middle of the 18th century some very fine tablewares were produced, including plates, dishes and some interesting tureens in the shape of large fish. These early tin-glazed wares were decorated in high-temperature colours, and the later ones, in-fluenced by Sèvres porcelain, used a greater range of enamel colours. The production of porcelain was not successfully achieved at Le Nove until 1765. It continued in the family until 1773, when the widow of Paquale Antonibon leased the factory to Francesco Parolin who remained there until 1801. Then the concern was continued by Giovanni Baroni. In 1825 it reverted to the Antonibon family who continued production until the late 19th century.

It is very difficult at times to differentiate between the porcelains of Cozzi and those produced at Le Nove. The latter were probably influenced more by French and English styles than the Venetian wares, but from 1780 Le Nove porcelain was of a finer white material and decorated in a far wider range of colours, which included a rose-pink, as seen on Chinese *famille-rose*, and the gilding which was also of a fine quality was often tooled in the popular Sèvres fashion.

A further, rather obscure undertaking was set up at Vinovo, near Turin, in 1776 by Giovanni Brodel and Pierre-Antoine Hannong; but very little success was achieved until the concern was taken over in 1780 by Dr Gioanetti whose tablewares were of a hybrid creamy-coloured porcelain—but they showed very little originality, imitating both the form and decoration of French wares.

Capodimonte & Naples

Despite the fact that the Buen Retiro porcelain factory was situated outside Madrid, in Spain, it was closely associated with the Italian factory of Capodimonte, the soft-paste porcelain factory of Naples founded by Charles IV of Bourbon in 1743. Production there flourished until 1759, when the king succeeded to the throne of Spain and moved the entire porcelain undertaking to the new premises of Buen Retiro.

Capodimonte is best known for fine porcelain figures, modelled in most instances by Guiseppe Gricc; but it also produced an excellent range of tablewares, intended primarily for court use, although public sales were also held annually.

The porcelain of Capodimonte was one of the most beautiful soft-pastes ever produced; the clays used were obtained from Fuscaldo in Calabria. For many years many of the tablewares produced at this early factory were attributed to the later Spanish factory, and it was only whilst carrying out research for his first edition of *Italian Porcelain* that the late Arthur Lane was able to accredit many examples to the earlier Italian concern. Marks were of no help, for when a mark was used it was the same at both factories, the *fleur-de-lys*, impressed, in blue or gilt.

The records concerning the early years of the factory are still available and wares for the tea-table feature prominently. The shapes were generally of a simple, late baroque form: tall beaker-like cups were popular, whereas the jugs and teapots tended, in complete contrast, to be of a squat pear-shape with rather thick, small handles; the plates were usually strengthened with a heavily moulded rim, probably to help prevent warping.

The enamel painting was usually of a very high quality and applied in a stippled manner, giving the appearance of a stipple-engraved print, rather than a brush painting. The palette invariably included a strong brick red and lavish, but well-applied gilding. The subjects chosen were usually of seascapes, mythology or battle-scenes involving cavalry. Flowers and fruit seem to have been a less popular form of decoration, but when used, were always applied in the same distinctive manner.

The early wares made immediately after the move to Buen Retiro were of the same high-quality paste as that used at Capodimonte; but when the supplies of the materials brought from Italy were exhausted, the local clays proved very inferior and the wares produced were much coarser: at times they looked more like a cream-coloured earthenware. The products were still basically reserved for court use, and it was only from about 1785 that the king permitted public sales to take place. These pieces consisted chiefly of figures or ornamental wares and it was not until after 1803, when Bartolomé Sureda became Director, that more humble, useful wares became generally available. Unfortunately the factory was occupied by the French during the Peninsular War, and destroyed, together with the factory records, in 1812 by the British forces.

Another soft-paste porcelain production was established near Naples in 1771 by Ferdinand IV, son of Charles IV. The first two years saw the work being carried out at the King's villa of Portici, moving to buildings adjoining the Royal Palace in 1773. The wares produced under Ferdinand were very much influenced by the nearby excavations at Herculaneum and Pompeii, which provided much of the inspiration for the neo-classical movement.

Many large table-services were produced making a feature of classical scrolls for border decoration and paintings after those found on the walls of the ancient Roman cities. The factory mark of a crowned 'N' was generally used.

GERMANY
Salt-glazed Stoneware

There is little doubt that the greatest contribution made by the Germans to the development of European pottery and porcelain was the independent discovery of the manufacture of a hard-paste porcelain, previously known only to the Chinese. Earlier they had developed salt-glazed stoneware—a very important material. In common with hard-paste porcelain, it is resonant and if fired at the correct temperature, non-porous. To produce this body, clays must be rich in silicic acid and capable of being fired at the high temperature of about 1000°C.

Although the introduction of salt-glazed stoneware is always associated with the Rhineland, it is most likely that the earliest decorative jars of this type were produced in Hessen, at the Dreihausen factory, where an interesting type of jug was produced during the early 15th century, known as *Willkomm* (welcome). This was a convivial drinking vessel, of baluster shape, with a spreading foot of Gothic metal form, and the typical grey stoneware body was covered with a brown clay slip. During the 16th century a more common sort of brown stoneware jug was made at Dreihausen known as a *Trichterbecker*; it was beaker-shaped with a flaring mouth and sometimes decorated with rings suspended from loop handles.

The Westerwald area was ideally situated for the development of salt-glazed stoneware due to the deposits of essential clays found in the vicinity of Höhr, Grenzhausen, Siegburg, Trechen and Raeren. Cologne became the obvious trading-centre, whilst the River Rhine provided easy transport to the majority of European countries. Siegburg was engaged in the manufacture of grey-bodied wares covered with a strong yellow salt-glaze as early as the 14th century, but the area is better known for a tall slender jug, known as a *Jacobakanne*, made from about 1400 onwards. Another Siegburg type is the long-spouted jug, or *Schnabelkanne*, where use was made of an 'S' scroll to strengthen the handle, similar to that used by the Chinese on their early European exports.

During the 16th century many potters moved from Frechen to Cologne, where they helped to establish a prolific manufacture of much finer wares. It was during this period that the well-known '*Bartmannskrüge*' (bearded-man jugs) were produced. These bottles of globular or pear shape were decorated with a moulded mask of a bearded man; in England the features were associated with those of the unpopular Cardinal Bellarmino (1542–1621) one of the leaders of the Counter Reformation, hence the term 'Bellarmine pots'. Another shape associated with the Siegburg potters is the *Schnelle*, a tall vessel which tapers towards the rim, usually decorated with three panels, featuring relief moulding of biblical or mythological subjects; they originally had pewter or silver lids, with a thumb-piece for easy opening.

One of the best-known potters of German stoneware was Jan Emens Mennicken, who worked at Raeren during the last decades of the 17th century. His fine dark-brown tankards were decorated with highly original relief work, featuring various biblical and mythological subjects, sometimes together with bands of carved ornament and lion-mask handles. Jan Emens was also the first potter to decorate his grey stoneware with cobalt, a fashion which later became popular throughout the Westerwald.

Some excellent tankards were also produced by the Vest family at Kreussen from about 1622. The glaze is dark chocolate in tone, showing to advantage the bright enamel painting depicting such subjects as the planets, the Apostles or hunting-scenes.

(For colour illustration, see p. 12)

Fayence

The first use of tin-glazed earthenware in Germany appears to have been by the Nuremberg and South Tyrolean stove-makers, but a few dishes bearing dates between 1530 and 1555 and painted in a similar style to that seen on Venetian *maiolica* are attributed to Nuremberg.

From the early 18th century in Germany, there had been fierce competition amongst the rulers of the principalities; each wanted his particular factory to produce the most successful wares and, unable to produce porcelain such as was being made at Meissen in Saxony, they were content to decorate their coarser wares in imitation of Meissen. The influence of the wares made at Delft, in Holland, can also be traced over a long period. Dutch potters came to Germany in large numbers, persuading many heads of states and rich merchants to become proprietors of a 'porcelain' factory. The term 'porcelain' was in common usage to describe fine tin-glazed earthenware painted in the manner of porcelain.

Amongst the earliest, and rarest, drinking vessels were those in the form of an owl with a detachable head to form a cup, naturalistically painted in high-temperature blue. These are attributed to the South Tyrol, and date to about the mid-16th century.

Jugs with pewter lids can be dated as from the early 17th century. The recorded examples with the initials 'LS' can be regarded as the work of Lorenz Speckner, who worked at Kreussen. The bulbous form is much akin to the contemporary salt-glazed stoneware and use was made of both high-temperature blue and manganese.

The factory established at Hanau in 1661 was under the direction of two Dutch potters and although the undertaking continued until 1806, the later years were very unproductive owing to competition from numerous rival concerns and the importation of English creamware. Some well-authenticated jugs with long narrow necks (*Enghalskrüge*) were produced similar in form to the Delft vessels. The decoration was usually confined to the basic blue, green, yellow and manganese and the full range of enamel colours were only used for a short period during the mid-18th century.

It is at times difficult to distinguish the wares of Hanau from those made between 1666 and 1772 at Frankfurt-am-Main, where large numbers of plates and jugs were produced. Many of these pieces were painted in the Chinese style of the Ming dynasty, and the usual high glaze indicates the addition of a clear translucent glaze over the opaque tin-glaze and decoration. Many of the dishes decorated in such a manner were formed with nine lobes. Such examples sometimes bear the initials 'KR' (Johann Kaspar Ripp). Ripp worked at the factory from 1703 to 1708. The fine painting of this same painter is also to be seen on the early wares of Ansbach, the factory founded in 1710 by the Margrave Wilhelm Friedrich, although its best-known productions are those decorated in the Chinese manner of the *famille verte* between about 1724 and 1749. The initial 'L' is usually associated with the painter von Löwenfinck.

Some fine colourful tankards were produced at Nuremberg during the middle decades of the 18th century, where one of the best painters at the factory was G. F. Kordenbusch, who signed his work with a simple 'K', sometimes together with 'NB' for Nuremberg.

German *fayence* (this spelling rather than *faience* is generally used in the German connection) was particularly popular with the independent decorators, or *Hausmaler*, one of the earliest being Abraham Helmhack, who was working at Nuremberg in about 1680. He used bright enamel colours to illustrate biblical scenes together with flowers from contemporary prints.

(For colour illustration, see p. 13)

Porcelain

Meissen (Dresden)

The first true porcelain to be produced outside China was the result of many years' experiments by Ehrenfried Walther von Tschirnhaus and Johann Friedrich Böttger. For a long time large sums of money had been spent on the purchase of Oriental porcelain to satisfy the passion that Augustus the Strong, Elector of Saxony, King of Poland, had for this luxury, which prompted Tschirnhaus to comment 'China is the bleeding-bowl of Saxony'. In 1707, Böttger, who claimed to know of the secret of producing gold from base metal and had been working upon his hopeless project in the Albrechtsburg castle twelve miles north-west of the city of Dresden since 1705, was called upon to assist Tschirnhaus in his researches into the manufacture of porcelain, in a laboratory built upon the city walls of Dresden.

Their first success resulted in the fine red stoneware which was inspired by the Chinese teawares produced at Yi-hsing during the reign of the Emperor K'ang Hsi (1662–1722). The Meissen production was of a much harder body and of a finer texture, and capable of being polished to a brilliant glaze-like finish. Many of the stoneware forms were in the style of the Yi-hsing wares, but newer and more original shapes were produced under the influence of the court silversmith, Johann Jakob Irminger (d. 1726), who produced designs entirely divorced from any Oriental influence, in some cases direct imitations of the silver prototypes.

The difficulty Böttger experienced in controlling his kiln temperatures resulted in these early red-wares being occasionally underfired, necessitating the application of a black glaze, derived from cobalt and manganese, to which unfired gold, silver or enamel colours were added by Schnell, the court lacquerer.

Tschirnhaus died in October 1708, just after he and Böttger had produced a form of white porcelain from white Colditz clay and alabaster. The clay was replaced with true *kaolin*, or china-clay, by about 1711, but alabaster continued to be used instead of the feldspathic flux of china-stone (*petuntse*) until nearer 1720. The wares attributed to the Böttger period (1710–1719) are of a distinct ivory tone. It is worth noting that the Royal Saxon Porcelain Manufactory was established in March 1710 in the Albrechtsburg, where Böttger was once virtually a prisoner.

The early red stoneware proved to be too costly and unsuitable for the manufacture of complete table-services and from 1715 the redwares were gradually replaced by white porcelain, often embellished with moulded or modelled applied decoration in the form of flowers or foliage. Owing to the high firing temperature of about 1400°C, little success was initially achieved with underglaze-blue decoration and difficulties were also encountered in the fusing of the enamel colours to such a hard glaze. In consequence, use was made of gilding, sometimes coupled with an attractive mother-of-pearl lustre which Böttger produced from gold in about 1716. The tablewares made prior to the death of Böttger often comprised complete services for tea, chocolate or coffee; the difficulty of overcoming the warping of plates and dishes prevented the manufacture of dinner services for many years.

Following the death of Böttger in 1719, the King was persuaded to provide more financial aid for the factory and the 1720s saw the manufacture of greatly improved wares in both paste and decoration, due mainly to the arrival from Vienna of the outstanding painter and chemist, Johann Gregorius Höroldt (d. 1775), who was responsible for the painting of the many fantastic *Chinoiseries* and the direct imitations of the Oriental wares which had for so long been desired by Augustus.

Many of these *Chinoiseries* were inspired by the engravings of Peter Schenk, which were among the 147 engravings purchased in 1720, to help inspire the decorators. Höroldt's skills were quickly recognised and in 1723 he was made Court Painter. At this time the factory was employing approximately forty workers. When he retired in 1765 no less than 731 were employed.

The Painting Era (*die malerische Periode*) of Höroldt came to an end in about 1731, when the famed modeller Johann Joachim Kändler was appointed as a court modeller. Augustus II died in 1733, by which time Kändler had been responsible for the production of no less than 439 large-size figures of animals, requested by the King for the decoration of the Japanese Palace, a building which he had purchased in 1717 for conversion into a 'Porcelain Castle' to house both his fine collection of Oriental wares and examples from his own factory.

Meissen (Dresden)

Kändler, who must be regarded as the finest porcelain modeller of the baroque period, was at first concerned solely with porcelain in the form of miniature sculpture, but following the succession of Augustus III in 1733, his scope was to be extended to tablewares. Augustus III's primary artistic interest was his great collection of pictures, and this resulted in the appointment of Count Heinrich von Brühl as the director of the porcelain factory. Count Brühl obviously preferred Kändler's talents to Höroldt's and large unique dinner-services were soon to be produced by Kändler, on which relief decoration was to take precedence over painting.

One of the earliest services produced by Kändler was for Count Hennicke in 1735. This was decorated with applied flowers and mask-like handles. In the same year, production was started on a very large service for Count Sulkowski, decorated with the early four-strand basketwork-moulded border (*Ozier*) together with fully modelled figures forming the handles of tureen lids, painted in enamel colours with simple Kakiemon style decoration and the arms of Count Sulkowski. Not to be outdone, Count Brühl then had made for himself the world famous 'Swan Service', which took four years to produce (1737-41). The entire service comprised 2200 pieces, involving thirty different shapes. The theme throughout was the swan, accompanied by naiads, tritons, dolphins, shells, etc. in many instances based on designs inspired by such outstanding silversmiths as J. A. Meisonnier.

During these years, when Kändler was so much in favour, painting, which had been used on so many earlier tablewares, came to be regarded as of secondary importance, and now consisted merely of small sprigs of stylised Oriental flowers and coats-of-arms with rich gilt borders in the extravagant baroque taste. There was a pleasing revival of painted decoration from about 1740, when use was made of engravings by Melchior Kysell after J. W. Baur, resulting in some charming miniature-style landscapes and harbour-scenes, often attributed to the hand of Christian Friedrich Höroldt.

In 1741 a very beautiful service was made for the Elector Clement Augustus of Cologne, decorated with a new type of European flower-painting (*deutsche Blumen*). These botanical specimens were copied from engravings and were frequently depicted with a grey shadow, which seemed to lift the flowers from the surface. A signed tankard dated 1742 accredits work of this type to the painter J. G. Klinger, but there were doubtless other painters who were directed to paint in a similar manner. During this decade wares were sometimes painted with naturalistic, but rather lifeless birds. These decorations were at times applied to reserves within coloured grounds of yellow, sea-green, red-violet, claret, or a rare iron-red—a style referred to as *Fondporzellan*.

Following the death of Köhler in 1725, the factory had very little success with its productions decorated with underglaze-blue, but the difficulties appear to have been overcome by about 1732. From this date many tablewares were decorated in this colour, often employing the so-called 'onion-pattern' (*Zwiebelmuster*), a pattern undoubtedly influenced by the Chinese painting of stylised peaches and other plant forms.

The influence of Kändler was much in evidence on tableware during the rococo period (c. 1745-1763). New varieties of basket-work moulding were introduced for plates and dishes, along with S-shaped ribbing and trellis patterns with raised flowers. Plates often had borders decorated with rococo scroll-work panels filled with painted scenes or dotted trellis.

Where plain surfaces were available for more colourful painting, use was made of scenes after Watteau or Teniers, surrounded by lace-like rococo frames.

(For colour illustration, see *pp. 14 and 23)*

Opposite: CHOCOLATE JUG *and* TEAPOT *of hard-paste porcelain, painted in enamel colours, and marked 'MOL' in underglaze-blue. Dutch (Oude Loosdrecht), 1774-82; ht. (jug) 14.2 cm/5½ in.*

Overleaf: COFFEE-SERVICE *of hard-paste porcelain, painted in blue. This design was first introduced at the Royal Copenhagen factory in about 1780, it was redesigned by Arnold Krog during the early years of this century, since which time it has remained popular.*

Höchst

Overleaf: TUREEN *of tin-glazed earthenware (faience), made and decorated in high-temperature blue, and marked 'No—1' in blue. Norwegian (Herrebøe), c.1765; lgth. 42.2 cm/17 in.*

Opposite: TUREEN *of tin-glazed earthenware (faience), made and decorated in high-temperature blue and white enamel* (bianco-sopra-bianco). *Swedish (Röstrand), date mark of 1767; lgth. 40 cm/16 in.*

Many European porcelain factories owe their initial success to J. J. Ringler, who, having acquired the secret of the manufacture whilst working at the Vienna factory of the Empress Maria Theresa, went off to Höchst, near Mayence, in 1750, to turn his knowledge to financial advantage.

The factory at Höchst was founded in 1746 by A. F. von Löwenfinck, who had previously worked at both Meissen and Fulda. Löwenfinck was a fine painter but knew little about the making of hard-paste porcelain and, until the arrival of Ringler, the concern almost certainly made only *fayence* (tin-glazed earthenware). By this time J. G. Göltz had become the sole owner of the factory.

The dating of Höchst tablewares is difficult. Its porcelain was of a creamy tint when compared with that of Meissen and the talents of its artists seem to have been devoted to the production of figures, in preference to useful wares. The early rococo forms of about 1750 to 1765 show very little originality and were obviously based on those of Meissen and Frankenthal. Helmet-shaped jugs were a popular form, as were tea- and coffee-pots with moulded spouts and 'J' shaped handles.

These early wares were painted in the popular styles of the day: naturalistic flowers, *Chinoiseries*, or harbour-scenes including figures in gay rococo frames. Engravings after the paintings of Boucher, Teniers or Chodoweicki were frequently used.

Production was not helped during these early years by the continual change of workers, caused primarily by the dishonesty and quarrelsome nature of Göltz, who even dismissed his own son-in-law. Ringler had left for Strasbourg by 1752, followed in 1753 by Benckgraff, who had arrived from Vienna in 1750 to take up the post of Director. The work of Johannes Zeschinger, Göltz's son-in-law and a painter at the factory, is by no means uncommon,

identifiable on both the early *fayence* and the porcelain by the initials 'I Z', or his full name. Despite the engagement of new and talented workers, the competition forced Göltz into bankruptcy in 1756, and he died a year later. Production continued under the Trustees in Bankruptcy of Mainz until 1759, when the Elector of Mainz arranged for the concern to be put under the ownership of J. H. Maas, with Adam Bergdoll as Director.

In 1765 the factory was enlarged and some skilled painters engaged. Louis-Victor Gerverot was working at Höchst by 1771 and is known to have executed some extremely fine work, including a large service, the coffee-pot belonging to which is in The Metropolitan Museum of Art, New York, signed '*Gerv*' on the base and 'LVG' on the cover. W. B. Honey, in his *Dictionary of European Ceramic Art,* says that Höchst painters 'occasionally decorated Ansbach, Nymphenburg or Chinese porcelain' during the difficult years when production was sometimes suspended.

Some of the most pleasing Höchst tablewares were made between 1770 and 1796, when neo-classical styles were so popular; cameo-heads and other current classical motives were depicted in circular or oval panels, surrounded by wreaths or ribbons.

The basic factory-mark consists of a six-spoked wheel, taken from the arms of the Elector of Mainz; it was first applied in an enamel colour, and from about 1762 in underglaze-blue. An Electoral hat was added above the wheel in about 1765.

Fürstenberg

Whilst porcelain figures can often be attributed to a particular German factory with a fair degree of accuracy, owing to the distinctive characteristics of the modellers, it is far more difficult to recognise the hand of a porcelain painter. Fortunately for the collector, the majority of German factories adopted recognised factory-marks, which were used fairly consistently, except on pieces left in the white.

When the impostor Johann Christoph Glaser offered to produce porcelain for the Duke Karl of Wolfenbüttel in 1748, he was given the use of the old castle of Fürstenberg and it is said that the Duchess Philippine Charlotte was so excited at the prospect, that she threw out all her old wares under the impression they could be melted down to make new. Glaser's claim proved false, and there is little doubt that, prior to the arrival of Benckgraff in 1753, only *fayence* was produced. The ill-fated Benckgraff died within four weeks of his arrival, but fortunately his son-in-law Zeschinger had gained sufficient experience at Höchst to enable him to organise the production of a true porcelain by December 1753. The factory flourished until the outbreak of the Seven Years War, which brought production to a halt in 1762. The factory enjoyed little prosperity until 1795, when Louis-Victor Gerverot completely reorganised the concern, ensuring good production and profits during his stay until 1814.

Fürstenberg is best known to the porcelain collector through the fine figures modelled by Simon Feilner, but some good work was carried out by a talented group of painters during the late 1760s, when dated and signed examples can help to identify with certainly the work of such people as Georg Heinrich Holtzmann, who painted pastoral scenes, Johann Friedrich Berger, a flower painter working in 1767, and Wilhelm Christoph Ruth, also painting flowers a year later. C. H. Albert can be identified as a painter of birds in 1768, Ernst Wilhelm Jungerblut as a figure painter in 1767, A. J. Stahn as a painter of mythological scenes at the same period. The work of the above and other painters appears on a series of plaques, which Honey (*op. cit.*) suggested were probably painted as 'demonstration or test-pieces'.

Great use was made of the large collection of engravings from the Fürstenberg library, and flowers after Vauquier and Tessier, and landscapes by Waterloo and Weirotter can be readily recognised. Some interesting landscape views of Brunswick are attributed to the Court Painter, Johann Friedrich Weitsch. These landscapes were only rarely framed, the more popular style calling for a heavy foreground of rocks and plants, giving a pleasing illusion of depth to the scenes.

An early form of Fürstenberg plate has a pierced border which would normally be considered later than the underglaze-blue date of 1758 indicates. The figure and landscape painting on these plates is attributed to J. F. Metzsch, after the engravings of L. G. Hertel. Metzsch was the leading painter at the Brunswick Academy of Painting.

This factory also produced some forms of extremely heavy rococo between about 1760 and 1765, from which time the majority of its tablewares were in the neo-classical taste, with a distinct tendency to over-simplification, probably influenced by the contemporary fashions of the new and important factory of Berlin.

From about 1790 to 1814, the entire factory output was devoted to the antique, soon to be followed by the geometric metal forms popularised by the Empire styles of Sèvres and Vienna, coupled with profuse gilding. The mark throughout the life of the factory was an '*F*' in underglaze-blue, with an additional crown added in more recent years. The factory continues to the present day.

Frankenthal

Although the factory of Frankenthal only existed from 1755 to 1799, many of its early moulds are still being used at the current Nymphenburg concern to this day. If Paul-Antoine Hannong had succeeded in reaching agreeable terms with the Vincennes authorities concerning his manufacture of a hard-paste porcelain at Strasbourg, the productions of Vincennes and Sèvres might well have been a lot different, and certainly a lot less beautiful. Forced to discontinue his production, Hannong was granted a privilege by the Elector Palatine at Frankenthal, where, having set up his manufactory, he left his son Charles-François-Paul in charge as Director. Owing to the early death of the latter in 1757, another son, Joseph-Adam Hannong continued in charge of the factory until 1762, when the entire establishment was purchased by the Elector, Carl Theodor, for about one third of the actual value. The factory continued until 1799.

The wares produced from about 1755 to 1775 were made of a paste and glaze far superior to that used in later years. There was a great similarity between the wares of Strasbourg and Frankenthal, and it is known that some examples were in fact produced at Strasbourg and decorated at Frankenthal after the transfer of the porcelain manufacture. More attention was again paid to the production of porcelain figures than tablewares, but those that were made were of a fine quality, even if at times the rococo theme was interpreted a little too extravagantly for such a fine material.

The tablewares of the early Carl Theodor period continued to have a great deal in common with those of Sèvres. This is particularly evident in the breakfast sets made for a single individual, the *Solitaires,* which comprised a lozenge-shaped tray, cup, saucer, cream-jug with three feet and a small teapot with an ear-shaped handle. A similar service in an American collection is painted in the manner of Ostade, Teniers and Brouwer. The figure painting on Frankenthal was of a very fine quality up to about 1780, due in most instances to the talents of such painters as Winterstein, J. Osterspey and J. B. Magnus. Winterstein favoured subjects after Teniers, Osterspey, who signed his work *'J O pinxit',* or 'O S', preferred mythological subjects, whilst Magnus, who signed his work with 'B M', or in full, was an ac-complished painter of battle scenes. In his book *German Porcelain and Faience,* Dr Ducret illustrates a unique plate, showing a battle-scene attributed to the engravings of Rugendas, and thought to be the the work of Magnus. The plate bears the Frankenthal mark of 'C T' in monogram under a crown, and the date '77' (1777). The border bears the monogram 'C A' under a ducal crown, and is from a service made for the Duke of Pfalz-Zweibrücken, Carl II.

During the 1770s the Frankenthal painters favoured many other Sèvres patterns, such as diapered grounds and borders, but preferred heavier tones, like deep crimson or green, to those used in France. Gilt-striped grounds with flowers or figures in a crimson monochrome were also popular, together with 'chintz' patterns. Their use of some rather gay *Chinoiseries* in plain gilding would have been considered a little out-moded at that time.

From the 1780s the rather more severe classical forms were frequently decorated with the French *oeil de perdrix* (partridge eye), a diaper of dotted circles on a coloured ground, or figures painted in monochrome brown or another colour.

Honey mentions (*op. cit.*) two rare Frankenthal plates in the Historisches Museum at Spires decorated by Pierre Berthevin in 1769, with underglaze-blue transfer-prints.

Nymphenburg

The importance of Meissen as the fashion centre for Europe was eclipsed during the Seven Years War, not only by the new fashionable rococo porcelains of France, but also by newly established German factories, such as Nymphenburg, a factory known best for the outstanding figures modelled by Franz Anton Bustelli, who must be regarded as superior to Kändler in this new age of porcelain.

As early as 1747, Franz Ignaz Niedermayer, a designer of tiled stoves, was experimenting with the manufacture of hard-paste porcelain. The Elector Joseph Maximilian III, was interested in the project and enlisted the aid of skilled workmen from Vienna, including the painter Jakob Helchis. It is likely, however, that the earlier wares were of tin-glazed earthenware, rather than of porcelain, which apparently was not produced until after the nomadic arcanist Ringler arrived in 1753 at Neudeck, where the production was first established. Ringler stayed for three years after having helped in the production of a hard-paste porcelain, which was marked with an impressed shield from the arms of Bavaria. He was replaced by J. P. Härtl, who became sole manager, and the factory flourished to such an extent that in 1761 it was moved into new premises at Nymphenburg.

The figures attributed to the modeller Bustelli, who was appointed in 1754, are easier to recognise than the tablewares, which, we know, he also helped to design. A tureen decorated with landscapes, in the Zurich collection of Dr Siegfried Ducret, is considered to be the work of Bustelli on account of the close similarity between its rococo modelling and that of some of his figures. The quality of this example, dating from about 1757, is poor both in body and glaze but much finer tablewares were being produced by 1760, sometimes coupling crimson monochrome painting—*en camaieu*—with the full polychrome palette and high quality rococo scrolls in gilt.

Life at the Electoral Court of Munich was very gay. There was entertainment by the Italian Comedy, games, concerts, the opera, tournaments, hunting, boating, parties, and fireworks—all activities which called for lavish banquets, and in consequence, lots of porcelain services. One fine service made for the Count in about 1760 is decorated with boldly painted flower sprays, considered to be the work of Josef Zächenberger, who was a chief flower-painter from about 1760 to 1770. Even on this service, with richly gilded borders, there is evidence of the difficulties that still prevailed and colours sometimes tended to flake off from the glaze. The majority of the Nymphenburg plates were moulded, much in the fashion of contemporary Meissen.

Teapots with snake-head spouts, and food-warmers (*réchauds*) were among the most favoured forms produced at Nymphenburg and some very simple cylindrical mugs with pewter-lids and base rims also appear in the price list which makes surprising reading—a beer tankard or teapot cost about three times that of an Italian Comedy figure.

Flowers remained the main feature of the painted decoration for many years, but, whilst the main source of inspiration appears to have been the engraving of J. D. Preissler, the individual work of painters such as G. C. Lindemann, Josef Zächenberger, and Josef Reiss cannot unfortunately be identified. Some very pleasing landscapes appear on food-warmers which are sometimes considered to be the work of Johannes Klein but most of his signed work must be considered *Hausmalerei* of a later period.

State ownership of the factory ceased when it became a private company in 1862.

(For colour illustration, see p. 24)

Ludwigsburg

As early as 1759 good quality porcelain was being produced here for Duke Charles-Eugene and followed slightly earlier experiments at Württemberg. The skills of J. J. Ringler were again enlisted to help in the manufacture of some very fine porcelains and he remained Director at Ludwigsburg for forty years. Even with the Duke's patronage, the factory was not self-supporting—at one period the staff were compelled to take a proportion of their wages in the form of slightly faulty wares.

The best examples were produced between 1764 and 1775, and despite attempts by Frederick, King of Württemberg, to restore the prosperity of the factory in the early 19th century, production finally came to a halt in 1824.

G. F. Riedel (d. 1784) was a painter concerned with both figures and useful wares. He was the designer of some very fine services in the early rococo styles, including a fifty-piece supper-and toilet-service made for the Marchesa Giovanelli-Martinengo of Venice.

Apart from the use of extreme rococo modelling, very much in the Frankenthal style, Riedel is credited with such innovations as enclosing small panels within raised rococo scrolls on the borders of plates, and on all-over scale patterns, somewhat similar to that seen on some of the early-18th-century soft-paste porcelain of Saint Cloud. He also often used the popular basket-work moulding around the tops of pear-shaped coffee-pots which were usually supported on three curved feet. Classical styles were adopted comparatively early and by 1770 the straight cylinder was in common use for teapots, coffee- and chocolate-pots, the latter often having a turned wooden handle inserted into a porcelain socket, at rightangles to the spout.

From 1758 to 1793 the factory-mark consisted of various forms of two back-to-back interlaced 'C's, under a ducal coronet (that of Charles-Eugene, Duke of Württemberg)—the neater marks suggesting the earlier years. The mark of three stag's horns in a shield, from the arms of Württemberg, was sometimes used from the late 18th to the early 19th century. 'L' under a crown indicates the period of Duke Ludwig (1793 to 1795), 'F R', or 'F' for 'Friedrich Rex' appearing under a coronet, in red, gold or impressed, indicated the period 1806 to 1816 and the last period, 1816 to 1824, can be identified by the 'W R' monogram of Duke Wilhelm.

COFFEE, TEA *and* CHOCOLATE SERVICE *of hard-paste porcelain, painted in enamel colours, and marked with two interlaced 'C's under crown. German (Ludwigsburg),* c. *1765; ht. (coffee-pot) 24.8 cm/9¾ in.*

Berlin

The first ventures into the making of a hard-paste porcelain in the Prussian city of Berlin were of short duration, lasting from 1753 to 1757. The owner of the Berlin concern was Kasper Wegely, a woollen merchant, who is known to have had the assistance of such people as the arcanist Niklaus Paul from Höchst, E. H. Reichard, modeller, and I. J. Clauce, painter. Wegely's porcelain, which is comparatively rare, was of good quality both in colour and glaze, but was rather opaque, probably due to being fired at too low a temperature, even though he suffered high kiln wastage. Wegely's enamels are also at times liable to flake off from the glaze.

The rather well-painted landscapes, with 'Watteau-like' figures, applied in the full palette or in purple monochrome, are attributed to I. J. Clauce. The simple factory mark of a blue 'W' might well be confused with that used at Wallendorf, but the Wegely pieces are usually additionally marked with three impressed numbers, one above the other, a triple fraction.

In 1761 a new porcelain factory was built in Berlin by Johann Ernst Gotzkowski, aided by E. H. Reichard, with J. G. Grieninger as manager—a post he retained until his death in 1798. Owing to financial difficulties Gotzkowski was forced to sell the entire undertaking to Frederick the Great of Prussia in 1763. It had always been the ambition of Frederick to transfer the Meissen establishment and the majority of the workers to Berlin during the Seven Years War but this had proved impracticable, and so he was especially pleased to become the owner of a going concern which from 1763 to the present day has been State property. The mark normally used by Gotzkowski was a script 'G' in underglaze-blue but wares are sometimes seen with both this mark and the later Berlin 'sceptre' mark, suggesting wares which were made in the early period were decorated after the factory changed hands. The King went to great lengths to ensure the financial success of the concern: it was given the complete monopoly of porcelain sales throughout Prussia; wood for fuelling the kilns was supplied free; there were no tariffs of any kind, and the large Jewish community were forced by law to spend an allotted amount of money on the purchase of factory wares each year. The workers, who toiled for very long hours, were paid very highly.

COFFEE-POT *of hard-paste porcelain, painted in enamel colours, and marked 'G' in gold. German (Berlin, Gotzkowsky's factory), 1761-63; ht. 21 cm/8¼ in.*

The Berlin factory is best known for the very fine table-services made for the King or as presents for his court favourites. Most of these services were made prior to 1770. Frederick died in 1786. Many of the early wares of Gotzkowski were influenced by Meissen but from 1763 onwards new forms and styles of decoration were introduced, including the popular scale, or *Mosaik,* pattern attributed to the painter C. J. C. Klipfel.

Between 1765 and 1766 a thirty-six place service was ordered by the King for the Neue Palais at Potsdam, moulded in a new popular style, *Reliefzierat mit Spalier* (Relief-pattern with trellis-work). This design proved so popular that it was imitated at numerous other German porcelain factories. Another equally important service was made for the Breslau Palace of Frederick, between 1767 and 1768 known as the 'Blue Service', fashioned in a simplified 'Antique' manner with the emphasis on flutes and reeding, rather than scrolls. In all instances the scale-pattern was included as a ground, in a variety of different colours. From 1770 onwards a new source of china-clay resulted in wares of a much whiter, but rather cold, tone that none-the-less lent itself readily to the more severe classical forms.

Minor factories

By the mid-18th century it had become fashionable for each head of a state to be the owner of a porcelain factory. Knowledge of the manufacture of the material was no longer a problem and new sources of the essential clays were constantly being discovered.

A factory was established at ANSBACH in 1758 to meet the needs of the Margrave Karl Alexander, who was aided by J. F. Kändler (almost certainly the nephew of the more famous Meissen modeller, J. J. Kändler), the painter J. C. Gerlach and the modeller C. G. Laut. In the beginning the factory prospered and in 1762 it was moved to Bruckberg. Many of the early tablewares made at Ansbach were beautifully decorated with *Chinoiseries* which in some instances were direct copies from the illustrations in Johann Nieuhof's book, originally published in Amsterdam in 1666. (An English edition followed in 1669 by J. Ogilby, entitled *Embassy to the Grand Tartar Cham*.)

There was a pleasing combination of moulded decoration and Watteau-like figures amid landscapes used on all kinds of tablewares in about 1766, which owes a great deal to the styles of Berlin. The factory ceased production in 1806.

Porcelain was made at KELSTERBACH from 1761 to 1768 and again from 1789 to 1792. The first owner was the Landgrave Ludwig VIII of Hesse-Darmstadt but upon his death in 1768, the factory produced only *faience* until 1789, when the manufacture of porcelain was resumed under J. J. Lay for a period of three years.

The wares produced were of a fine quality and included breakfast sets, coffee-pots, teapots, jugs, sugar-bowls and cups, but apparently no large wares, such as dinner-services, trays or dishes.

The factory established at OTTWEILER in the Rhineland in 1763, was patronised by Prince Wilhelm Heinrich of Nassau. The porcelain produced there was rather grey in tone, but the forms and styles of decoration were very pleasing. The tablewares included many jugs and tureens in rococo style, with scroll handles of square section and mask spouts. Landscapes were often painted in purple monochrome which was a style favoured by the painter Jean-Pierre Vaquette.

The Prince Bishop of Fulda, Heinrich VIII, engaged the services of Niklaus Paul, from Weesp in Holland to supervise the establishment of a porcelain factory at FULDA in 1764. The venture was a great success and continued until 1789. The figures produced at Fulda number among some of the most beautiful ever produced in a hard-paste porcelain, whereas the tablewares show very little originality. The earlier wares were decorated with Meissen-style flowers or landscapes, whilst the later pieces in classical styles were often decorated with medallion heads in relief in the biscuit, or painted in a monochrome tone with ribbon or wreath frames.

During the 18th century there were four factories engaged in the manufacture of pottery and porcelain in CASSEL but only one was concerned with the production of a hard-paste porcelain, lasting from 1766 to 1788 and patronised by Friederich Landgrave of Hesse. Niklaus Paul who, as we have already seen, was involved with the establishment of the Fulda factory was appointed as arcanist at Cassel and other skilled workers were recruited from neighbouring concerns. The operation was never a commercial success and was in constant need of subsidies from the Prince until it eventually closed in 1788.

The majority of Cassel tablewares were decorated in the less costly blue-and-white styles, and the more colourful ones owed much to the influence of Fürstenberg. There was a lot of rococo relief scrollwork, moulded in a rather haphazard fashion, but nevertheless often enclosing some rather attractive landscapes painted in an uncommon green monochrome. The factory mark was a lion *rampant,* with two tails (the familiar Frankenthal lion has only one).

The factory patronised by Duke Christian IV of PFALZ-ZWEIBRÜCKEN was first established in the castle of Gutenbrunn in 1767, moving to Zweibrücken two years later. Production was very short-lived and ceased upon the death of the Duke in 1775.

The factory produced wares of a poor quality porcelain, mostly decorated in underglaze-blue, but there are records of some finer quality tablewares, such as tureens with pierced rococo handles and knobs in the shape of cauliflowers. K. F. Wohlfahrt painted some fine landscapes during his short stay in the first year or so of the concern. The factory-mark consisted of a 'P Z' monogram in either underglaze-blue or an enamel colour.

An equally short-lived porcelain factory was established at WÜRZBURG in 1775 by J. C. Geiger who was granted a privilege by Franz Ludwig von Ertal, Prince Bishop of Würzburg. The factory came to a

Minor factories

halt in 1780. The rare tablewares known to exist can be identified by the mark C G/W (Caspar Geyger/ Würzburg), or an unexplained device within a circle over 'W', for Würzburg.

Both the body and the glaze of wares attributed to this concern are of extremely poor quality but the landscape decoration, surrounded by gilt rococo scrollwork, is often very pleasing. Use was also made of *Mosaik* (scale-pattern) sometimes in crimson enamel, as introduced at Berlin.

Many unidentified German wares have at times to be rather vaguely attributed to the forest region of the Thüringerwald where there was an abundance of the necessary clays and fuel essential for the manufacture of porcelain and the skilled labour already conversant with the manufacture of *fayence* and glass.

A factory was started at GOTHA, in Thuringia, in 1757 by W. T. von Rothberg and continues to this day. This concern which in 1775 was only employing twelve workers, was nevertheless successful in every way and in its early years produced some pleasing, useful wares in the rococo style from a cream-toned body. Production was stepped up in about 1772 and from this date the majority of wares were in the new classical forms, often designed to order. One pleasing shape consisting of a small tray to hold two cups was made from about 1780 and referred to as a *tête-à-tête*. The graceful classical styles also included some tasteful flower-sprig and figure decoration, but towards the close of the 18th century the hard cylindrical forms with angular handles were far less attractive. From 1804 to 1881 the factory was owned by the Henneberg family, and from then onwards by the Simson brothers.

By far the most important of the many Thuringian factories was that established in 1760 by Prince Friedrich Wilhelm Eugen von Hildburghausen at KLOSTER-VEILSDORF. In 1797, following the death of the Prince, the factory was taken over by the Greiner family who was already involved in porcelain manufacture at Limbach and Rauenstein.

The tablewares in rococo styles produced there until about 1780 had pleasing scrolled handles; shell-edges were popular on trays and cups and many borders featured Meissen-type basket-work patterns. Friedrich Döll (mark 'D' in enamel), the painter who was employed at the factory for at least twenty-five

years excelled in the painting of fruit and flowers of outstanding quality. The most common factory-mark consisted of the initials 'C V', as written, or in monogram form.

Another Thuringian factory was established in the same year at VOLKSTEDT by G. H. Macheleid and is still in operation today. Its early wares were of a soft-paste porcelain but within a short period, the more common German hard-paste was being produced. This was of a grey hue with many minor imperfections. Its many tablewares showed a preference for clumsy relief rococo decoration, usually inspired by contemporary silver forms or were direct copies of Meissen. The painted decoration was of a higher quality. The painter Franz Kotta is credited with some good figure subjects in an iron-red, after Chodowiecki, the Berlin engraver (1726–1801). The mark of crossed hayforks was obviously used as a direct jibe at the crossed swords of Meissen and, despite the latter's official protest in 1787, the hay-forks continued in use for many more years.

The Thuringian factories which started during the 18th century and are still in production today include Wallendorf, Limbach, Gera, Rauenstein and Grossbreitenbach. The majority of the porcelain tablewares produced at these factories were very modestly decorated and the less expensive under-glaze-blue was very frequently used, often on export wares for Turkey, whose thirst for coffee-cups appears to have been unquenchable.

Opposite: TEAPOT, CUP and SAUCER, and JUG *of hard-paste porcelain, decorated with enamel colours, and marked with* 'Z' *in underglaze-blue. Swiss (Zurich), 1770-80; ht. (teapot) 10 cm/4 in.*

Overleaf: DISH *of lead-glazed earthenware, decorated in coloured glazes. French, modelled by Bernard Palissy (or followers), 1550-1600; lgth. 53 cm/21 in.*

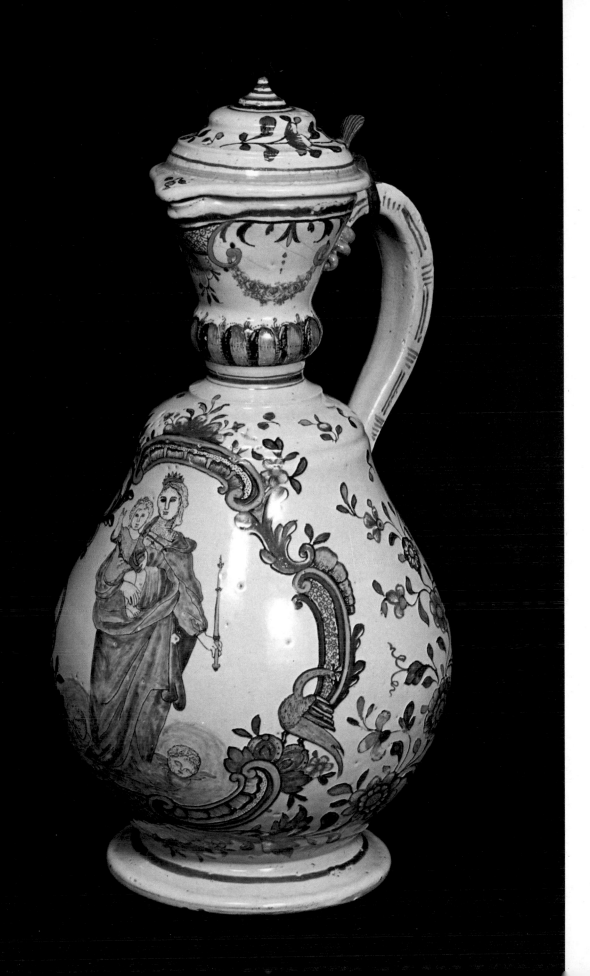

AUSTRIA
Porcelain

Vienna

The success of an early porcelain factory and the popularity of its wares can often be judged by the number of reproductions produced by later concerns and independent decorators. This is certainly true of the hard-paste porcelain produced at the Vienna factory between 1719 and its closure in 1864.

Claudius Innocentius Du Paquier had been endeavouring to produce a porcelain similar to that of Meissen from 1717, but it was not until 1719, when he was aided by C. K. Hunger, a gilder, and Samuel Stölzel, a kiln-master (both had deserted from Meissen) that Vienna started to produce some attractive porcelain in the current baroque silver forms. The early wares were very much influenced by Meissen, although the porcelain body was of a distinct greyish tone whereas by this time Meissen was producing a fine white material. The early Vienna wares also lacked the professional finish of Meissen; their foot-rims were usually rough and unglazed. Full relief figures, of both human and animal forms, were particularly popular for handles and knobs, and typical baroque masks were used together with relief floral decoration.

The unique documented piece of Vienna porcelain is a tall two-handled chocolate-cup and saucer, undecorated apart from moulded fluting, dated 1719. Cups of this form, often with two handles, were produced at the factory for many years, the matching saucer often having a raised gallery to house the cup-rim (*trembleuse*). Coffeewares, teawares, tureens and jugs were among the most popular wares produced; there was, it seems, little demand for table-services of the proportions produced at Meissen from the 1730s.

Du Paquier's wares were decorated in all the styles popularised by Meissen. Oriental-type flowers were probably the earliest form of decoration in coloured enamels, but by about 1725 some excellent *Chinoiseries* in the full polychrome palette were being used on a large variety of tablewares, which would appear to owe nothing whatever to the better-known painting of Johann Gregor Höroldt who was only at Vienna for a short period, 1719 to 1720. A further early document as to styles of decoration, in the Hermitage Museum, Leningrad, is a tureen and cover, signed with the initials of Christian Frey. The subject-matter shows *putti* working in a porcelain factory. *Putti* and mythological scenes were especially popular as decoration in about 1730. Similar decoration can at times be attributed to the painters Jacobus Helchis, C. F. von Wolfsburg, H. G. von Bressler and Ignaz Bottengruber. Some very attractive black enamel painting (*Schwarzlot*), with occasional additional gilding is attributed to the painter Carl Wendelin Anreiter von Zirnfeld, who was engaged from the start of the factory until 1737, when he moved to the Doccia porcelain factory in Italy.

The Vienna porcelain undertaking was taken over by the State in 1744, at which time the well known Vienna shield with two cross-bars (*Bindenschild*) was adopted as a factory-mark. The Vienna tablewares made during the State period (1744-84) favoured rococo forms but showed very little originality, due in part to the hiring of several painters formerly employed at Meissen.

In 1784 the Vienna factory came under the direction of Konrad von Sorgenthal, and remained prosperous until its closure in 1864. During these years the richly decorated tablewares were produced, for which Vienna is best known. Beautiful miniature paintings feature on fine gilt grounds and on typical neo-classical shapes.

The new collector should avoid wares with printed decorations, 'signed' by Kauffmann or Boucher together with a fake enamel mark; these are all of comparatively recent manufacture.

(For colour illustration, see p. 25)

HOLLAND
Delftware

Dutch potters had been producing tin-glazed earthenware in Italian styles for many years prior to Delft becoming known as an important centre of production. The term Delftware has nevertheless today been adopted generally to indicate the technique, rather than the place of manufacture.

Throughout the 17th century the Dutch East India Company imported huge quantities of Chinese blue-and-white porcelain to Europe, and it is not surprising that the Dutch potters endeavoured to produce comparable wares in their own earthenware in order to protect their livelihoods. One of the reasons for Delft becoming the major centre of this new manufacture is that, owing to a decline in the brewing industry, many ideal premises became available at that time. In addition the town was ideally situated near major waterways for the export of the wares and the import of many necessary raw materials.

The potters of Delft enjoyed at least one hundred years of prosperity, from about 1650 to 1750; their finest reproductions of Chinese porcelains were made during the second half of the 17th century. The earliest examples were imitations of wares made during the reign of the Chinese Emperor Wan Li (1573–1619). It was the aim of the Delft potters to reproduce the Chinese wares perfectly down to the finest detail, except, of course, for the material itself. Finer potting and more delicate painting became necessary and, in order to acquire a brilliant porcellaneous glaze, a second clear glaze *(kwaart)* was often applied over the tin-glaze and the high-temperature blue painting.

Most of the early Delftwares were large, ambitious productions such as vases, but dishes, plates and jugs were also produced in direct imitation of the Oriental wares. In the third quarter of the 17th century the Delft potters began to adopt more original styles of decoration which included European landscapes, often used on large plates with plain wide rims. Some excellent jugs were made during the late years of the 17th century at 'The Young Moor's Head' factory of Rochus Hoppestyn; they were sometimes enhanced by the addition of gold and red decoration, probably inspired by the mid-17th century Chinese 'transitional' porcelains.

The teapots produced in imitation of the Chinese *famille noire* or lacquer, never attained the high-quality of the French wares soon to follow, whereas the Dutch red-stonewares made to imitate the Chinese Yi-hsing tea wares, were of a very high quality. These red stonewares, considered to be essential for the successful brewing of tea, were certainly being made by Lambertus Van Eenhoorn at the 'Metal Pot Factory' before the end of the century and, following the order of 1680 which required redware potters to register their mark, no less than seven complied, including Arij de Milde whose mark of a running fox is the one most frequently encountered.

The majority of these Dutch redware teapots were small and had the typical small loop handle and short straight spout seen on so many of the Chinese prototypes. They were often decorated with applied prunus sprays or similarly raised decoration of other Far Eastern styles. It is interesting to note that even at this early date it was considered necessary for a teapot to have a stand, very often octagonal in shape.

It is appropriate here to mention that English creamwares which were imported into Holland during the second half of the 18th century, were often decorated on arrival in the Dutch taste with enamel colours. This is particularly the case with many plates and teapots.

(For colour illustration, see p. 26)

Porcelain

Familiarity with Chinese porcelain appears to have had little effect upon the porcelains produced by the Dutch potters, other than to delay the manufacture of this material until about 1760. Unlike the majority of other European concerns the Dutch factories were entirely commercial ventures, rather than status symbols of wealthy patrons, or undertakings subsidised by the State purse.

The earliest Dutch porcelain factory was established in 1757 at WEESP, near Amsterdam, by D. McCarthy and was taken over in 1759 by Count Gronsveld-Diepenbroick-Impel who enlisted the aid of several well-known German workers to enable him to produce a fine quality white porcelain. The form and decoration of the wares showed hardly any originality and the German influence can be clearly seen on the majority of tablewares which were decorated with Watteau-like scenes, birds, or naturalistic flowers.

In 1771 the factory was purchased by Pastor Johannes de Mol who transferred the undertaking to OUDE LOOSDRECHT where the moulds and plant, formerly used at Weesp, were put to use for a further short period after which some original shapes in *Louis-Seize* style were introduced. These later pieces showed greater charm, often having pleasing smooth surfaces giving ample areas for some very commendable landscape paintings, sometimes applied in an unusual brown monochrome.

Following the death of Mol in 1782, the concern was again taken over, this time by his backers, who, in 1784, arranged for yet a further move, to OUDER AMSTEL where the manufactory was put under the direction of Friedrich Däuber. The business then flourished until Däuber died in 1800, when it was purchased by G. Dommer and Co. who transferred it in 1809 to Nieuwer Amstel where it continued until 1820.

The quality of the tablewares made at Amstel cannot be criticised technically, but in both form and style they showed even less originality than the previous two factories already discussed. They were completely under the influence of the contemporary Parisian hard-paste porcelain factories. The late-neo-classical styles were soon followed by the Empire fashions and the straight cylinder became the standard cup shape, together with long-outmoded pear-shaped jugs and pots, brought up-to-date with sunken lids. The mark of 'Amstel' was written in either underglaze-blue or an enamel colour.

Prior to making a hard-paste porcelain of his own, Anton Lyncker, a German, was engaged at THE HAGUE, dealing in Thuringian and Meissen porcelains. It occurred to him that it would be financially worthwhile to import undecorated wares and add the decoration in his own workshop. The original underglaze-blue marks of the German factories of Meissen, Höchst or Ansbach, were then disguised by overpainting in enamel colours the accepted mark of The Hague—a stork with an eel in its beak, the emblem of the town. Lyncker also managed to acquire examples of the soft-paste porcelain then being produced at Tournai, which, when decorated with charming landscapes within frames of gold scrolls or trellis, are particularly attractive.

The wares produced from Lyncker's own hard-paste showed hardly any more originality than the other Dutch porcelain factories. He too was a slave to the contemporary factories of Germany and France, the late rococo style of Berlin and Meissen and then the neo-classical taste of the many French factories. One name worthy of note is that of Leonhardus Temminck whose purple monochrome Cupids owe much to his having been trained by a pupil of Boucher.

(For colour illustration, see p. 35)

SCANDINAVIA
Faience & Porcelain

The tin-glazed earthenwares produced in Sweden, Schleswig-Holstein, Norway, and Denmark are too often entirely overlooked. These countries produced wares of great originality in both form and decoration and of a style which, in many instances, was rarely seen elsewhere.

Johann Wolff, born in the Duchy of Holstein, started a manufacture of tin-glazed earthenware at STORE KONGENSGADE in Copenhagen in 1722, but he himself only stayed until about 1725, when he moved to Stockholm where he was involved in setting up the factory at Rörstrand. The wares associated with Wolff's stay at Copenhagen are too few to warrant lengthy discussion; they would almost certainly have been decorated only in blue, in a similar style to the contemporary wares of Nuremberg, Delft and Rouen.

The RÖRSTRAND factory had rather difficult beginnings, due mostly to poor leadership. Wolff was dismissed in 1728 and was succeeded by the equally incompetent C. C. Hunger who was replaced in 1733 by A. N. Ferdinand who remained manager until 1739. Real success was not enjoyed until 1753 when Elias Magnus Ingman became Director, with Andus Fahlström as technical manager. It was unfortunate that the importing of English creamwares caused Rörstrand to begin manufacturing a similar body from as early as 1771, with the manufacture of faience virtually coming to a halt before the end of the century.

From about 1745 the earlier blue-and-white wares gave way to those decorated in high-temperature colours, applied in a manner more usually associated with enamels and porcelain. The tin-glaze ground was usually tinted, which showed to advantage the use of a white pigment (*bianco-sopra-bianco*, white-upon-white) which was attractively used to produce lace-like borders or grounds of diaper pattern to blue flower-painting. A further attractive style of border-painting, consisting of foliage, fruit, graceful scrollwork and pendant ornaments, is referred to as the 'Rehn' border, after J. E. Rehn, Superintendent of the furniture at the Royal Palace. In common with other Scandinavian factories,

Rörstrand produced some well-painted large tea-table trays, which fitted into a wooden base, to form a tea-table. Another shape peculiar to Rörstrand is a sauce-boat, or cream-jug, fashioned exactly after contemporary Swedish silver. Both of these two specialities were also produced at Marieberg.

The MARIEBERG factory was started in 1759 by J. L. E. Ehrenreich, a German who was a dentist by profession. The first factory was devoted to the making of porcelain, but within a month the building was burnt down and the second factory, erected within the same year, was concerned only with tin-glazed pottery. Marieberg did not rely as much upon painted decoration as Rörstrand did and many of the early wares were left with just the fine white glaze and no painted decoration. The decorated tablewares included tureens, moulded in rococo fashion with shell-forms, flowers, fruit and leaves, which were in most instances decorated in a palette which included rich emerald green, crimson, purple and a good black.

In 1766 Ehrenreich was succeeded by Pierre Berthevin who had previously been a modeller at Mennecy, in France. Before Berthevin left, three years later, a softer range of colours was being used on neo-classical forms and black enamel transfer-printing had been introduced. This latter method of decoration was continued under Henrik Sten, who followed Berthevin. Marieberg, whose factory-marks usually included the triple-crown device, was taken over by the Rörstrand owners in 1782.

A less well-known but quite important faience factory was started in 1757 at STRALSUND by Johann Buchwald who had previously gained experience at several German factories. From about 1766 many good workers arrived at Stralsund from Marieberg, including J. L. E. Ehrenreich who took over the lease of the factory. The tablewares included many rococo-style tureens with both low relief and enamel decoration of a very high quality, and openwork plates and dishes with basket-work moulding.

Besides faience, Pierre Berthevin was producing a creamy soft-paste porcelain at Marieberg between 1766 and 1769. One of his most common shapes was the small lidded custard-cup with closely reeded decoration, painted in soft enamel colours with typical German-style flower-painting. In 1769 the factory was taken over by Henrik Sten who produced a chalky hybrid hard-paste porcelain. Custard-cups were also made from this new material, together with tureens, teapots, bowls and *tête-a-tête* sets, nearly all being copies of contemporary French or German wares.

Following the departure of Johann Wolff from the Store Kongensgade factory in Copenhagen, the factory enjoyed twenty-two years of prosperity under the management of J. E. Pfau. After Pfau left the factory declined and finally closed in 1769. In accordance with the privilege granted to Pfau in 1722, the faience produced during his direction was decorated only in high-temperature blue, or occasionally manganese (purple) on what were usually simple shapes of baroque-formed plates, dishes and table-trays.

Peter Hoffnagel was the owner of a short-lived factory at ØSTERBRO where his faience owed much to both the form and decoration of the wares of the Herrebøe and Schleswig factories. His rococo shapes were mostly decorated in blue and manganese-purple, to which gilding was sometimes added.

The manufacture of faience was started in the two Duchies of SCHLESWIG-HOLSTEIN in 1754. J. C. L. von Lücke was granted a Royal privilege in that year which gave him numerous financial advantages to ensure the success of the undertaking, but he proved to be totally incompetent and was succeeded in 1756 by other managers. From 1758 to about 1800 the factory operated very successfully under Johann Rambusch and his son. The concern finally closed in 1814.

The principal market for the earthenwares produced at Schleswig was Copenhagen, and in complying with an order which prohibited the importation of blue-and-white faience, the majority of their wares were decorated in only high-temperature blue, manganese-purple, with the occasional addition of green. One of the popular Schleswig forms was a bowl in the form of a bishop's mitre, made especially for a popular punch drink, known as 'bishop'.

Some quite attractive tablewares were produced at ECKERNFÔRDE between 1765 and about 1771 under the ownership of J. N. Otte. The early wares were simple and teacaddies, coffee-pots, etc. were usually painted in only high-temperature colours, but from the time of the arrival at the factory of Johann Buchwald and Abraham Leihamer, more ambitious shapes were produced, decorated in a palette which included a range of strong primary colours.

J. S. F. Tännich set up a thriving faience factory at KIEL in 1763, which enjoyed the patronage of the Duke of Holstein. Between 1763 and 1768 some excellent tablewares were produced, including plates, with pierced basket-work rims or wave-like edges, sometimes decorated with enamel flower-painting as good as the best seen on the faience of Strasbourg. Following the departure of Tännich and the arrival of Buchwald, his daughter, and son-in-law Abraham Leihamer, the early pleasing shapes gave way to wares with too much applied and vividly coloured leaf and flower decoration.

The only major concern manufacturing faience in Norway was established by Peter Hoffnagel in about 1758 at HERREBØE, which he sold to a company in 1762 who produced faience for a further period of ten years. The Herrebøe interpretation of the rococo style is unique in its pleasing, but wild, approach.

Louis Fournier produced some soft-paste porcelain in COPENHAGEN between 1759 and 1765, but his productions are very rare consisting primarily of small tablewares decorated in French styles.

In 1779 King Christian VII took over the hard-paste porcelain manufactory started in 1775 by F. H. Müller; this became the 'Royal Danish Porcelain Factory' which is still in operation to this day. The early wares, which were of a cold grey tone, were mostly decorated in simple underglaze-blue patterns owing much to Meissen. The majority of the 18th-century tablewares were of a more severe classical character, sometimes more appropriate for earthenware than porcelain. Many complete tea- and coffee-services were produced in shapes which were well over-shadowed by the excellent painting of birds, flowers, landscapes or figures, mostly by painters who had previously worked for the factory in Berlin.

(For colour illustration, see pp. 36, 37 and 38)

SWITZERLAND
Faience & Porcelain

Zurich & Nyon

Some of the most pleasing tablewares were produced at ZURICH where, between 1763 and 1790, both porcelain and faience were made under the direction of Adam Spengler.

The early soft-paste porcelain was made for only a very short period and is consequently exceedingly rare. The pieces which have been recorded include the usual range of small tablewares, all marked with a 'Z' either painted in underglaze-blue or incised.

From about 1765 the necessary clays were obtained from Lorraine, enabling Spengler to produce some really beautiful wares, despite the fact that the available raw materials resulted in a rather smoky-hue glaze. The productions consisted mostly of well-proportioned tablewares which, although rather thickly potted, were of pleasing rococo forms including globular teapots, pear-shaped jugs, shallow cups and plates with shell-moulded rims or moulded basket-work.

The painted decoration included typical Swiss landscapes—in most cases the work of Salomon Gessner who occasionally signed his work—Meissen-type flower-painting with shadows and insects as associated with Klinger, and the earlier Meissen stylised flowers in the Oriental fashion (*indianische Blumen*). In order to cater for all classes of customer the factory also produced considerable quantities of tablewares decorated only in underglaze-blue, with the popular 'onion' pattern (*Zwiebelmuster*) and the 'aster' pattern (*Blaublümchenmuster*). The engravings of Johann Esaias Nilson (1721-1788) were used to inspire other talented decorators, such as Heinrich Thomann and J. H. Bleuler, both of whom specialised in landscapes.

There was a great similarity between the decoration used on Zurich porcelain and on its faience, but use was also made on the coarser ware of transfer-prints, engraved in most instances by Heinrich Bruppacher.

The manufacture of a hard-paste porcelain at NYON, in Switzerland, did not start until 1781, surviving until 1813. Jakob Dortu from Berlin and Ferdinand Müller of Frankenthal were partners until about 1786 when, for a short period, the concern came under the direction of J. G. Zinkernagel, who built new premises in the rue de la Porcelaine. Dortu returned to the factory in 1787 and remained in charge until its closure.

The porcelains of Nyon were of a cold white material, produced from Limoges clays. The forms and decoration of all their wares showed hardly any originality, and pieces without the well-known factory-mark of a fish, painted in underglaze-blue, are very difficult to distinguish from the contemporary wares of the many Paris factories. Diaper grounds, butterflies, sprigs, garlands, trophies and all the usual classical motifs were applied in a monotonously dull manner, albeit with great competence. Sèvres-like coloured grounds and the popular underglaze-blue patterns of Meissen were frequently imitated.

In his book *German Porcelain and Faience* Dr Ducret illustrates what he describes as a unique *trembleuse* (covered cup and saucer) painted and signed by Etienne Gide, a famous Geneva miniaturist, who worked at Nyon from 1789 to 1804. Other well-painted landscapes and figures in polychrome, or *en camaieu,* are attributed to this exceptional artist.

The mark of a stylised fish must not be considered sufficient evidence of Nyon manufacture, for this same mark has been copied a great deal by many more recent German concerns on very good imitations of genuine Nyon.

(For colour illustration, see p. 47)

FRANCE
Earthenware

Henri Deux

A class of early French pottery not likely to come the way of the average collector is known as Henri Deux or Saint-Porchaire ware. For many years pottery was ascribed non-specifically to various areas of France and it was not until the late 19th century that E. Bonnaffé produced evidence of the name Saint-Porchaire being used during the mid-16th century in relation to cups, goblets, basins, ewers, etc. in a black-and-white earthenware. In addition Bonnaffé discovered the names of potters working in Saint-Porchaire (near Bressuire, Deux-Sèvres) at that same period.

It is not possible to decorate clay with a clay of a contrasting colour and still retain the crisp detail if the ware is to be covered with a lead-glaze; there is always the tendency for the colours to mingle in the very fluid glaze during the firing. This leaves two alternatives: firstly, the very heavy-handed process of slip-trailing, practised by the Staffordshire potters from the second half of the 17th century; secondly, the method of inlaying the contrasting colour into prepared sunken areas, produced with the aid of metal stamps or roulette wheels, as used by book-binders when 'tooling' leather covers. The second method was used at Saint-Porchaire. These inlaid clays were usually black, brown or red, inlaid into a creamy coloured ground, somewhat similar to an English cream-coloured earthenware, but low-fired. Occasionally coloured glazes of blue, purple or green were sparingly added.

The earliest Henri II wares were in typical Renaissance shapes, mostly derived from metal prototypes, but during the second half of the 16th century a large variety of tablewares were produced including salt-cellars, ewers and goblets. The majority of the sixty-four, or so, examples of this rare ware known to exist, was made during the third quarter of the century, the earliest even predating King Henri II. Some interesting reproductions of these wares were made from about 1875 by the Staffordshire firm of Mintons.

Another type of early French pottery which prompted with justification the production of many 19th-century fakes, is known as Palissy ware. Bernard Palissy was born at Saintes (Charente-Inferieure) in about 1510 and he lived to about eighty years of age. He was trained as a glass painter, but it has been suggested that he was so impressed by what was most probably a Saint-Porchaire cup, that he became a potter.

Palissy became best known for his tablewares which were moulded after nature—fishes, lizards, snakes, shells, rocks and grass—although the style of decoration limited their use as practical tablewares in most instances. The beauty of Palissy's earthenware is in the clear coloured glazes of blue, brown, purple, yellow and green, the like of which did not appear again until used by the Wood family of Burslem, Staffordshire from about 1770.

There seems little doubt that Palissy had many imitators, both contemporary and later; this is almost certainly the case with many examples moulded after Renaissance silver forms. In order to cater for the tastes of 19th century collectors, many reproductions of Palissy wares were produced in France and elsewhere. Charles Avisseau of Tours, Georges Pull of Paris, Lesme of Limoges, and Mafra and Son from Caldas, Portugal, all made copies of these popular wares. Most of the reproductions were unmarked, like the originals, but can usually be detected by their greater weight, 'muddy' colours, and if made from moulds taken from originals, they are proportionately smaller, owing to the shrinkage of the clay.

(For colour illustration, see p. 48)

Faience

Nevers

Italian potters were producing tin-glazed earthenware in Nevers from the late 16th century, but their wares are very difficult to distinguish from those being made in other early French centres. Large ewers, similar both in form and painting to those of Urbino, were certainly being produced at Nevers, usually of a fairly high-fired reddish-clay, with dragon-like handles, painted in blue, greenish-yellow and manganese-purple.

It was during the first half of the 17th century that the very fine large dishes were produced at Nevers, painted in a more original style with a pale manganese which was often used as an outline to other soft-shades of high-temperature colours. The Urbino style of filling the entire upper surface of a dish with a picture was replaced by the more traditional painting of a distinct border-pattern of either figure subjects or flowers, framing the main subject matter, which was often mythological or biblical. Jacques Conrade is particularly associated with painting of this type.

During the second half of the 17th century a new style of decoration was introduced referred to as *bleu Persan,* a somewhat doubtful term, as there is little doubt that it was Chinese porcelain of the Ming dynasty which suggested the use of a dark-blue ground with opaque white, yellow, and orange decoration. The painting of flowers and foliage, with occasional birds, can be quite attractive, but the forms of some of the wares tend to be rather heavy and clumsy. It should be noted that other factories also decorated their wares in a somewhat similar manner, including Delft, Saint-Omer, Rouen and Lambeth, the latter usually using only white decoration. It has also been suggested that this style of decoration could also have been inspired by 16th-century Limoges enamels.

The late-17th-century faience potters provide the silver collector with good records of just what the contemporary silver would have looked like. The majority of the original metal unfortunately went into the melting-pots to help King Louis XIV pay for his costly wars. In his book on *French Faience* Arthur Lane stated that the potters of Nevers were producing excellent wares inspired by Chinese porcelain before the potters of Delft. The French certainly did 'borrow' many Chinese styles of decoration, but they were usually applied to typical baroque metal forms.

Although production continued throughout the 18th century and to the present day, Nevers never again produced the beautifully decorated wares which had won it fame during the 17th century. Plates, jugs and pilgrim-bottles were rather clumsily made and painted in a rough manner with patron-saints *(faience patronymiques),* or emblems, sometimes accompanied by the owner's name.

The potters of Nevers rarely adopted recognised factory-marks, so the only guide is the occasional name, or initials, of a recorded potter or painter.

TAZZA *of tin-glazed earthenware (faience), painted in white and yellow on a dark-blue ground (décor persan or bleu de Nevers). French (Nevers), 1650–80; dia. 24 cm/9½ in.*

Opposite: TUREEN *and* COVER *of soft-paste porcelain, painted in enamel colours. French (Saint-Cloud), c.1750; dia. 34 cm/13½ in.*

Overleaf: CUP *and* SAUCER *of soft-paste porcelain with tin-glaze, decorated in the Japanese 'Kakiemon' manner with enamel colours. French (Chantilly), 1730–55.* COFFEE-CUP *and* SAUCER *of soft-paste porcelain, painted with underglaze-blue sprigs. French (Chantilly), c.1770.* MILK-JUG *of soft-paste porcelain, decorated in enamel colours. French (Mennecy), c.1760.*

Rouen

The earliest tin-glazed earthenwares produced in France were primarily intended for the use of the apothecary, or as tiles; this also applied to the Italian potters. These wares are best referred to as maiolica rather than faience, because of their close association in every way with the Italian wares.

Very few tin-glazed wares appear to have been made in Rouen during the early years of the 17th century. It was not until 1644 that Nicolas Poirel obtained a privilege for the manufacture, which he in turn passed to Edmé Poterat, the potter whom we know best as being associated with early French soft-paste porcelain. The early wares of Poterat included some dishes on which the only decoration was the owner's coat-of-arms.

Rouen is probably best associated with the so-called *lambrequin* style of decoration which became so popular from the last decade of the 17th century. Louis Poterat, the son of Edmé, is given credit for the introduction of this style of decorating pottery, but his Rouen monopoly expired in 1696 and many other potters then began to operate in the same city, making similar wares which were decorated in the same manner.

The term *lambrequin* is related to hanging draperies, designs which were used together with festoons, lacework, diapered panels and formal scrolls, in a high-temperature blue painted on to the tin-glaze prior to firing. These designs owe much to the engravings of Jean Bérain. It is sometimes difficult to distinguish between the *'style rayonnant'* and *lambrequin*, the former style generally being applied in a radiating manner to dishes, the latter usually suspended from the borders of upright wares. These designs were occasionally, and not too successfully, enriched with a high-temperature red, derived from iron-oxide. Another style of decoration consisted of tracery which had much in common with the decorative ironwork of the period, known as *'ferronerie'*. These decorations are shown to advantage on some of the large dishes which could hold as many as twenty partridges, or fifteen chickens. Once the King had given his blessing to faience by using it in the building of the *'Trianon de Porcelaine'*, the material became acceptable at the court as an alternative to silver for tablewares. Many tablewares were produced including complete armorial services which were usually only decorated with blue—ice-pails, salt-cellars, sugar-dredgers (a form of large pepper-pot) for powdered sugar and spice-boxes. From about 1740 copies of the work of such artists as Watteau and Boucher were often used on small plates with borders of rococo style enclosing pastoral scenes, some of which would have been considered rather *risqué* at that time.

From the early 18th century Rouen produced a well-known class of large cider-jug, which might well be considered a form of 'peasant-art' and was often decorated with the name of the recipient, a date and a landscape or a figure of a patron saint. The 18th-century Rouen decorators were never very successful in their attempts at portraying the delicate style of asymmetrical curves associated with the new rococo styles, their designs were definitely painted in a much too heavy style. One type of decoration which has remained popular with Rouen tablewares from about 1745 to the present day, is the *décor à la corne*, the cornucopia. The boldly painted cone-shaped device is still used on many 'souvenir'-type wares, often showing a tell-tale type of 'crazing' that can best be likened to a dried-up pond, the glaze completely parting, leaving sunken lines between the fragments.

(For colour illustration, see p. 49)

Moustiers & Marseilles

The small town of Moustiers, about sixty miles north-east of Marseilles, came into prominence as a faience centre as early as 1679 when Pierre Clérissy started to manufacture some large dishes and basins, painted in high-temperature blue, with subjects taken from engravings by Tempesta, Leclerc and Frans Floris. The shapes were simple on the whole with large areas decorated with excellent copies of the original engravings, often coupled with border patterns of *lambrequin* or *ferronerie*.

Moustiers faience is, however, much better known by the wares made at the factory set up in 1738 by Joseph Olerys and Jean-Baptiste Laugier. They favoured a style of decoration which was used generally from about 1710, the designs being based on a revival of the Renaissance grotesques, but used in a more delicate and fanciful manner, often combined with frames of arabesque scrolls. These designs were inspired by the engravings of Jean Beráin (*d.* 1711), who, as Designer to the King in the Department of 'Occasional Expenses', was responsible for the settings to the various court festivities including firework displays and *masques*. The same decorations often featured on faience table-services, which by this time were becoming popular with all classes of society. Plates and large dishes appear to have been the most common wares produced, but *écuelles* (individual covered soup-bowls with stands), coffee-pots, *biberons* (feeding-cups), helmet-shaped ewers and sugar-casters were among other popular wares made for the dining-table. The dominant colour used on those pieces was a high-temperature orange-yellow, to which was often added green or purple. The monogram 'O L' is attributed to Olerys and Laugier but somewhat similar wares were produced by Fouque and Pelloquin (1749–83). The later wares of Gaspard Féraud (1779–92) shows a preference for mythological and pastoral scenes, or naturalistic flowers, all painted in the high-temperature palette.

Although faience was made at Marseilles from the late 17th century onwards, the reputation of this centre is concerned with the many tablewares made during the third quarter of the 18th century, nearly all of which were decorated with enamel colours. This new and popular fashion of decorating faience in a style normally associated with porcelain, was adopted by several different potters in the area. The

TUREEN *of tin-glazed earthenware (faience), painted with enamel colours, and marked 'VP' monogram. French (Marseilles, factory of Veuve Perrin), c.1770; wdth. 35.5 cm/ 13⅞ in.*

style is best described as an 'unlaboured composition'—the flowers painted as if the actual blooms had been carelessly dropped upon the ware. Credit for the introduction of such painting is given to the factory of Veuve Perrin (Widow Perrin), where Honoré Savy was in partnership prior to starting his own production in about 1764. Flowers, fishes, fishing equipment, insects, birds, fruit and vegetables were all treated in this manner—the subject matter often suggesting the geographical location of the city itself. Painting of this quality has been much harder to reproduce successfully than the equally popular interpretation of Pillement's engravings in typical rococo *Chinoiseries*.

The forms of the majority of later Marseilles wares were fully sympathetic to the style of decoration, although the rococo theme is less evident than in either Strasbourg or Niderviller ware. Borders of plates and dishes tended to have wavy edges, whereas moulded fruit, vegetables, animals, and fishes served usefully as knobs, handles of tureens, and so on.

Joseph-Gaspard Robert started a factory in 1759 and is credited with the introduction of decoration outlined in black and washed over with a pleasing translucent green enamel.

Strasbourg

By far the most important of the 18th-century French faience factories was that established in Strasbourg by Charles-François Hannong in 1721, with a second concern being opened at Haguenau in 1724: both were in the hands of his son Paul by 1737. Until about 1740 all the wares produced at Strasbourg were decorated in the usual limited range of high-temperature colours, but from that time onwards the greater range of enamel colours were used with great success.

The majority of the wares produced during the active years of the founder were painted in under-glaze-blue, in styles very closely related to those used with such success at Rouen. Plates and dishes with thick moulded edges appear to have dominated the output. The tureen invariably was the centre-piece of the French dining-table so an interesting raised plat-form, a *surtout de table,* was produced, about twenty-inches in length, with four candle-holders around the edge, decorated with an original version of the stylised Oriental flower-painting with insects first used on Meissen porcelain.

Paul Hannong's success owed a great deal to the help he enlisted from various German porcelain workers and it was following the arrival of Adam Friedrich von Löwenfinck's family that such success-ful use was made of the deep rich crimson enamel—the 'purple of Cassius'. It was Andreas Cassius of Leyden who first discovered how to achieve this colour by using chloride-of-gold. The same colour was later used on Chinese porcelain decorated in the palette of the *famille rose.*

Following the death of Paul Hannong in 1760, the Strasbourg and Haguenau factories were under the direction of his son Pierre-Antoine who proved a poor successor and in 1762 both factories were purchased by another son, Joseph-Adam Hannong. Joseph-Adam ran into financial trouble with both the French tax-collectors and creditors who withdrew their loans and he was forced to close both factories in 1782.

The arrival of Löwenfinck coincided with the beginning of a new period of unsurpassed flower-painting, the Oriental-type flowers were replaced with those which had again originated at Meissen, the naturalistic *deutsche Blumen.* A Strasbourg barber's bowl in the Historisches Museum at Basle is painted in this manner, and signed by Adam von Löwenfinck.

The fanciful rococo shapes used at Strasbourg owe a great deal to the skills of Paul Hannong who suc-ceeded in producing a range of wares which in many instances equalled the same delicacy normally only possible with the finer material of porcelain. Some remarkable tablewares were produced, dishes moulded with vegetables and fruits and a great variety of tureens made in the form of cabbages, cauliflowers, boar's heads, etc.

The factory-mark during the years of Paul (*c.* 1740-60) consisted of slightly varying forms of a 'PH' monogram in high-temperature blue, some-times with green or purple additional marks, usually the initials of the painter.

The faience produced during the ownership of Joseph Hannong was very similar to that made by his father, but the naturalistic flower-painting *(fleurs fines)* and the stylised Oriental flowers were all painted in a less organised manner, at times having a great deal in common with those on the wares of Veuve Perrin. The coarser type of Strasbourg painting with black outlines has been reproduced during recent years.

(For colour illustration, see p. 50)

Minor factories

The success of the faience factories at Strasbourg was responsible for the setting up of other neighbouring concerns, the most important being that at NIDER-VILLER, which was founded in 1754 by Baron Jean-Louis de Beyerlé who had the assistance of a number of workers who had previously been with the Hannongs at Strasbourg, including the painter and chemist Antoine Ansett, later to take over as Director. The factory was purchased in 1770 by the Comte de Custine who was active in the American revolution and beheaded in the French. The factory eventually closed in 1827.

The early Niderviller wares had a great deal in common with those of Strasbourg, but their rococo forms were less successful, tending to be over-decorated in a rather fussy manner, resulting in confusion between moulding and painting. These features are especially noticeable on tureens and pierced basket-work plates.

Jacques Chambrette established a factory in 1731 at LUNEVILLE, with a branch factory at SAINT-CLÉMENT; both factories are better known for their biscuit figures of either 'terre-de-pipe' (pipe-clay) or hard-paste porcelain, but they also produced a wide range of tablewares of extravagant rococo forms.

The factory of Luneville was under the direction of Keller and Guérin and their descendants for most of the 19th century and during this time a fairly common kind of plate seems to have been made in large quantities, painted in crimson and green enamels with rather 'blowsy' flowers or stylised cockatoo-type birds.

A small factory at SCEAUX, founded in about 1748 by de Bey, produced some very superior wares, as might be expected of a factory producing a fine soft-paste porcelain. As the factory was very near to Paris, its manager, Jacques Chapelle, responded to current court taste and as a result many of its early wares show great similarity to the beautiful porcelains of Mennecy and Vincennes. The later tablewares favoured the Louis-Seize styles.

Faience was being made at SAINT-AMAND-LES-EAUX as early as 1718 by P. J. Fauquez in whose family the concern remained until the French Revolution. Some very pretty tablewares were produced from about 1760, when the glaze was stained to a bluish-grey and lace-like opaque white decoration (bianco-

PLATE *of tin-glazed earthenware (faience), painted in purple and marked 'S' in purple. French (St. Omer), 2nd half of 18th c.; dia. 24 cm/$9\frac{3}{8}$ in.*

sopra-bianco) was used together with blue or manganese-purple painting of flowers or landscapes. Sometime around 1800 the factory was acquired by the Bettignies family, best known for their many reproductions of wares of an earlier date.

A factory which continued to produce a popular form of faience well into the 19th century was set up in 1785 at LES ISLETTES, near Verdun. The wares were obviously influenced by the earlier Strasbourg pieces but have no similarity as far as quality is concerned, being extremely coarse in every way. Their wide variety of painting, which included birds, flowers, and Chinese figures were usually applied in vivid colours, with outlines of black or brown.

Porcelain

Rouen & Saint-Cloud

Serious attempts to produce a porcelain comparable to that which had been made in China since the 9th century were not really justified until, during the second half of the 17th century, the upper classes throughout Europe adopted the new social habit of tea-drinking and it was in France that we find potters experimenting with the production of an artificial porcelain in imitation of the Oriental material.

There seems little doubt that Louis Poterat of Rouen did produce what must have been a very limited quantity of soft-paste porcelain. He was granted a patent relating to both porcelain and faience in 1673, but at that period the word 'porcelain' was used very loosely, and in 1694, when he applied for a renewal of his patent, he stated that the secret (of porcelain manufacture) was very little used, the petitioners devoting themselves rather to faience making. The tablewares attributed to Poterat all show a thin potting of a glassy-type, thin paste; the underglaze-blue painting, in Rouen faience style, is a dark inky blue, whilst the brilliant glaze has a slight greenish tint.

The first patent taken out in Saint-Cloud in 1667 named Claude and François Réverend as the potters manufacturing 'faience and counterfeiting porcelain equalling and even surpassing in beauty that which

comes from the Indies of the East'. Unfortunately their porcelains have not been identified with any certainty.

'As perfect as the Chinese' was also claimed for the porcelain produced at Saint-Cloud, and even though this claim must be considered a little rash, the descendants of Pierre Chicaneau did produce some beautiful soft-paste porcelain tablewares until the factory closed in 1766. The factory was on the estate of 'Monsieur', the Duke of Orleans, brother of the King, and so enjoyed both his patronage and protection. The writings of Dr Martin Lister tell in a very flattering way of the fine porcelain being produced at Saint-Cloud in 1698, but he does complain of the high cost, 'Chocolate Cups, askt Crowns apiece', and 'Furniture of Tea Tables at four hundred Livres a Sett'.

The creamy soft-paste porcelain was an extremely difficult material to work with, necessitating thickly thrown or moulded shapes, made less apparent by careful selection of forms and appropriate decoration.

Despite the fact that a mark of a *fleur-de-lys* or a sun-face, usually in blue, was supposedly used as a mark from 1696, and a 'St C' over 'T', for Henri Trou from after 1722, it is difficult to date accurately the tablewares of Saint-Cloud, except when they are fitted with obviously contemporary silver mounts, with appropriate year marks.

The *lambrequin* pendant decoration (*see* p.63) must obviously be an indication of an early date. This form of decoration was often accompanied with attractive reeding or gadrooning which had the effect of producing a much less bulky appearance.

The Saint-Cloud designers were influenced by the so-called *blanc de Chine,* the type of milky-white porcelain produced in the Fukien province of China from the early 17th century. Cups, saucers, jugs and teapots were frequently produced with moulded scale-patterns, most probably suggested by the artichoke, rather than the pineapple. Many of these various forms had one thing in common, very substantial handles of square or rectangular section. The saucer with a raised ring, to fit the base of the matching cup (*trembleuse*) was also a popular Saint-Cloud feature.

ICE-PAIL *of tin-glazed earthenware (faience), painted in high-temperature blue and red in the* lambrequin *style. French (Rouen), 1725–40; ht. 16.5 cm/6½ in.*

(For colour illustration, see p. 59)

Chantilly

The soft-paste porcelain factory at Chantilly was founded in 1725 by Louis-Henri de Bourbon, Prince de Condé, under the direction of Ciquaire Cirou. The factory continued under various directors of little account until 1792 when it was taken over by Christopher Potter, an Englishman. It finally closed in 1800, but several 19th-century factories continued to make wares which were similar in form and decoration but in a less attractive hard-paste porcelain, usually decorated in underglaze-blue.

The Prince de Condé was a great admirer of the 17th-century Japanese porcelains made at Arita and decorated in the so-called Kakiemon manner. The Typical creamy soft-paste porcelain of Chantilly was entirely unsuitable for decorating in the same manner as the hard-paste porcelain of Japan and, in order to remedy this, tin-oxide was added to the glaze to make it white and opaque, and so providing a much more accurate ground colour for Japanese designs, which at that period were called 'décor Coréen'—a misnomer caused by the common belief that much Japanese porcelain originated in Korea. The majority of the forms used together with Kakiemon-style painting were also suggested by the Japanese, although often simplified into softer, more delicate forms to cater for the French taste.

Teapots often took the shape of melons or pomegranates; cups and dishes were often of peach form, whilst many cups, saucers and bowls followed the popular Japanese octagonal forms.

Following the death of the Prince in 1740, the wares fashioned and decorated in the Japanese manner gradually gave way to the silver forms which were being popularised by the new factory of Vincennes, although new and original shapes were also introduced. One particularly pleasing shape made at Chantilly was the shallow quatrefoil écuelle, cover and stand, with a very distinctive knob formed from three open flowers of the convulvulus type. The painting on these mid-18th-century wares was applied in defiance of the strict monopoly granted to the Vincennes and Sèvres factories, which endeavoured to restrict the use of polychrome enamel decoration on the wares of rival French porcelain factories. A dull crimson monochrome enamel was sometimes used to portray chubby cupids, painted in the Boucher manner.

ICE-PAIL *of soft-paste porcelain, painted in purple enamel, and marked with a hunting-horn in red enamel. French (Chantilly), 1750-60; ht. 14.5 cm/5¾ in.*

Between 1755 and 1780 large quantities of very pleasing tablewares were produced including an abundance of plates decorated with roses, tulips, or pinks, in underglaze-blue. Even better known by today's collectors are the so-called 'Chantilly sprigs' copied at about the same time on the wares produced by Thomas Turner at Caughley, in Shropshire, England.

(For colour illustration, see p. 60)

Mennecy

One of the most beautiful soft-paste porcelains ever produced was made at the factory first set up in 1734 by Louis-François de Neufville, Duc de Villeroy, under the direction of François Barbin. The factory was first established in Paris, moving to Mennecy in 1748, and to Bourg-la-Reine in 1773, where production was continued by Joseph Jullien and his descendants until 1806. It is almost certain that the last twenty years or so were spent only on the manufacture of English-type cream-coloured earthenware and faience.

The 'milky-white' porcelain was usually covered with a 'wet-looking' brilliant glaze, an ideal surface to absorb the enamel decoration which, in the early period, often consisted of Kakiemon patterns as used at Chantilly, but now looking rather unfamiliar on a creamier-coloured ground. Chinese *blanc-de-Chine* relief patterns of the prunus blossom and other similar relief decoration were often used on tablewares left in the white.

The early styles of decoration soon gave way to those currently in production at Vincennes and Sèvres; the protection of the Duc de Villeroy obviously prevented the monopolies of those factories being applied too harshly, although, it is interesting to note, the rule forbidding the application of gilding was complied with, and even more pleasing rose-pink or bright blue enamel was used for edging.

One of the most popular Mennecy forms was the simple upright cylinder, used for cups and covered boxes of varying heights. Teapots were either globular, or egg-shaped, with a low foot rim and a typical early French ear-shaped handle.

The same close spiral reeding was used on some small attractive custard-cups as also made at Marieberg in Sweden; fine basket-work moulding took on a pleasing appearance under the soft glaze. One of the most pleasing products of Mennecy was the shell-shaped sugar-basin, with cover and stand.

The enamel decoration used at Mennecy can hardly be considered original and it was only the way it was applied that made it so attractive. Effective use was made of Meissen's naturalistically styled flower-painting *(deutsche Blumen)*, together with a liberal use of Mennecy's own characteristic rose-pink and bright blue. The bird-painting and figures amid lightly sketched landscapes were also obviously inspired by the wares of Vincennes and Sèvres.

Mennecy was among the many factories which produced some very attractive, but rather unpracticable, porcelain handles for cutlery. Examples are known, painted in Kakiemon and marked with the 'D V' factory-mark (Duc de Villeroy), but it is very difficult to attribute any unmarked handles with any degree of accuracy, although certain forms of moulding or painting do sometimes help.

(For colour illustration, see p. 60)

TEAPOT *of soft-paste porcelain, painted in enamel colours, and marked 'D' incised and 'M' in purple. French (Mennecy), 1755–60; ht. 12.5 cm/5 in.*

Vincennes & Sèvres

Some of Europe's finest soft-paste porcelain was produced in a royal château at Vincennes which is still standing today. It was in about 1738 that Orry de Vignory and Orry de Fulvey were granted permission from Louis XV to start experiments at Vincennes aided by Gilles and Robert Dubois who had previously worked at Chantilly, but the earliest production of porcelain at the château was due mainly to the knowledge and industry of François Gravant, assistant to the Dubois brothers.

There does not appear to have been a regular production of porcelain from Vincennes until about 1745, from which time some really beautiful wares were produced until 1756 when the undertaking was transferred to a new factory at Sèvres, near Madame de Pompadour's Château de Bellevue, between Paris and Versailles.

Apart from a few early examples, the wares produced in this new beautiful soft-paste porcelain were entirely unrelated to the hard-paste forms and decorations popularised throughout Europe by Meissen. Vincennes made much more use of coloured grounds and superior quality gilding, seen at its best on the early underglaze-blue (*bleu lapis*) which was introduced in about 1749 by the factory chemist, Hellot. These blue-ground wares were at first decorated in reserved panels with some fine gilt silhouettes of birds, attributed to the painter and gilder, Mutel. Many of the early figure paintings after Boucher or Watteau, were painted in crimson monochrome.

The fashion for using porcelain figures as table-decorations was not popular in France and more attention was paid to the actual wares which in themselves were so finely decorated and generally designed to serve a specific function, making any further decorative porcelain entirely unnecessary. It is recorded that what might well have been the first complete dinner-service made for King Louis XV in 1754, included two soup-tureens (one for stew), eight plates for *hors d'oeuvres*, eight fruit dishes, two oval sugar-bowls, two cheese-dishes, two butter-dishes, four jam-pots, six mustard-pots, eight salt-cellars, eighteen individual wine-coolers, various platters and three dozen dishes. The entire service was decorated in enamel colours with flowers and cost 15,144 livres. The wares of Vincennes were expensive and in the luxury class—a breakfast-set

comprising cup and saucer, milk jug, covered sugar-bowl and a small tray was priced at 204 livres. Small ice-pails were particularly popular and were usually only sparsely decorated leaving large areas of the fine porcelain showing to advantage.

The transfer from Vincennes to Sèvres in 1756 was not in any way marked by any distinct changes in forms or decoration and many of the early styles remained popular for many years.

The work of the painters and gilders employed at Sèvres is well authenticated by the factory records. The painted wares are usually marked with a device, or the painter's initials; we also know when most of these workers were employed at the factory and what type of decoration they specialised in. Similarly, gilt marks can often be traced to particular gilders, and so it is often possible to decide just which year an item was made and who was responsible for the decoration. This detailed information often makes it very easy to recognise a 19th-century fake or a piece of genuine 18th-century Vincennes or Sèvres porcelain which has been subjected to new or additional decoration during the 19th century.

It was appreciated at quite an early date that a large area of a strong ground colour was offending to the eye and so a series of attractive designs were introduced to tone these colours down. Gilding was often used on the *bleu-lapis,* or later *bleu de roi* enamel in a variety of styles, the most popular being a form of 'crazy-paving', where the entire ground was broken into a network of gilding enclosing pebble-like shapes, called '*caillouté*'. Another variation was

Opposite: *A group of veilleuses.* CHINESE MANDARIN *and* COMPANION FIGURE *of hard-paste porcelain. Bohemian (Schlaggenwald, Slavkov), c.1840.* PERSONNAGE *in the form of a Marquise, of hard-paste porcelain, marked 'JP' in underglaze-blue. French (Fontainebleau, made by Jacob Petit), c.1840.* TEA-WARMER *in the form of a tower, of hard-paste porcelain. Russian (Moscow, made by A. Popoff at Gorbunovo), c.1835.* FOODWARMER *of soft-paste porcelain, probably painted by Sioux âiné. French (Sèvres), undated but made c.1770.* FOODWARMER *of hard-paste porcelain, marked 'B' in underglaze-blue. French (Boisette); ht. (Personnage) 35 cm/ 14 in.*

Overleaf: DISH *and* POSSET-POT *of lead-glazed earthenware with slip-trailed decoration. English, the dish made by Ralph Toft and dated 1677, the posset-pot dated 1696.*

Vincennes & Sèvres

Overleaf: *Part of a* TOY TEA-SERVICE *of tin-glazed earthenware (Delftware), decorated with high-temperature blue. English (probably Liverpool), c.1760; ht. (teapot) 9.5 cm/ 4 in.*

Opposite: *A selection of Staffordshire lead-glazed earthenware. Whieldon type* CUP *and* SAUCER *with variegated glaze, c.1755. Astbury-Whieldon type* TEAPOT, *c.1760. Whieldon-Wedgwood type* SUCRIER *and* COVER *in the form of a cauliflower, 1755-60. Whieldon type* CREAMER, *c.1760. Whieldon type* DISH, *1750-60; ht. (teapot) 12.7 cm/5 in.*

termed '*vermiculé*' 'worm-like'. Sometimes gilding or another coloured enamel was used to cover a large area of coloured ground with small dotted rings around a central dot, this was referred to as '*oeil-de-perdrix*', partridge-eye. This class of decoration was especially popular on the *écuelle*, a shallow covered bowl with two handles and a saucer-like stand—a slightly deeper version is at times referred to as a *bouillon* cup. A later and less attractive ground effect was the *briquette* where the whole area around a reserved painting was painted to simulate bricks, laid in the contemporary Flemish bond: all the bricks being laid length-wise. One of the most admired ground colours introduced at Sèvres is said to have been invented by the enameller Xhrouet in 1757, this colour has for many years been referred to as *rose Pompadour* but in the factory records only the simple term '*rose*' is used.

The wares made at Vincennes were occasionally marked with the crossed 'L' cypher of Louis XV which was adopted as a factory-mark in about 1750. From 1753 a letter was included denoting the year of manufacture, 'A' for 1753, 'B' for 1754, etc. and a second alphabetical cycle starting with 'AA' continued until the factory was taken over by the French Republic in 1793 (PP).

Tea-drinking was one of the many social pastimes of the French Court and nobility and so *cabaret* services were made in large numbers. The term '*cabaret*' originally referred to a tea-table but it was adopted to refer to a set of vessels composing a small breakfast or tea-service, depending upon the number of pieces, and so the name varies. The largest service would include a tray *(plateau)*, with teapot, coffee- or chocolate-pot, a stand for the latter, milk-jug, creamer, sugar-bowl—usually with cover—caddy, jam-pot and cups and saucers. A smaller, less complete

range was termed a *déjeuner;* the single items for tea for one, a *solitaire;* and 'tea-for-two', a *tête-à-tête*. By about 1763 these sets were being produced in about twelve different forms, named according to the shape of the tray. The shapes of the various items tended to differ slightly, with the exception of the the teapot which remained fairly consistent—ovoid, with curving spout, ear-shaped handle, and an almost flat lid with a tight flower-shape for a knob. This shape was named '*Verdun*', after one of the main shareholders of the factory. The original drawing of the '*thèyere Verdun*' (Verdun teapot) is still preserved at Sèvres, dated 1753.

The Wallace Collection in London includes some of the finest and most decorative Sèvres ever produced, including an example of the table-centrepiece referred to as *vaisseau à mât* (ship with mast). The table-like stand with four scrolled legs supports the main body of the vessel, which has bowsprits at either end in the form of lion-masks. The cover is in the form of the ships rigging and sail, topped with a furled banner decorated with small gilt *fleur-de-lys*. This vessel, of which there are about eleven now known to exist, was most probably intended as a *pot-pourri*, but could be used for other purposes.

Until about 1772 all the wares produced at Vincennes and Sèvres were of a soft-paste porcelain (hence no hard-paste porcelain should normally bear a date-letter prior to 'T'). The materials essential for the manufacture of a hard-paste were discovered at Saint Yrieix, near Limoges, and used to produce the first '*Porcelaine Royale*' in about 1770, but not in any quantity until 1772. This means that most so-called 'jewelled Sèvres' should, if genuine, be of a hard-paste porcelain for 'jewelled porcelain' did not feature in the factory records until 1773 and was not popular until several years later. Cups and saucers are the most common wares to be seen decorated in this way; translucent enamel colours were fused over gilt or silver foil, giving the necessary radiance to the colour-glaze to simulate inlaid jewels, such as emeralds or rubies. Opaque enamels were also used to simulate turquoise and other opaque gems. Fakes of these pieces can usually be detected because they bear an earlier, incorrect date-letter.

In his excellent book on *Veilleuses* Harold Newman illustrates several examples of tea-warmers, or

Vincennes & Sèvres

veilleuses. The earliest wares of this type were apparently made as egg boilers *(coquetières);* one example in the Wallace Collection bears the date-letter for 1758 (F). The Sèvres records also tell of a *veilleuse* being sold to Madam de Pompadour in 1762.

The new hard-paste porcelain of Sèvres became available at about the same time as rococo and Louis Seize styles were giving way to the newly fashionable 'antique' style, as introduced by the younger Lagrenée, a painter. The pleasing rounded shapes were replaced by much more severe, geometrically balanced shapes, applied more to the large vases, than the tablewares. Decoration was to play a less important role and the attractive broken grounds were no longer so essential. New ground colours were introduced including brown, black, tortoise-shell *(fond écaille)* and a dark-blue enamel, sometimes marbled.

These colours were sometimes accompanied by some rather belated *Chinoiseries* by Sinsson, Le Guay, or other painters working in about 1780. Use was also made of scrolls and grotesques after Pompeiann frescoes or Raphaelesque designs. The Raphaelesque designs appear on the cups, saucers and bowls made for the use of Queen Marie-Antoinette at her Trianon and Rambouillet dairies.

From 1793, when the Sèvres factory was taken over by the French Republic, until the end of the 18th century, no new styles of either form or decoration were introduced, apart from a few large dinner-services and tea-services sometimes decorated with paintings of birds in reserves on a pale-yellow ground, copied from engravings from Buffon's *Natural History.* They were painted in some instances by Evans, who was employed at the factory from 1752 to 1806. Revolutionary emblems were also a popular form of decoration during these years.

The Consulate and Empire periods (1803-1814) saw the factory restored to a comparative state of prosperity and the Emperor Napoleon kept the factory busy with orders for large services both for his own use and for diplomatic gifts to heads of foreign states, including the Tsar of Russia, Pope Pius VII and the Count of Livourne, King of Etruria. An important service, now in the Louvre, Paris, is known as the Egyptian coffee-set. It was made in 1810 as part of Napoleon I's service at the Tuileries and was painted by Robert, Lebel and Béranger. The ground colour is of royal-blue, covered with gold hieroglyphics, the reserves contain Egyptian landscapes and monuments taken from the actual sketches made on site by Vivant Denon. The service was just finished in time to grace the table at the wedding of Napoleon to Marie-Louise.

During the last decades of the 19th century many French porcelains were faked, the kinder word 're-produced' is not appropriate here as not only were the forms and decorations imitated, but fraudulent marks were also added. The most common initials used as part-decoration on these later wares is the crowned 'N' for Napoleon, or 'L P' monogram for Louis-Philippe. The marks generally include not only the date of manufacture and the date of decoration but also the name of the royal residence for which they were supposedly made. The Tuileries is the most common, but Bizy, Breteuil, Dreux, Eu, Fontainebleau, Neuilly, Pau, Saint-Cloud or Trianon also occur. Many of these faked versions tend to have a series of unnecessary turned circles on the base in addition to the unglazed foot-rim. The crowned 'N' is not only seen on fakes of course: the Campbell Museum collection of tureens includes a tureen and soup-plates with acceptable marks for between 1861 and 1867 for wares made for Napoleon III, and these pieces are of such a simple and practical shape and form that they could well pass for a good modern continental factory's ware.

(For colour illustration, see *pp. 61 and 62)*

TEA-CADDY *of hard-paste porcelain, painted in enamel colours and gilt, marked 'JP' in underglaze-blue. French (Fontainebleau, factory of Jacob Petit), c.1835; ht. 19 cm/7½ in.*

From about 1770 onwards many factories were set up in Paris for the manufacture of a hard-paste porcelain from the clays discovered at Saint Yrieix, near Limoges. In many cases these concerns were only allowed to operate because they enjoyed the protection of a member of the royal family.

Among the most flourishing of these Paris factories was CLIGNACOURT, protected by Louis-Stanislas-Xavier, later to succeed to the throne as Louis XVI. The porcelain tablewares were of a very high quality with decoration occasionally signed by George Lamprecht who also worked at Sèvres and Vienna.

The Paris factories

Porcelain made at the RUE THIROUX was known as *porcelaine de la Reine,* since the factory had been protected by Queen Marie-Antoinette from the time of its establishment in 1775 by Leboeuf. It continued under different owners until the second half of the 19th century. The finest wares, made there during the 18th century, were decorated in the popular Paris styles.

The factory of RUE DE BONDY was established in 1780 by Dihl, under the patronage of the Duc d'Angoulême. The name of the protector is a constant reminder of the type of decoration seen on a great deal of the porcelain produced by this factory—the popular sprig pattern of stylised cornflowers. The same design appears on the wares of other French and some English factories, including Derby and Pinxton.

A highly productive Paris porcelain factory was established at LA COURTILLE in 1771 by Jean Baptiste Locré de Roissy. Its tablewares were once more the usual Paris styles and showed very little originality. Porcelain from La Courtille was obviously exported to other countries as several examples are known to have been decorated by William Billingsley, the Derby painter, who eventually set up his own factory at Nantgarw in South Wales.

There are several French hard-paste porcelain wares decorated in the extravagant, revived rococo style which is generally associated with the English factory of Rockingham (Swinton, Yorkshire). It is therefore essential to check carefully whether the material is typical hard-paste Continental porcelain or the creamier coloured English bone-china. Many of these French pieces were the work of Jacob and Mardochée Petit, who, in 1830, took over an earlier factory at FONTAINEBLEAU. These wares are sometimes marked with 'J P' in underglaze-blue.

From the time the necessary clays were first discovered in the area Limoges became the centre of the French porcelain industry, and since the beginning of the 19th century numerous factories have been engaged in the manufacture of very dull tablewares. The initials of the proprietor often accompanies the word Limoges, while the word 'France' indicates a date after 1891.

(For colour illustration, see p. 71)

ENGLAND
Tin-glazed Earthenware

The term 'Delftware' seems hardly fair when applied to the English potters who were in fact producing tin-glazed earthenware from the middle of the 16th century, and the town of Delft did not become the centre of the Dutch industry until about 1620.

Among the earliest wares produced by the Flemish and Dutch immigrant potters working in England were some jugs, the so-called 'Malling' jugs, named after an example preserved in a church in Malling, Kent. These jugs were far from original in shape and were fashioned after those first made of salt-glazed stoneware in the Rhineland.

The majority of English tin-glazed wares produced up until the first-quarter of the 18th century, were intended to serve a practical purpose rather than to be merely decorative and nearly all were for table use. The earliest dish, dated 1600, in the London Museum, is painted in high-temperature colours with what looks like a view of the Tower of London and inscribed 'The Rose is Red. The Leaves are Grene. God Save Elizabeth Our Queene'.

Many 17th-century London wares were drinking vessels; barrel-shaped mugs were especially popular, as were spouted posset-pots with two handles, enabling the imbiber to 'sup' the hot spiced and herbed drink through a spout which terminated in a strainer on the base. Many of these pots were decorated in blue with birds and rocks, in the manner of Chinese porcelain of the Wan Li period (1573–1619). Globular wine-bottles with narrow-necks were produced as alternatives to the Rhenish salt-glazed bottles, the contents being written in blue, together with a date: 'Whit' (White-wine), 'Sack' or 'Claret' were the most common names. Dates between 1629 and 1672 have been recorded.

In the middle of the 17th century the London potters were producing dishes up to about fifteen inches in diameter, in contemporary pewter or silver forms, as parts of dinner-services, which would in some cases also include rose-water dishes for rinsing the fingers at table, prior to the general use of forks. Shallow porringers with two flat handles were also produced for the table, these are at times confused with 'bleeding' bowls, as used by the barber-surgeons.

By the beginning of the 18th century the manufacture of tin-glazed earthenware had spread from London to other areas and wares were being made at Brislington, near Bristol; the city of Bristol itself; Wincanton and later at Liverpool, Dublin and Glasgow.

The 18th-century English potters engaged in the industry were becoming more acquainted with both coloured and blue-and-white Chinese export wares; this is constantly reflected in their styles of decoration, but happily they did not attempt to slavishly imitate the Oriental originals like the Delft potters of Holland did.

The popularity of tea-drinking also encouraged these same potters to endeavour to produce tea-cups, saucers, sugar-bowls, tea-caddies, cream-jugs, and teapots with matching stands, but these inevitably clumsier forms offered very little competition to the Chinese imported porcelains. Other 18th-century wares took the form of punch-bowls, ladles and monteiths (bowls with wave-like rims intended to retain the base of glasses, which were suspended in cold water). Excavations on sites of potteries have proved that the simple plate was the most common of all tablewares produced by the English galley-potter.

Slipware

Since about the middle of the 17th century North Staffordshire has been recognised as a pottery centre of great importance to England. The area was ideally situated both geographically and physically, all the necessary clays required were readily available and so were the ample supplies of coal for firing the kilns which were formerly fuelled by the rapidly diminishing supplies of timber. Water was also available in large quantities.

The term 'slipware' is self explanatory and basically refers to the low-fired earthenwares which were decorated with applied liquid clay (slip), in the same manner as a pastry-cook would ice a cake. A rich lead-glaze was then applied, giving a warm, pleasing effect to what would otherwise be a very dull material. It is also a fact that without a glaze, low-fired earthenware remains porous and is consequently of little use as table- or kitchenware. The early forms of slip-trailing seen on some 16th-century wares was very primitive and the potter appeared to have had very little control of the applied liquid clay, but the skill of the Staffordshire potters was soon to convert this crude peasant art to a degree of technical excellence that was not matched in any other country.

The country potters were primarily concerned with producing the everyday necessities for the more humble table. Burslem, known as the 'Mother of the Potteries' was also referred to as the 'Butter-pot Town', due to the fact that it specialised in producing large cylindrical jars for the farmer to convey his butter in to the local markets. When the occasion arose these same potters were well capable of producing wares in a much more highly decorated style.

The names of Thomas Toft is synonymous with fine slipware dishes which he was producing in the third quarter of the 17th century. These dishes vary in size from twelve to twenty-two inches in diameter. They are unglazed on the reverse, have no footrims and have a wide rim which normally would be intended for condiments, but not in this case because of the heavy raised decoration, which usually took the form of a close trellis pattern. The body of the clay was a deep red: a white slip was applied to the upper side; contrasting slips of black, orange or brown clays were then applied by an instrument

CUP *of buff-coloured earthenware with slip decoration, inscribed with initials and date, 'IB 1700'. English (Staffordshire), dated 1700; ht. 8 cm/3¼ in.*

somewhat similar to an oil-can and the flow of the slip was controlled by placing the finger over the air-vent. Various potters would have devised their own 'gadgets' for this stage of the decoration.

Posset-pots, mugs and jugs were produced by the same technique. They were often dated and sometimes inscribed with the name of the owner. The posset-pots are a guide to the versatility of the potter: marbling, feathering, incising and stamping over pads of clay were all used to good effect.

Slipware can sometimes be identified as the work of other slipware pottery centres, such as Tickenhall in Derby, or the West Country, but the most important centre outside of Staffordshire was Wrotham, in Kent, where some excellent slipware was being produced from as early as 1612 until about 1740. Apart from all the usual domestic requirements, including dishes and jugs, Wrotham specialised in what are referred to as 'tygs', usually of beaker-shape with three or four sets of double handles, a practical convivial drinking vessel.

(For colour illustration, see p. 72)

Stoneware

John Dwight

If John Dwight, the English potter, had achieved his ambition, England might well have produced a hard-paste porcelain before the Saxon factory at Meissen.

John Dwight was granted a patent as early as 23rd April, 1672, to manufacture 'transparent earthenware commonly known by the names of porcelain or China and Persian ware'. Unfortunately there is as yet no certain evidence of his having produced any translucent porcelain, although some of the salt-glazed stoneware he did manufacture is so thin that a slight degree of translucency is at times apparent.

It was while he was Registrar and Secretary to the Bishop of Chester at Wigan, that Dwight started his experiments which may not have had the approval of his employer, for he eventually quarrelled with the Bishop and moved to Fulham, in West London where he set up his manufactory in about 1673. The site only recently ceased to be occupied by a working pottery.

According to reports of the time Dwight's experiments with porcelain achieved little success; the material apparently blistered and sometimes turned black. It is doubtful if he was aware of the true essential ingredients—china-clay and china-stone—which at that time had not been located in Europe. However, Dwight's salt-glazed stoneware was highly successful from the start and as early as 1673 he had not only produced figures but 'Several little Jars of several colours all exceeding hard as a flint, very light, of very good shape', which, coming from Robert Hooke, the scientist, was indeed a compliment.

John Dwight's production of salt-glazed stoneware wine-bottles of the Rhenish type proved so popular that he was awarded contracts by the Glass-Sellers Company who undertook to buy only his wine-bottles in preference to those made on the Continent of Europe.

In 1866 the discovery of a bricked-up kiln on the Fulham pottery site revealed a great deal of material which has helped in the identification of Dwight's productions. Apart from bottles, he produced some well-shaped mugs, or cups, fashioned after those made during the 17th century in Fukien, south-east China, where the so-called *blanc de Chine* was manufactured for export to Europe. One cup can be dated by an engraved silver-mount to about 1682.

In 1693 Dwight started a lengthy law suit against

MUG *of salt-glazed stoneware. English (Fulham, John Dwight's factory), c.1680; ht. 12 cm/$4\frac{5}{8}$ in.*

other potters whom he accused of infringing the renewed patent granted to him in 1684. Among the potters cited were John and David Elers. David, the elder brother, was born in Amsterdam, and John the younger, in Utrecht. In their defence they claimed they had acquired their knowledge of the Rhenish salt-glazed stoneware whilst living in Cologne. They both admitted to making brown mugs and red teapots in England from about 1690. All we know of them later is that they were declared bankrupt in 1700 but their precise movements are undetermined. There is little doubt that they were involved in the pottery at Fulham and in the potteries around Newcastle-under-Lyme, where they at least produced some excellent red stoneware mugs, teapots, cups and saucers, fashioned after those made at Yi-hsing in China.

Excavations on the site of the Elers pottery at Bradwell Wood, Staffordshire, have revealed very little material which makes the recognition of their wares easier. Credit must be given to the Elers for introducing to Staffordshire a type of refined stoneware acceptable to those wishing to enjoy tea.

Staffordshire (Salt-glaze)

It was during the late 17th century that the Staffordshire potters began glazing their wares in a manner which had been used on the stonewares of Germany since the early 14th century—salt-glazing. The technique, which is only possible on highly fired stonewares, is comparatively simple and cheap, enabling a glazed pot to be produced at a single kiln firing. Salt is thrown into the kiln at a temperature of between 1200° and 1400° C, the salt volatises and the sodium from the salt combines with the alumina and silica in the clay forming a thin 'tight-fitting' vitreous glaze over the surface. This same process was used in Fulham (*see* p 80) and Nottingham before it became popular in North Staffordshire, but credit must be given to the Staffordshire potters for introducing a refined and well-decorated range of salt-glazed tablewares.

In his excellent book *Staffordshire Salt-glazed Stoneware* Arnold R. Mountford, Director of the City Museum and Art Gallery, Stoke-on-Trent, reproduced a list, first compiled in 1765 by Josiah Wedgwood, of Burslem potters known to have been working between 1710 and 1715. This list includes many 'Stone ware' potters who at this early date were primarily engaged in producing thrown and turned tankards or cups, with occasional incised or 'rouletted' decoration. A rare teapot of about 1710 is also illustrated in the above-mentioned book.

The earliest white salt-glazed stonewares were produced by applying a thin layer of white pipe-clay over a drab-coloured body, but with the introduction of white clays from Devon and Dorset, in the South-West of England, and the use of flints which were first calcined in a flint-kiln and then ground to a fine powder, a thin near-white body became possible. This manufacture of stoneware occurred at a most opportune time for the Staffordshire potters who were able to produce comparatively fine wares to cater for the new social habit of tea-drinking. The early 'drab-ware' teapots, bowls and three-footed cream-jugs of about 1725 often had 'crabstock' handles and spouts of the white clay and applied decoration taken from moulds, in either white clay, or clay of a contrasting colour. These were rapidly developed into more refined wares and, by about 1730, punch-pots, teapots and mugs in several pleasing shapes were being produced, with intricate lace-like decoration taken from metal dies and applied, or 'sprigged' on the surface. At about this time not only tewares, but some excellent plates, dishes and tureens were being produced, with basket-work of relief foliage decoration, made by pressing thin sheets of clay into prepared plaster-of-Paris moulds.

Between about 1740 and 1780 many attractive tablewares, often dated, were produced with so-called 'scratch-blue' decoration. While the clay of the unfired ware was still 'green' or 'cheese-hard', the decoration was incised, and a mixture of clay and cobalt-oxide was rubbed into the incisions, resulting in clear-cut blue designs, sometimes similar to contemporary fabrics. A further use was made of cobalt when tablewares, including coffee-pots, teapots and jugs, were dipped into a thin clay wash, rich in ground zaffre (cobalt) resulting in an all-over blue glaze, known today as 'Littler-Wedgwood' blue.

From about 1750 the Staffordshire potters were decorating their wares with enamel colours to compete with English and imported porcelain.

Earthenware & Stoneware

Astbury &Whieldon

There is often a great deal of confusion concerning the names of well-known Staffordshire potters, due to so many having the same surname. For instance, John Astbury was potting at Shelton in Staffordshire and died in 1743 and his son began potting in 1725 but today the name Astbury is used to give an indication of a particular type of ware and style of decoration, rather than an attribution to a particular potter.

Astbury refers to a type of lead-glazed earthenware, made from about 1735 to 1740, with a refinement of body and glaze of a quality somewhat akin to the earlier stonewares of the Elers. The clay used for the body of the Astbury-type wares can vary from a red to a pale chamois tone, the sprigged (applied), or stamped decoration is of a white pipe-clay. These wares, if left in the biscuited earthenware, would have remained porous and would have been very unattractive but the thin lead-glaze not only rendered the material non-porous, but also imparted rich colours to otherwise drab clay; the red body was converted to a rich dark brown and the white pipe-clay to a pleasing yellow. The most common Astbury wares to have survived are teapots and jugs, decorated with small relief harps, animals, and shields of arms. Another cruder, but attractive type has trailing vine decoration, sometimes in light clay on an almost black glaze, or all black, with the decoration picked out in unfired gilding. Some of the teapots have three silver-like feet in the shape of masks or claws while others (probably the earlier pieces) have crabstock handles and spouts, with the knob in the form of a bird with outstretched wings. The later examples are less 'rustic' and sometimes have faceted spouts and Chinese-type 'Dog of Fo', or acorn-shaped, knobs.

There is still a tendency to call all the near-black wares 'Jackfield' which is not correct since pieces attributed to this later Shropshire factory have a much higher glaze and 'slicker' forms.

Thomas Whieldon, with whom Josiah Wedgwood was in partnership from 1754 to 1759, was born in 1719 and died in 1795. Excavations on the site of his factories have proved that he made all types of Staffordshire earthenware and stoneware, including 'Astbury' type. The name of Whieldon is today associated with cream-coloured earthenwares covered with a lead-glaze under which various metallic oxides have been applied to give either the variegated, mottled-coloured effect or the so-called 'tortoiseshell' effect, where only manganese has been used. Similarly decorated wares were not only made by other Staffordshire potters, but also at various Yorkshire concerns and at Melbourne in Derby.

During excavations at Whieldon's earlier factory site at Fenton Low Works evidence as to the kinds of wares produced there was found and was discussed by the late A. T. Morley-Hewitt in a paper read to the English Ceramic Circle in 1950. The 'wasters' discovered were mostly of the earlier types of comparatively common Staffordshire wares, and there was a clear lack of later coloured types. More recent excavations have proved that these were mostly produced at Fenton Vivian, where Whieldon was working from about 1747.

The site wasters revealed the wide range of Whieldon and Whieldon-Wedgwood (1754–59) tablewares, including plates, butter-tubs, baskets, which in some cases were made from the same moulds being used to make both stonewares and creamware.

(For colour illustration, see p. 74)

Opposite top: *A group of Wedgwood stoneware.* SUCRIER and COVER *of multi-coloured jasperware,* 1790–1800. CHOCOLATE-POT *of green jasper-dip, c.1785.* CUP *and* SAUCER *of lilac jasper-dip, c.1785.* PUNCH-POT *of black basaltes, late 18th century.* TEAPOT *of cane-coloured stoneware, c.1790.* SUCRIER *and* COVER *of white stoneware with 'smear-glaze', 1820–30.* COFFEE-CAN *and* SAUCER *of red stoneware* (Rosso Antico), *c.1805. All English (Wedgwood); ht. (chocolate-pot) 14.6 cm/6 in.*

Opposite bottom: *A selection of English cream-coloured earthenware.* Wedgwood DISH *with transfer-printed decoration added at Liverpool, c.1768. Pair of* CANDLESTICKS, *marked 'Wedgwood', c.1795.* Wedgwood TUREEN *and* COVER *with painted decoration, c.1780.* Pearlware CUP *and* SAUCER, *c.1775–80.* Wedgwood COFFEE-POT *with transfer-printed decoration, c.1770; dia. (dish) 39.5 cm/16 in.*

Overleaf: *A group of Yorkshire pottery.* BOWL *of salt-glazed stoneware, painted with enamel colours. English (Rotherham), c.1760.* COFFEE-POT *of red earthenware, decorated with manganese glaze and gilding, marked 'Rockingham' impressed. English (Swinton), c.1830.* SAUCE TUREEN *with* STAND *and* LADLE *of pearlware decorated with enamel colours and gilding. English (Swinton), 1806–25.* TERRINE, *one of a pair, of cream-coloured earthenware painted with enamel colours. English (Leeds), c.1780; ht. (coffee-pot) 22 cm/8½ in.*

Josiah Wedgwood

Overleaf: TUREEN *and* STAND *of lead-glazed earthenware, decorated with underglaze-blue transfer-prints depicting incidents in the Mexican War, probably based on the lithographs issued by N. Currier. This 'Texian Campaigne' series is attributed to the Staffordshire potter, Anthony Shaw, who was active from 1851 to 1900; lgth. (stand) 36.1 cm/14 in.*

Opposite: *A group of Chelsea soft-paste porcelain, painted in enamel colours. Large oval* MEAT DISH, *c.1755.* TUREEN *and* COVER, *in the form of a melon, marked with a red anchor, c.1755.* MILK-JUG, *marked with an incised triangle, c.1745-50.* Silver-pattern *DISH with 'Kakiemon' decoration, marked with a raised anchor, c.1750. All English (Chelsea); wdth. (meat dish) 42 cm/17 in.*

The excavations on the Fenton Vivian site, provided evidence of the type of wares made during the 1754-59 period, when Josiah Wedgwood was in partnership with Thomas Whieldon.

Josiah Wedgwood was born in 1730, the twelfth, and youngest son of the potter Thomas Wedgwood of the Churchyard Pottery, Burslem. Following the death of his father in 1739 Josiah started to work in the family pottery inherited by his elder brother Thomas. He was apprenticed at the age of fourteen to learn 'the Art, Mistery, Occupation or Imployment of Throwing and Handleing'.

During his five years with Thomas Whieldon, Josiah had ample time to experiment on his own behalf and the results were all recorded for future use in his *Experiment Book*. This book also revealed Wedgwood's aims for the future which encompassed improvements in the manufacture of earthenware, which at the time stood in great need of it. He also recorded that the factory's principal article of manufacture, white salt-glazed stoneware, was fetching such low prices that the workmanship was suffering and that the buyers had grown weary of agate-ware, tortoiseshell and variegated coloured glazes.

It was towards the end of the partnership that a new range of tablewares were produced with a fine green glaze. This glaze featured in his *Experiment Book* as number 7. It was acquired by using very refined copper and enabled them to produce a wide range of tablewares in imitation of cabbages, cauliflowers and pineapples. The idea of tablewares in such naturalistic forms originated at the Meissen porcelain factory, and Wedgwood would have been conversant with the copies of Meissen being made at about that time

at the London factory in Chelsea. These naturalistically shaped and coloured wares were soon produced by other rival potters, both in Staffordshire and elsewhere. The moulds of many of these early Wedgwood shapes are still preserved at the Wedgwood Museum at Barlaston, Staffordshire, and are important evidence to the precise shapes of many unmarked wares.

Josiah Wedgwood became a master-potter in 1759, when he leased the Ivy House Works from his uncle at an annual rental of £10.

The green glazes already mentioned were applied to a near white body, similar to that used for salt-glazed stoneware, but fired at a lower temperature, thus producing an earthenware which called for a lead-glaze. It was soon after the move that Josiah started a production of cream-coloured earthenware, a colour resulting basically from the high content of lead in the glaze rather than the clay. His trade flourished to the extent that in 1764 he moved to the larger factory, 'Brick House', later known as 'Bell House' owing to the fact that the workers' hours were regulated by the sounding of a bell, instead of the customary blowing of a horn.

By 1763 he had perfected the creamware body to 'a species of earthenware for the table quite new in its appearance, covered with rich and brilliant glaze bearing sudden alterations of heat and cold, manufactured with ease and expedition and consequently cheap, having every requisite for the purpose intended'.

Wedgwood continued to use his coloured glazes on wares modelled for him by William Greatbach, who was working at Lane Delph from 1764. Existing correspondence lists such items as teapots, leaf-dishes, melon-shaped sauce-boats with stands and numerous tablewares in the form of cauliflowers, pineapples, apples, pears, quinces and other fruits.

In 1765 Wedgwood received an order for a tea-service from Queen Charlotte: it was to have a gold ground with raised flowers in green. This tea-service does not appear to have survived but wares are known with a green ground and relief flowers in gilt. Following orders from the Queen for more cream-coloured earthenware, Wedgwood was permitted to take the title of 'Potter to the Queen' and the popular cream-ware became known as 'Queen's Ware'.

Josiah Wedgwood

The early creamwares are of a rich buff tone and the glaze, which is inclined to craze, shows a greenish tone where thick, such as under the foot-rim. By 1768 the introduction of Cornish china-clay and china-stone resulted in wares of a much paler colour than that being produced by his Staffordshire and Yorkshire rivals. At the same time the Wedgwood glaze became noticeably thinner and less prone to crazing.

The growing popularity of Wedgwood cream-wares, led to a simplicity in form. Teapots were orange-shape with the sunken lids appearing as if cut from the globular form. The demand for his wares was so great that he was at times forced to purchase similar wares from neighbouring potters, who were imitating his styles, in order to fulfil his own orders.

The moulded sections have helped to identify a great many examples of unmarked creamwares. The earliest Wedgwood teapot spouts and handles were almost certainly among those modelled by Greatbach, they are hexagonal, or faceted, with finely moulded decoration. One of the most popular forms of spouts—again probably the work of the outside modeller—has cabbage-, or cauliflower-leaf moulded decoration.

In 1763 Wedgwood had an arrangement with the Leeds firm of enamellers, Robinson and Rhodes who were advertising, as early as 1760, that they were prepared to decorate wares to match Chinese or Meissen porcelain or to add enamel coats-of-arms to wares. Robinson retired from the business in 1763, whereafter the firm became D. Rhodes and Co. and David Rhodes moved to London in 1768 to work for Wedgwood as an enameller until he died in 1777. Documented orders from Rhodes to Wedgwood from March 1763 show he was buying melon-shaped and pineapple-shaped teapots, fruit-baskets, and tea-pots in red stoneware and the new creamware.

Rhode's London decoration on Wedgwood's creamware is some of the most attractive to be seen of its type; it included designs that had a lot in common with contemporary textiles, and were painted in red, black, green, yellow and purple. Rhodes also used an opaque rose-pink for attractive flower-painting, sometimes using the same colour over the entire spout and handle.

From 1761 Wedgwood also came to an arrangement with the firm Sadler and Green of Liverpool (Green was not actually a partner until 1763) who decorated so many Wedgwood wares with prints taken from engraved copper-plates. These were printed in either an Indian-red, black, or lilac enamel with a variety of subjects including pastorals, coats-of-arms, figure subjects, landscapes, birds or flowers.

The largest service ever produced by Wedgwood in cream-coloured earthenware was commissioned by Empress Catherine of Russia in 1773. This dinner- and dessert-service totalled 952 pieces, each decorated with a painted English landscape, house or garden, the location being inscribed on the reverse. This service was known as the 'Frog-Service', after the palace for which the service was made, the emblem of a frog was also transfer-printed on the pieces.

It was in 1762 that Josiah Wedgwood first met Thomas Bentley but it was 1769 before their mutual ambitions to produce wares fashioned after the classical treasures being excavated at Herculaneum and Pompeii were fulfilled. These Grecian wares were originally thought to be Etruscan, hence the name Etruria was given to the factory first opened in 1769 for the production of these currently fashionable wares. Many of these pieces were produced from a new black stoneware which Wedgwood had perfected by about 1767, which he called 'black basaltes'. This material was used primarily for decorative wares, but some tea-services were also produced.

Drinking from an unglazed black basaltes cup must have been far less pleasant than from his contemporary creamware. Teawares were also produced from the Jasperware introduced in 1774 to 1775 but for the table this texture must have been equally un-pleasant.

(For colour illustration, see p. 83)

Wedgwood's contemporaries

Competition was so great among the potters of North Staffordshire that it was almost impossible for a potter to produce an entirely exclusive ware or style of decoration. This was certainly the case with the large range of wares introduced and first popularised by Josiah Wedgwood. Today's collectors consider that some of the wares of such firms as Neale and Co. of Hanley and John Turner of Lane End, surpassed those of the famous Josiah Wedgwood.

John Neale became a partner of Henry Palmer, who, by 1776, was a well-established potter with a reputation for good black basaltes and Jasperware. On the death of Palmer in 1778, Neale engaged Robert Wilson as manager until 1786, when he became a partner of Neale and Co. Neale produced creamware, black basaltes and pearlware, but it was his creamwares which were mostly used for his extensive range of tablewares.

Neale's creamwares were of excellent quality showing a perfection in both body, glaze and decoration, often superior to those of all his English contemporaries. He made some charming dessert-services, with feathered edging in enamel colours. Many of these wares were decorated with a variety of well-engraved transfer-prints covering a wide range of subjects.

John Turner was potting at Lane End on his own account from about 1760; his range of wares were eventually to include all those popularised by Wedgwood. His creamwares were often exported to Holland where they were decorated in enamel colours to the Dutch taste. Other marked 'Turner' wares were of cream-coloured earthenware and used by the independent painter Absolom of Yarmouth, who painted some most attractive botanical specimens in black and green enamels. Turner's blue Jasperwares decorated in white reliefs in the Wedgwood manner are usually of a distinctive slatey blue.

From about 1781 to 1792 John Turner and his sons were in partnership with Andrew Abbott, during which time they had a retail and decorating shop in London. In their advertisement of 1785 they list the wares in stock including 'a great variety of table-services, dessert setts, dejeunes' and 'a very general assortment of Egyptian Black, and Bamboo, or Cane Colour Tea-Pots, some elegantly mounted with silver spouts and chains and Mugs and Jugs, with silver rims and covers'. The concern closed in 1806.

A similar range of wares were produced from about 1773 to 1805 at Hanley, Staffordshire, by Elijah Mayer. His creamwares were light in weight and had a distinct greenish-tinted glaze. He produced many tea-services that had straight-sided teapots with globular knobs to the lids; his attractive pierced openwork baskets were often rimmed with brown enamel and copies of Wedgwood's border-patterns. Mayers' creamwares were well produced and often lined with enamel colours, whereas his large range of black basaltes teawares were very inferior and, unlike the earlier Wedgwood, were usually glazed on the inner surfaces.

The Wood family of Burslem is best known for its production of good earthenware figures, but during the late 18th century, Enoch Wood made some excellent creamwares for the table, including some very fine, large fruit-baskets in imitation of those made from twigs.

Another well-known family of potters were descendants of the early master-potter William Adams, who worked at Tunstall from 1777 to 1805 where he produced many fine quality creamwares for the table, often painted in underglaze-blue. His later pearlwares were usually decorated with underglaze-blue prints.

DISH *of cream-coloured earthenware, painted in purple in a style attributed to Bakewell, marked 'Wedgwood' impressed and 'B' in purple. English (Staffordshire, Josiah Wedgwood's factory at Etruria), c.1770; lgth. 33 cm/12.⅞ in.*

Yorkshire

For many years knowledge concerning the potteries of Yorkshire has been very vague and there is little doubt that many examples attributed in the past to Staffordshire were in fact made by the northern potters. In a recent book *Yorkshire Pots and Potteries* Heather Lawrence has thrown new light on and revived interest in many 18th- and 19th-century factories in the county of Yorkshire. The majority of potters worked in the West Riding of Yorkshire, close to the coalfields, which provided a cheap supply of fuel and a good market for their wares, being the most densely populated area of the county.

Identification of the cruder kitchenwares made during the 18th century by the country potter has been difficult, but marked examples and excavations on the sites of the larger factories have provided evidence of many finely produced tablewares. Probably the most important revelation of Mrs Lawrence's research is that the well-known Leeds Pottery was not established until 1770, not in about 1757 as was previously thought. Good creamware was certainly being made before 1770 in Yorkshire, of the type previously attributed to the Leeds Pottery, and it can only be conjectured that the factory either moved from somewhere else, or, probably more feasible, that the Leeds Pottery took over the moulds and stock of a neighbouring pottery, such as Dennison's which appears to have closed by 1769.

The wares produced at the Leeds Pottery from 1770 until its final closure in 1881, were great in variety and quantity. Among the earliest wares known to have been made at Leeds are some well-produced engine-turned red stonewares of the Wedgwood type. The most important productions were undoubtedly of cream-coloured earthenware. The earlier examples are of a deep cream tone, with a thinly applied yellow glaze which has a tendency to craze when thick such as within the foot-rims. The Leeds handles and spouts would have been considered decidedly rustic by Josiah Wedgwood; they consisted of intricate reeding or rope-twists, usually with moulded terminals, the details of which are often a sure aid to attribution. Their attractive, but often impractical knobs were usually in the form of a flower, mushroom or acorn. It is interesting to note that the Leeds Pottery also used Whieldon-type

SAUCE-BOAT *of cream-coloured earthenware, decorated in high-temperature colours. English (Yorkshire, the Leeds Pottery), 1770-75; lgth. 20.5 cm/8 in.*

glazes and 'Whieldon-Wedgwood' shapes, such as teapots in the form of cauliflowers.

With the paler coloured creamwares of about 1775, greater use was made of intricate pierced decoration, coupled with neo-classical forms, and wares were often decorated with transfer-prints, first in enamel colours and later, on early-19th-century pearlwares, use was made of underglaze blue.

Wasters recently found on the site of the Rothwell factory, near Leeds, has thrown new light on a previously little-known production. The factory started in 1767 and continued under various owners until about 1788. The evidence of the wasters has proved that apart from the usual range of coarsewares and bricks, fine salt-glazed stoneware, creamware and pearlware were also produced. The sherds of plate rims have enabled complete examples to be attributed to this pottery; they have distinctive variations of popular styles of moulded or pierced decoration, somewhat similar to those known elsewhere. The moulded rims were often further decorated in a green enamel.

The Rothwell Pottery produced a wide range of tablewares including plates, dishes, teapots, tureens, basins and jugs. Another pottery was established at Rothwell in 1774 by Samuel Shaw, a Staffordshire potter, who made wares similar to those of the earlier concern.

(For colour illustration, see p. 84)

Derbyshire (Melbourne)

One of the most important discoveries of recent years concerns a hitherto unknown production of cream-coloured earthenware near Melbourne, a small town about eight miles south of Derby. The excavations originated at Furnace Farm, thought to be associated with early blast furnaces, but the 'dig' was to produce ample evidence in the form of 'wasters' of a prolific earthenware manufacture. The lower, earlier levels revealed creamware and the higher, later levels revealed country-type brown-glazed earthenware and salt-glazed stoneware. In addition, evidence in the form of saggers and kiln-furniture provided ample proof that this was indeed a site and not merely a dump. Later research also brought to light a newspaper advertisement of 1776, in which the Melbourne proprietor was seeking a sober journeyman potter who could 'throw' and 'turn' creamware.

The fragmented wasters which were found on the site were nearly all unglazed but have provided good evidence as to the types of creamware produced at Melbourne, and have furthermore enabled many excellent examples of creamware to be re-attributed without question to this newly discovered works. The wares were produced by 'throwing' or moulding and the production was devoted primarily to table-wares. The fragments indicate that cups and saucers, plates, various sized bowls, teapots, coffee-pots, pepper-pots, sauce-boats, creamers and jugs were all produced in quantity.

Among the many fragments found were a variety of border-patterns used on plates, some of these are similar to those used on plates made elsewhere and so it is only by careful, detailed study that one can attribute wares to Melbourne with confidence. This is the case with the 'feather' border where the correct number of barbs and the spacing must conform exactly to the finds. Recognition of this border enabled many plates, decorated with rich green enamel, to be attributed to Melbourne, rather than to Leeds where a somewhat similar form of decoration was used. Other border-pattern finds have helped collectors to recognise an attractive form of purple monochrome painting as belonging to the factory. Many of the plates have two clear adjacent 'nicks' in the edge of the foot-rim, apparently a plate-maker's mark.

The popularity of lobed edges and the patterns of pierced work has helped us to identify many plates, dishes, tureens and baskets as the work of this factory. Apart from two varieties of green enamel flower-painting and the distinctive purple monochrome, use was also made of transfer-printing in black or red enamel. These prints were at times copied from those made by the company of J. Sadler in Liverpool, the source of others have yet to be identified.

The exact section of reeded handles and the leaf and berry terminals have also helped in the recognition of both teapots and coffee-pots. Teapots were made in at least two shapes, globular and cylindrical; handles were either of the plaited-strap or twisted-rope variety, while most knobs were in the form of a convolvulus flower.

Many wares previously attributed to various Staffordshire or Yorkshire factories can now be attributed to Melbourne, and additionally the fragments have proved that many varieties of form and decoration were introduced at Melbourne which have not as yet been recognised as complete examples in many public and private collections; but knowledge of this kind takes a long time to circulate.

Transfer-printed wares

Until recently the entire field of 19th-century transfer-printed earthenware had attracted very little attention from the more serious collector of pottery and porcelain, but today, with ever increasing numbers of collectors, and new research being made available concerning the production and recognition of these humbler pieces, early marked examples are now very difficult to find and getting increasingly expensive to purchase.

The earlier examples are decorated in underglaze-blue derived from the metallic oxide of copper mixed with oil. The subject-matter is line-engraved into a copper-plate—on rarer occasions a form of stipple-engraving is used. The prepared 'ink' is then rubbed into the engraving and the surplus colour removed from the surface of the plate with a large palette knife—the engraving retaining the colour. A thin wet tissue paper is then placed upon the copper-plate and protected by a flannel 'blanket'; the plate and paper are then 'ironed' under a roller, thus transferring the ink from the copper-plate to the tissue. This transfer is then carefully trimmed and placed on the ware to be decorated which has been fired once; a flannel pad and soapy water is then used to ensure close contact between the ware and the paper, thus transferring the design to the earthenware (or porcelain). The paper is then washed off and the applied design is ready to be fired at a low temperature to 'fix' it to the surface, after which the ware is immersed in a liquid glaze and after drying fired again to the full 'glost' kiln temperature. The process varies very little from that first used on Italian porcelain in about 1743.

Transfer-printing on porcelain was already well known at many earlier English porcelain factories, including Bow, Worcester, Caughley, Lowestoft and several Liverpool concerns, but credit is given to John Turner of Lane End for introducing underglaze-blue prints to earthenware in about 1783, the year in which Josiah Spode managed to obtain the services of some Caughley workers who were already well versed in this technique.

Identification of unmarked examples of underglaze printed wares is made more difficult owing to the fact that, from the early years of the 19th century, many skilled engravers moved to the 'Potteries' (Staffordshire) and set up independent engravers'

shops, with the result that nearly identical subjects can be found on the wares of different factories. It was usually only the larger and more prosperous potteries who could afford to hire their own engraver or buy exclusive patterns engraved to order. The engraver Thomas Sparks is known to have been supplying copper-plates to Josiah Wedgwood II, Spode, Ralph Stevenson, Ridgway and others in about 1815.

The bulk of these wares consisted of plates, averaging about 9-10 inches in diameter, mostly circular, others with various wavy or scalloped profiles. Tureens of all sizes, complete with lids, stands and ladles have survived in surprising quantities, whereas cups and saucers are harder to come by. Spode produced some interesting plates which are 'double-walled' enabling the hollow chamber to be filled with hot-water, thus keeping the food warm.

The shapes and manufacturing characteristics, rather than the patterns, are often better indications of a particular factory and hence foot-rims and bases on marked wares should be carefully studied and used as a guide for those which are unmarked. Among the most attractive wares decorated with underglaze-blue prints are the miniature services, which were at one time often wrongly termed 'travellers' samples'. In his book *Blue and White Transfer Ware, 1780–1840* A. W. Coysh discusses wares of well over one hundred potteries engaged in this form of manufacture.

Victorian decorative jugs

Some of the most impractical and useless jugs ever produced were made during Victorian times by the English potters mostly from the Staffordshire area. These highly decorated jugs are nevertheless important documents, as they can often be dated to the very day the designs were patented. Wares made between 1842 and 1883 can often be seen with a 'diamond' or 'lozenge' mark, printed, impressed, moulded, or applied in relief on the base. If the mark is clearly legible, the numbers and letters in each corner can be deciphered to give the exact information deposited with the Patent Office: the day, month, year, and parcel number relating to the design or the form of the ware. If no maker's name is present this can be found by consulting the Class IV Index which relates to pottery and porcelain. If one knows the exact date, one can find out the name of the potter and his location. Sometimes it was a wholesaler or a dealer, who registered the design (see my Pocket-Book of British Ceramic Marks).

The majority of these Victorian jugs were simply moulded in extravagant forms, with rarely any added decoration. They were, therefore, cheap to produce and were made in a variety of economic bodies. The most common ware used was an off-white stoneware, which in the past has often been mistaken for salt-glazed stoneware. The effect is achieved by placing lead-glaze into the kiln, which volatises and produces a so-called 'smear-glaze'; the interiors were usually well and thickly glazed in the normal manner. On some occasions the background can be seen to have been painted out in a 'Wedgwood blue', leaving the white decoration in relief in a vain endeavour to suggest applied decoration of the Jasper-type.

The firm of W. Ridgway Son and Co. of Hanley were producing jugs with this heavy relief decoration as early as 1838. The profile of the earlier jugs had much in common with the contemporary porcelain but from about 1850, the straight-sided jug, which was to remain popular for many years, became fashionable, with only slight variations being made to the basic form.

The firm of T. and R. Boote made relief jugs in a wide range of styles. One of the most popular styles of decoration, inspired by the current revival of Gothic taste, displayed biblical figures in Gothic niches. The best-known of all Gothic jugs was that produced by Charles Meigh of the Old Hall Works, Hanley. These have a biblical figure in each of eight niches and are sometimes called 'Apostle' jugs.

Cork and Edge of Newport Pottery, Burslem, were also producing a wide range of comparable jugs between 1846 and 1860. Some of the jugs they advertised in the catalogue of the 1855 Paris Exhibition were fitted with metal lids which are often mistaken for pewter; they were much thinner and were in fact made of a newly introduced alloy known as Britannia metal. They were advertised under such titles as 'Vine', Lily', 'Grape Gatherer 'and 'Babes in the Wood'. Samuel Alcock even registered a design in 1859 entitled 'Daniel in the Lions' Den'.

The association of jugs with alcohol gave rise to the portrayal of Bacchanalian scenes, but all the characters usually appeared clothed to cater for the prudish Victorian taste. Even the 19th-century reproductions of the famous Portland Vase, which was sometimes modelled to form a jug, were modified with the addition of a few more draperies than seen on the glass original or on the copies made in 1790 by Josiah Wedgwood.

Porcelain

Chelsea

Although we know that experiments concerning the manufacture of materials for the production of porcelain were taking place at Bow in 1744, and that William Steers also produced a limited amount of soft-paste porcelain at Newcastle, in Staffordshire, from 1745, the only English factory producing a soft-paste porcelain in commercial quantities by 1745 appears to have been the Chelsea factory.

Nicholas Sprimont, a Hugenot silversmith from Liège, established the Chelsea factory and was probably assisted financially by Charles Gouyn who, in 1749, was described as 'The Late Proprietor and Chief Manager of the Chelsea House'. The Chelsea porcelains divide very well into four distinct periods, related to the type of marks sometimes present on the wares within a period of years. From about 1745 to 1749 (the incised triangle period) the Chelsea porcelain was a highly translucent 'frit' porcelain containing about 10% lead-oxide – used as an alternative to china-stone to produce translucency. Although this early Chelsea porcelain paste was not ideal for tablewares due to it being prone to cracking with sudden changes of temperature, Sprimont still managed to produce some most attractive pieces, sometimes modelled in the form of his earlier silver, including salts decorated with fully modelled crayfish, moulded teapots, coffee-pots, beakers and shallow strawberry dishes, sometimes left in the white, sometimes decorated in enamel colours with rather poor imitations of Meissen flower- and insect-painting.

In about 1749 Chelsea adopted a new mark in the form of an anchor in relief on an applied medallion and it was at this time that Chelsea began to add a small quantity of tin-oxide to the glaze, which imparted a much whiter tone to tablewares and figures up to about 1758. Throughout the 'raised-anchor' period (c. 1749–52) Chelsea wares rarely showed any originality in form or decoration, the influence of the hard-paste porcelains of China, Japan and Meissen being very apparent. Some more original painting is sometimes seen on the early teawares; illustrations of Aesop's Fables for instance, attributed to the painter William Duvivier from Tournai. Similar painting on 'red-anchor' wares (c. 1752–58) is more probably the work of Jefferyes Hamett O'Neale.

It was during the 'red-anchor' period that Chelsea produced many tablewares decorated with paintings of botanical specimens. Services decorated with these detailed illustrations were obviously made over a long period and are often still to be seen on porcelain of the 'gold-anchor' type (c. 1758-70). Research has proved that many of the original engravings of plants copied by the Chelsea painters was the work of a German botanical painter, Georg D. Ehret who settled in Chelsea in 1737.

Many of the Chelsea tablewares made during the 'red-anchor' period reflected the Germans' passion for decorating the table with naturalistic scenes in porcelain. Besides the porcelain figures and animals that graced the table, tureens and stands were fashioned in the form of full-size hens with chicks, rabbits, fighting-cocks, swans, or boar's heads. Smaller dishes and pots with covers were made to resemble apples, melons, cauliflowers, pigeons and fish.

From about 1756 and throughout the 'gold-anchor' period (c. 1758-70) Chelsea looked more towards the fashionable rococo porcelains of Vincennes and Sèvres for its ideas. Although Chelsea porcelain became rather thick and clumsy, and the clear glaze very prone to 'crazing', one cannot deny the very high quality of the decoration. A very fine underglaze-blue, comparable to the *'bleu lapis'* of Sèvres was often used, known at Chelsea as 'Mazarine blue' which, when coupled with flower- and figure-painting and lavish gilding, soon became the popular taste of the day.

(For colour illustration, see p. 86)

Opposite: *A group of Bow soft-paste porcelain, decorated in underglaze-blue.* DISH, *c.1760* CHOCOLATE-CUP, COVER *and* STAND, *c.1762.* SHELL CENTRE-PIECE, *c.1755* DOUBLE-HANDED SAUCE-BOAT, *c.1755* KNIFE *and* FORK *with porcelain handles, c.1755-60. All English (Bow); ht. (centre-piece) 13 cm/5 in.*

Overleaf: *Selection of Lowestoft soft-paste porcelain, decorated in underglaze-blue or enamel colours.* COFFEE-POT, *c.1790.* CREAM-JUG, *known as the 'Curtis style' pattern, c.1780o-1800.* MUG, *painted in enamel colours by the 'Tulip painter', c.1774.* TEAPOT, *painted in enamel colours by the 'Tulip painter'.* TEA-CADDY, *with moulded decoration and underglaze-blue painting, 1761-64.* TEA-BOWL *and* SAUCER, *painted in enamel colours and underglaze-blue with a 'Redgrave-style' pattern, 1780-1800. All English (Lowestoft); ht. (coffee-pot) 27.9 cm/11 in.*

Bow

Overleaf: Group of Pinxton soft-paste porcelain, painted in enamel colours. All three examples date from 1796 to 1800 and are unmarked, with the exception of the CREAM-JUG *which bears the pattern number '367'. All English (Pinxton); ht. (teapot) 16.5 cm/6½ in.*

Opposite: Part of a TEA-SERVICE *of soft-paste (soapstone) porcelain, marked with a fretted square in underglaze-blue. English (Worcester, Dr Wall period, 1751–76), most probably c.1775.*

This London factory was actually situated just beyond the bridge over the River Lea, and it was consequently in West Ham in Essex rather than Bow in Middlesex at that time. The first patent granted in 1744 to Edward Heylyn and Thomas Frye dealt only with the manufacture of porcelain materials, rather than the finished wares. According to Daniel Defoe's *Tour of Great Britain,* published in 1748, Bow was a flourishing concern making wares comparable (at least to his eye) to those being imported from the Far East. The actual patent relating to the manufacture of these wares was not taken out until 1749, this time by Thomas Frye alone.

Bow was, to our knowledge, the first English porcelain factory to have used bone-ash (calcined animal bone) as an ingredient, which, among other things, helped to reduce the high percentage of wastage experienced by factories which made the more glassy bodies. Some early documentary ink-wells are decorated in either underglaze-blue or enamel colours and inscribed 'Made at New Canton', '1750' or '1751'. According to Thomas Craft, a Bow factory painter, the style for the factory building itself was one in Canton in China.

The success of the Bow factory was largely due to the mass of good substantial tablewares which it produced and for which there was obviously a large demand. The appearance of early Bow varies a great deal, from a greyish-white to a creamish tone; the material often has a lot in common with the early soft-paste porcelain produced at Saint-Cloud in France. The waxen glaze is rather soft and very easily worn or scratched, and staining or discoloration around the bases or footrims is often apparent. The greater part of the early Bow tablewares were made in imitation of Japanese and Chinese wares, and many charming little cups were decorated with sprigs of prunus blossoms which were separately moulded and applied in relief (sprigging) because the thick glaze had a tendency to blur any crisply modelled detail.

Bow found the *famille-rose* Chinese manner of flower-painting very popular in England and used it quite frequently on tablewares, which were basically of typically English shapes and forms: sauce-boats, mugs and plates, teapots, coffee-pots and coffee-cups are among the most common tablewares. In common with some other English porcelain factories Bow produced many tablewares decorated with, or including, painting in the well-known Japanese Kakiemon styles. Probably owing to the lack of skilled painters, the designs were painted in a free style, which produced a freshness so often lacking in the more painstaking copies of Kakiemon seen on the wares of other English or Continental factories.

The Bow factory undoubtedly relied a great deal on its very large output of tablewares decorated with underglaze-blue painting in the Chinese manner; printing in this same colour was only rarely used from about 1760 onwards and only about six subjects are recorded. The painting at Bow was usually in a strong 'royal blue' and among the most popular and easily identified patterns are: peony, rock and pine-tree, peony and fence, banana tree, fence and bird, small cross-legged Chinese figure, and various Chinese landscapes.

Early Bow wares generally have a good translucency of a pale straw tone with a tinge of green, whereas the later wares were often so underfired that the material remained practically opaque. The opposite is often the case with the glaze, which, on the early wares, appears to have been deliberately underfired to preserve the crisp definition of the painting, but later a blurred image often resulted from the glaze being well fired.

(For colour illustration, see *p. 95)*

Lowestoft

The small, but important, factory of Lowestoft, on the East Coast of England, was established in about 1757 by four partners, with Robert Browne as manager. The Lowestoft body was a soft-paste bone-porcelain, comparable to that made from about 1747 at Bow and the early wares were all decorated with underglaze-blue which was also used for printing from about 1770. Until quite recently it was thought that the use of enamel decoration started at about this same time, but in a paper read to the English Ceramic Circle in 1974, John Howell discussed documented pieces which prove that enamel colours were being used at Lowestoft as early as 1766. Production ceased in about 1799.

Apart from a very limited production of small animals and figures, this factory concentrated on small tablewares and vases. Excavations on the site made at the beginning of this century provided ample examples whereby the majority of Lowestoft wares could be recognised further and documentary wares can be used to date these and other productions. The wares produced during the early years at Lowestoft are very rare and have much in common with Bow. Coffee- and chocolate-pots usually have a handle at right-angles to the spout; the spoon-trays are long and slender; sauce-boats were relief-moulded and painted in a rather naïve *Chinoiserie*; and bell-shaped mugs all had a typical Lowestoft handle. Many of these early wares have a small painter's number, usually on the wall of the foot-rim.

Teapots were obviously made in large numbers and, like early Bow, were mostly of globular form, with the simple Chinese-type loop handle, although a few early examples were made with the well-known Lowestoft-type handle with the slight protruberance, or 'kick', at the lower attachment to the body. Teapots were also made with close-reeded decoration (like early Saint-Cloud); this was achieved through moulding. The better-known Lowestoft moulded wares are of the so-called 'Hughes' type. James Hughes was almost certainly a modeller and designer at the factory and the initials 'J. H.' do occur on some wares produced during the 1760s, including teacups, covered sugar-bowls, jugs, sauceboats, oval butter-dishes and stands (today most have lost their lids), octagonal tea-caddies and small cream- or butter-boats. Teapots with the typical Hughes-type mould-

ing are very rare. Many of the teapots would originally most certainly have also had a matching stand of octagonal form, usually with a flat base.

Handles were only rarely applied to teacups, the normal Chinese-type tea-bowl being more fashionable, whereas the taller coffee-cups, often with moulded decoration, had either moulded or simple 'kick'-type handles.

Lowestoft butter-pots were made over a period of many years. An early rare form of butter-pot, now in the Victoria and Albert Museum and the Norwich Castle Museum is oval with curved walls, moulded with close reeding; it has underglaze-blue borders and the indicative bird-finial. The Victoria and Albert Museum also has a painted example of the more traditional butter-cooler with straight walls, and a lid cut away at both ends to fit the lugs attached to the cooler.

Jugs were obviously one of the most popular items produced at Lowestoft. The early examples painted in underglaze-blue have a comparatively narrow neck broadening out considerably in the body, the handles are well-moulded, with thumb-rests. One of the most popular types of border decoration seen on these jugs and other early wares is divided into panels in which a criss-cross trellis pattern alternates with clustered foliage.

Shapes of handles, spouts, knobs, forms of moulding and painted border-patterns are all major aids to the identification of Lowestoft wares and are dealt with in more detail in the later section of this book.

(For colour illustration, see p. 96)

Longton Hall

Recent research and excavations on the site of the Staffordshire porcelain factory of Longton Hall has helped the collector to be a great deal more certain of the wares made at this concern which was producing a glass-type porcelain between 1749 and 1760. The man most often associated with Longton Hall is William Littler. He was also known as a potter producing salt-glazed stoneware, which at times was stained to a dark rich blue, known as 'Littler blue'.

The actual founder of the factory was William Jenkinson, who, in 1751, took William Littler and William Nicklin into copartnership 'in making, burning (firing) and selling the said porcelain ware and all other sorts of ware which the said partners should agree to make or deal in and in painting, japanning, gilding and enamelling thereof'.

Attempts to produce tablewares, were soon made but the Staffordshire potters of that period obviously found it difficult to work in this new glassy type of porcelain since, despite thick potting, the early wares were often misshapen and, when decorated with a strong underglaze-blue, the colour often ran so profusely that even the low-fired gilding and enamel painting did little towards 'tidying' such wares.

Probably owing to the difficulty of 'throwing' the material, the majority of the wares made up to about 1753 were moulded, often showing a close relationship with the contemporary Staffordshire lead-glazed earthenwares, with a profusion of leaves, strawberries and natural foliage of many kinds. Cream-boats and sauce-boats were frequently moulded in the shape of leaves and tureens in the shape of melons. Basket-work, as seen on salt-glazed stoneware was also a popular feature.

By the mid-1750s the porcelains of Longton Hall were more competently produced in every respect, although the nature of the paste still made the process of moulding wares preferable to that of throwing on a wheel. The underglaze-blue was no longer so unruly and the loud 'Littler blue' was replaced with one of a greyish tinge. More use was made of a rather distinctive palette of enamel colours which included a bluish-green, a yellow-green, crimson, pink and an iron-red. Little is known of the actual painters, but some fine detailed landscape painting is attributed to John Hayfield, who paid meticulous attention to the painting of the buildings in a 'brick-by-brick' fashion, and so earned the name of 'the Castle painter'. (Very similar painting can sometimes be seen on Staffordshire salt-glazed stoneware punch-pots.)

Longton Hall mainly used very limited styles of decoration: a range of designs featuring exotic or Chinese-type birds, European-type flower-painting and Chinese *famille rose* where the colour tends more towards a dirty purple than a rose-pink. In his book *Longton Hall Porcelain*, Dr Watney christened the painter of one particular style the 'trembly rose painter', as the style gives the impression of having been painted by a rather shaky hand. This painting at times bears a close resemblance to the roses seen on the recently discovered class of 'Girl-in-a-Swing' Chelsea wares. There was, of course, a likely interchange of workers between these two factories who both produced an almost identical type of porcelain with a high percentage of lead-oxide.

It is not many years ago that evidence came to light proving that, when the Longton Hall factory was closed in 1760, William Littler went to West Pans in Scotland, where he apparently decorated some early Longton Hall wares in enamel colours for local residents and produced both creamwares and earthenwares.

Derby

The early Derby factory enjoyed a long, unbroken history: established in 1756, it finally closed in 1848. (The present-day Derby Crown Porcelain Company Ltd. was not established until 1876.) Within the first year of its establishment William Duesbury and John Heath, partners in the new factory, were advertising the sale by auction of a wide range of wares 'after the finest Dresden models'. Whilst many of their early figures were modelled after Meissen originals, their tablewares showed more originality in both form and decoration, but their early paste was light and chalky and frequently marred by a glaze to which cobalt had been added in an endeavour to make the material resemble the hard-paste of the Continent. Their coffee-cups showed many original styles in every way. Small bell-shaped cups with handles shaped like a pixie's ear were often painted with flower-sprays of the type attributed to the unknown 'cotton-stalk' painter who painted the stems of his flowers in a thread-like manner: this same style of painting is often seen on early square-shaped coffee-cups with a flute running down each corner.

The late W. B. Honey, a former Keeper of the Ceramic Department of the Victoria and Albert Museum, was the first to introduce many descriptive terms which have been generally adopted throughout the world of the collector. He wrote of Derby's 'dishevelled' birds being in direct contrast with the 'exotic' birds of Chelsea and Worcester, and of the 'dirty-turquoise' enamel, which on the early Derby wares and figures had a tendency to fire to a drab yellowish-brown, and of the 'moth painter', who often decorated tablewares solely with such colourful insects.

Unlike other English factories of that period, Derby produced comparatively few wares decorated in underglaze-blue. There are some sauce-boats and cream-jugs, but this form of decoration is mostly seen on less useful wares. Up to about 1770 many of the Derby useful wares can be identified by the three or more small discoloured areas on the bases, known as 'patch-marks' which were caused by the small pads of clay used to support the wares free of the inside base of the sagger in which the pieces were placed during the glaze firing.

Many of the early Derby tablewares were obviously fashioned after those produced during the 'gold-

TUREEN, COVER *and* STAND *of soft-paste porcelain, marked with a crown, crossed batons and 'D' in blue enamel. The painting in enamel colours is attributed to William 'Quaker' Pegg. English (Derby), late 18th c.; lgth. 45.5 cm/18 in.*

anchor' period of Chelsea and at Sèvres, but after Duesbury took over the Chelsea concern in 1770, a new and attractive range of wares in neo-classical styles were produced throughout the 'Chelsea-Derby' period (1770-1784). The underglaze-blue grounds of Chelsea and Sèvres were replaced with a rich, lighter toned blue enamel, referred to as 'Smith's blue', often combined with the classical running honeysuckle pattern in gilt.

The shapes of the Chelsea-Derby tablewares were all pleasing, yet practical, and were usually marked with an anchor and 'D' in gilt, in either monogram form or side-by-side. Table-services had tasteful enamel and gilt decoration in the form of swags, garlands, sprigs of flowers, urns, classical figures or heads painted in sepia monochrome.

Following the death of William Duesbury in 1784, the factory passed to his son of the same name. He too died in 1797 and the factory continued under his partner, Michael Kean, until about 1810, when it was purchased by Robert Bloor, who is best known for the large output of poor quality porcelain decorated in Japanesque patterns.

Pinxton

The work, and travels of the famous flower-painter, William Billingsley has for many years fascinated collectors of English porcelain, but knowledge concerning Billingsley's years at the Pinxton factory in Derbyshire, was very slight, prior to C. L. Exley's book *The Pinxton China Factory.*

For many years Billingsley had been anxious to start his own business as a porcelain manufacturer, but lacked the necessary capital. In 1795 he made the acquaintance of a wealthy young man, John Coke, who agreed to supply the necessary financial aid for the new manufactory and Billingsley would receive his salary from the high profits he anticipated. As a result the Pinxton China Factory was built and in April 1796 the first kiln-firing took place. William Billingsley resigned his position as leading flower-painter at William Duesbury's Derby factory to take up his position at Pinxton in October 1796. During the three years of the partnership some very fine tablewares were produced from Billingsley's soft-paste porcelain recipe, but the costs were so high that during this three year period no profits were made and Billingsley presumably received no salary. In about April 1799 the partnership was dissolved and the business was continued by John Coke on his own account for two and a half years. In September 1801 Henry Bankes was taken into partnership but following many disagreements, this arrangement was dissolved in January 1803. Coke continued as proprietor until about 1806, when John Cutts, who had been in charge of the decorating during the Coke-Bankes partnership, took over the production until the final closure in 1813 when Cutts went to work at Wedgwood's Etruria factory in Staffordshire.

The majority of the wares produced at Pinxton had a great deal in common with the contemporary wares made at Derby, due to the fact that many of the workers had previously been employed at the earlier concern. Throughout the short lifespan of Pinxton the main output was concerned with tablewares, including teacups, coffee-cans, tea-and coffee-services, beakers, cabinet cups and saucers, dishes, plates, jugs, hors d'oeuvres sets, bowls and ice-pails.

The painting of the porcelain made during Billingley's three years at Pinxton was generally of a very high quality. For much of the time that Billingsley was at Derby (1774-1796) he had benefited from his association with the painter Zachariah Boreman, who had moved from Duesbury's Chelsea factory to Derby in 1783. Boreman was a particularly talented miniature landscape painter, and whilst Billingsley is better known for his naturalistic flower-painting, he also became a skilled painter of Boreman-type landscapes, which feature on many of the early examples of Pinxton tablewares. The most pleasing of these landscapes are in a limited palette of green, brown, yellow and light blue, without any restricting framing. Simple beaker forms were frequently painted with similar landscapes in a reddish-brown or bright purple monochrome enamel. The latter colour was later used by Billingsley when he was decorating at Mansfield.

Landscapes were often coupled with attractive ground decoration such as the small 'Angoulême sprig' similar to that frequently used at Derby. More original to English porcelain was the delicately painted arabesques and French Empire-style patterns, painted *en grisaille* (varying shades of grey) under a pale translucent canary yellow. Production of the fine Billingsley paste seems to have ceased after the inventor's departure, from which time a paste practically identical to that of contemporary Derby was produced, with a more opaque and thicker body.

(For colour illustration, see *p. 97)*

Worcester (Dr Wall period)

Most of the porcelain made at the Worcester Porcelain Company during the lifetime of the well-known Dr Wall (*d.* 1776), has always been comparatively easy to identify, although there has always been a little competition between Worcester and Liverpool porcelain collectors concerning certain classes of tablewares with enamel decoration of *Chinoiseries.*

Recent excavations on the site of the Warmstry House by Henry Sandon, Curator of the Dyson Perrins Museum, and the Worcester Royal Porcelain Company Ltd., have now helped to clear up the confusion between the very early wares made at Lund and Miller's Bristol factory and those made in the first years of Worcester, and between the Worcester porcelains of the Davis and Flight period and those made at Thomas Turner's rival concern at Caughley in Shropshire.

Although Dr Wall and his fourteen partners claimed credit for introducing a new type of soft-paste porcelain containing soap-rock, there appears to be little doubt that the originators of this very fine body were Lund and Miller who were producing some well-designed tablewares at Bristol between 1748 and 1752, when the entire Bristol concern was taken over by Worcester.

The finds on the Warmstry House site have proved that, apart from a very limited number of moulded wares and figures which have the word 'Bristol' or 'Bristoll' in relief, many of the earlier shapes could have been produced at either factory. Many of the forms of the so-called Bristol/Worcester wares were based on silver prototypes of sauce-boats, cream-jugs and teapots. The decoration used at both factories was mainly *Chinoiseries,* and use was made of both the popular Chinese palettes, *famille verte* (the green family) so popular during the reign of the Emperor K'ang Hsi (1662–1722), and the *famille rose* (the rose family) used in China from about 1720, when chloride-of-gold was first used in the Far East to produce colours ranging from a pale pink to a deep crimson.

The underglaze-blue decoration used on wares of the Bristol/Worcester period had a tendency to run, producing a rather blurred image, but many of these early pieces can be readily recognised from repetitive characteristics of the painters. In his book *English Blue-and-White Porcelain of the 18th Century,* Dr

Watney discusses many distinctive styles of underglaze-blue decoration used at these two factories, such as the 'three-dot' method, 'the swimming ducks', 'the zig-zag fence', the prunus-root' and the 'cormorant'.

Prior to about 1758 the only marks occasionally seen on Worcester underglaze-blue wares refer to the painter, but from that time onwards the well-known Worcester crescent or 'W' was often used. Wares decorated in enamel colours were less frequently marked and although the underglaze-blue mark of a fretted square intended to suggest a Chinese seal-mark was introduced in about 1760, it was by no means constantly used.

The Warmstry House excavations proved that Worcester produced some very fine porcelain during the Dr Wall period, but at the same time evidence came to light that many inferior pieces which had previously been 'blamed' on Caughley, did in fact originate at Worcester during the 'Davis and Flight' period; these are the wares decorated with poor-quality underglaze-blue prints, marked with numerals one to nine, painted to resemble a Chinese character. The wasters also indicate that there is no foundation for the belief that Caughley ever deliberately applied its 'C' mark in a manner resembling the Worcester crescent.

(For colour illustration, see *p. 98)*

Worcester (1776-1840)

In 1783 the Worcester factory was purchased by Thomas Flight for his two sons, Joseph and John, and from this time onwards there was a succession of partners. When John Flight died in 1791, the remaining brother took Martin Barr into partnership and from 1792 to 1807, the firm traded as 'Flight and Barr'. During this period their mark consisted of 'F & B'. A less conspicuous mark sometimes overlooked is an incised 'B'. In 1807 Martin Barr's son became a partner and the title changed to 'Barr, Flight and Barr' (1807-1813). Again, either the full name, place and address of their London showrooms was used as a mark, or an impressed 'B F B' under a crown. The last independent period was much longer and from 1813 to 1840, following the death of Martin Barr Senior, the title was again changed to 'Flight, Barr and Barr', when George Barr replaced the elder Martin. The firm was then amalgamated with that of Messrs Chamberlain.

The Flight factory seems to have concentrated mainly on large elaborate services with sparse neoclassical style decoration, using the more brassy-looking mercury gilding. Several of the popular Worcester patterns first introduced in the Dr Wall period (1751-1776) continued in use to the end of the Flight period (1840) including the pattern consisting of bands of stylised flowers alternately painted in a spiral fashion in underglaze-blue and red-enamel and gilt, known today as the 'catherine whorl', 'wheel' or 'Queen Charlotte' pattern. Another pattern which enjoyed similar popularity was the 'Royal Lily', a more formal pattern in underglaze-blue of stylised lilies, first introduced during the Davis and Flight period (1776-93), and almost immediately imitated at Caughley.

During the 1783-92 period, when Flights were in sole charge, they produced some well-designed tea- and coffee-services, which at times had much in common with early Chamberlain wares; they produced a similar spiral fluted moulding, but without the twin lines on the upper ridges, so indicative of Chamberlain's work. Handle-less tea-bowls were still popular, and teapot stands appear to have been considered a necessity, but just one dish sufficed.

Flight produced a very finely decorated dinner-service in 1792 for the Duke of Clarence who later reigned as King William IV (1830-37). The decoration in sepia monochrome was by John Pennington and depicts the mythological figure of 'Hope and the Anchor' in various scenes. Shells and feathers were frequently used as alternative styles of decoration during the Barr, Flight and Barr period. This was often the work of Thomas Baxter (d. 1821) who, after working in London as an independent decorator until 1814, spent his remaining years between Swansea and Worcester.

A rather less attractive pattern, also used at other major porcelain factories is known as the 'Bishop Sumner' pattern, named after a Bishop of Worcester. It is a rather fussy Chinese design including a kylin, phoenix, rocks, plants and fabulous animals. This pattern was popular on Worcester dessert-services from about 1780 onwards.

During the Barr, Flight and Barr period use was made of the newly invented process of bat-printing as a form of decoration: the oiled pattern is transferred from a stipple-engraved copper-plate to the surface of the glaze by means of a slab, or bat, of glue or gelatine, and the enamel powder is then dusted on and retained by the oil.

(For colour illustration, see p. 107)

Worcester (Chamberlains and Kerr & Binns)

Following the death of Dr Wall in 1776, the Worcester factory started to produce some very inferior wares. This situation continued until the works were purchased in 1783 by Thomas Flight, the London agent of the company, for his two sons Joseph and John who almost immediately restored the factory to a flourishing concern. Robert Chamberlain who started at the factory as an apprentice during the Dr Wall period, left in about 1786 to establish his own decorating establishment, where, for several years, he and some other former Flight workers were engaged in decorating porcelain made at Caughley by Thomas Turner.

In 1791 Chamberlain set up his own porcelain production which from the start was a great success, despite the comparative simplicity of much of his decoration which at times had much in common with Caughley, Coalport and the Flight partnerships of Worcester. Many early Chamberlain tewares were fluted and can be easily identified by the 'train-line' effect on the peak of the spiral flutes. Flight made similar wares without this feature.

These attractive early wares soon gave way to the louder and more ornate taste of the day. 'Japan' patterns, vaguely derived from Japanese Arita porcelain, and other heavily decorated services were produced, with superb painting all too frequently lost within a profusion of gilding and other enamelled decoration.

In 1840 the original Worcester factory, then under the partnership of Flight, Barr and Barr, was amalgamated with Chamberlain and Co. and the entire plant and stock removed from the site of the original Worcester factory at Warmstry House to Chamberlain's factory. Following further changes of partnership the factory changed hands in 1852, continuing until 1862 under R. W. Binns and W. H. Kerr, trading as Kerr and Binns, or W. H. Kerr and Co. In 1862 the present-day factory was started under the title of the Worcester Royal Porcelain Company. Kerr and Binns devoted themselves to restoring the factory to its 18th-century standing, with a whole succession of new styles and ideas, and more attention was paid to decorative ornamental wares than to services for the table.

In addition to this continuation of the Worcester factory, a further concern was established in 1800 by Thomas Grainger, which in 1812 became Grainger, Lee and Co. This undertaking made some high-quality dessert services from about 1840–1860 and it is known to have produced many wares for the London retailer John Mortlock, a firm which was in business from 1746 until about 1930.

Prior to 1850, Grainger produced only porcelain. From then onwards he made a new 'semi-porcelain' which was first publicised at the 1851 Exhibition. It was an ideal material for dinner-services, being hard, durable and able to withstand rapid changes of temperature without cracking and yet had the appearance of fine china. This concern was absorbed by the Worcester Royal Porcelain Company in 1889.

(For colour illustration, see *p. 108)*

Opposite: ICE-PAIL *with* COVER *and* LINER *of soapstone porcelain, marked 'FBB' under a crown, impressed, and probably painted by Thomas Baxter. English (Worcester, Flight, Barr & Barr period), c.1815.*

Overleaf top: TEA-CUP *and* SAUCER *of bone china. English (Worcester, Kerr & Binns period, 1852-62).*

Bottom: CABINET-CUP, COVER *and* STAND *of bone china, painted with the portrait of Charlotte Corday. English (Worcester, Kerr & Binns period, 1852-62).*

Caughley

Overleaf: *Collection of Caughley porcelain, decorated in underglaze-blue. Large moulded* JUG, *inscribed 'Edw. Jeffreys Salop'. Mask-spouted* JUG. *Transfer-printed* MUG, *with printed 'S' mark.* CREAM-BOAT, *marked with an impressed star.* PLATE, *decorated in powder-blue, marked with a pseudo Chinese character. Three small* SALTS, *marked with a painted 'S'.* TEAPOT, *marked 'C'. Small sparrow-beaked* JUG, *marked 'C'. All English (Caughley), all made between 1772 and 1799; ht. (moulded jug) 23 cm/9 in.*

Opposite: Selection of Liverpool soft-paste porcelain, decorated in underglaze-blue. DISH, *made by Messrs. Pennington & Part, 1769-99.* TEAPOT, *by Richard Chaffers, 1754-65.* SAUCE-BOAT, *by Pennington, 1780-85.* PATTY-DISH, *by Pennington, 1775-80.* SWEETMEAT-DISH, *by William Ball, 1755-69. All English (Liverpool); ht. (teapot) 12 cm/4½ in.*

The excavations on the site of the Worcester factory, (*see* p.104) and those on the site of Thomas Turner's factory at Caughley (pronounced Calf-ley) in Shropshire, have provided substantial evidence to help identify wares which have previously been wrongly attributed.

Thomas Turner (1749-1809) was initially trained as an engraver at the Worcester factory under Robert Hancock. In 1772 he moved to Caughley, near Brosely, Shropshire, where he started his manufacture of porcelain in a factory which had previously only been concerned with the production of crude earthenwares for domestic purposes. The evidence of wasters found on the sites of Worcester and Caughley suggested that for many years some rather inferior blue-and-white porcelain, previously attributed to Caughley, was in fact made at the Worcester factory during the so-called 'Davis and Flight' period (1776-93).

SPOON-TRAY *of soapstone porcelain, decorated with underglaze-blue and gilt, marked 'Salopian' impressed. English (Shropshire, Caughley, the factory of Thomas Turner), c.1785; lgth. 17 cm/6⅝ in.*

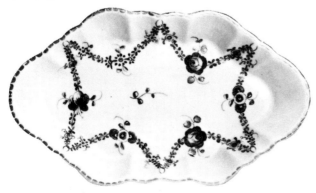

It would appear from Turner's early wares that it was his aim to compete with the mass of blue-painted hard-paste Chinese porcelain which at that time was being imported to Britain in great quantities via the East India Company. His early wares which were of an almost identical soapstone porcelain to that of Worcester, were nearly all modelled in the style of contemporary Chinese imports but decorated with underglaze-blue prints from engraved copper-plates, in place of the more lengthy Chinese painting which called for skilled decorators. Records of the engravings used have helped considerably in making possible many sure attributions to Caughley.

The entire output of Turner's factory was concerned primarily with tablewares and when the stock of the factory was eventually sold in 1799, the list included 'a great number of beautiful tea and coffee equipages of various much approved patterns ... richly executed in enamel and burnished gold together with a great variety of new and elegant blue-and-white tea- and coffee-sets, table- and dessert-services, muffin plates, butter tubs, mugs, jugs, egg cups and drainer, butter cups of different sorts and sizes, pickle-shells, eye baths, asparagus servers, toy table and teasets and candlesticks ... with a great variety of other articles'.

For many years, collectors were puzzled by the great variation in the types of decoration applied to Caughley wares. It is very rare that wasters which have been decorated with enamel colours are found on the site of a pottery but since about 1970, documents have provided evidence to prove that some of the fine enamel decoration seen on Caughley porcelain was added between about 1785 and 1790 at the Worcester workshop of Robert Chamberlain who left the Worcester factory to start an independent business of his own, initially as a decorator of mainly Caughley wares and later as a potter with a very successful pottery of his own which in 1840 was to absorb the Flight Barr and Barr Worcester factory.

Many of the Worcester and Caughley wares are very similar in form and decoration, and in the absence of a mark, it is only by careful study of the moulded features and the slight variation of underglaze-blue transfer-prints, that these pieces can be attributed with any certainty.

(*For colour illustration, see p. 109*)

Liverpool

It is only during recent years that research concerning the 18th-century Liverpool porcelain factories has enabled distinctive classes of tablewares to be recognised as the work of a particular factory.

The most prolific porcelain factory in the area was situated on Shaw's Brow, now William Brown Street, where the original works were established following the signing of an agreement in 1755 between Richard Chaffers, Philip Christian and Robert Podmore, formerly of the Worcester factory. By the end of 1756, Messrs Richard Chaffers and Company were advertising that 'all the ware is proved with boiling water before it is exposed for sale'. Owing to the involvement of Podmore the early wares had much in common with the 'Dr Wall' period at Worcester.

The porcelain first produced at Chaffers's factory was of a phosphatic paste (containing calcined animal bone) decorated with either *Chinoiserie* subjects in a very distinctive style or enamel prints applied by Sadler, of such subjects as Frederick the Great, William Pitt, or The arms of the Society of Bucks. For a short period Chaffers made both bone-porcelain and soapstone porcelain of the Worcester type. The underglaze-blue painting can be rather confusing as many of the designs used were copied from the earlier examples of Bow, Worcester or

Derby. Chaffers's best tablewares were produced during the 1760s, when large quantities of mugs, coffee-pots, teapots, coffee-cups and other teawares were in great demand. Richard Chaffers died in 1765, but his wife and children continued to have an interest in the factory until 1769, when Christian purchased their share of the business, which then became known as 'Philip Christian and Son'.

Some of the soaprock porcelain produced before Philip Christian sold the lease of his soaprock deposits to the Worcester Company in 1776, was decorated with some rather inferior versions of the underglaze-blue transfer-prints made from the plates Robert Hancock produced for Thomas Turner of Caughley. Christian made more use of enamelled decoration than Chaffers did, and often applied a Sèvres-like ground of underglaze-blue marbling with fine gilding on bowls, jugs and teawares.

James, John and Seth Pennington were potting during the late years of the 1760s, but the exact whereabouts in Liverpool of their manufactory is not known. It is known that Seth Pennington and John Part became partners and took over the Shaw's Brow works which were left unoccupied after the closure of Philip Christian's production in 1776. There is very little consistency in the quality of the bone-porcelain production by Seth Pennington up to the early years

Three leaf-shaped DISHES of porcelain, painted in underglaze-blue. English (Liverpool or Shelton, at the Reid/Baddeley factories), 1756-61; lgth. (approximately) 19 cm/7½ in.

Liverpool

of the 19th century. Certain forms are accepted as being good indications of his work, including poor reproductions of Worcester, cream-boats moulded with acanthus leaves, sauce-boats with a face moulded on either side, together with a bird thought to be the Liver bird from the crest of the City. Handles in the form of a snake biting the upper rim of sauce-boats are a sure indication, as are knobs in the form of birds or lions *couchants*.

Samuel Gilbody was producing porcelain in the same area as Chaffers from about 1754 to 1761. Many of his wares were decorated with Sadler prints and he is also accredited with a very distinctive style of heavily potted wares decorated with a combination of underglaze-blue and red enamel.

Other major Liverpool porcelain manufacturers were William Reid (*c.* 1755-61) and William Ball (*c.* 1755-69).

Another pottery whose wares have until recently been sadly overlooked is that set up at Toxteth Park, Liverpool, in 1796 by Samuel Worthington who took over facilities and premises which were originally constructed in 1772 in connection with copper-smelting. A very full account of the opening of his Herculaneum Pottery appeared in a local newspaper on 15th December, 1796. In order to attract some skilled labour the proprietor had invited a group of potters from the Staffordshire town of Burslem, to enjoy the merrymaking. (*See* 'The Herculaneum China and Earthenware Manufactory, Toxteth, Liverpool', a paper read to the English Ceramic Circle by Alan Smith—January, 1967.)

By 1798, Samuel Worthington and Co. were seeking orders 'for Cream Colours, Enamelled, printed and Fancy Ware Services, Enamelled in any pattern'. In common with so many other early-19th-century potteries, their trade was seriously affected by the Napoleonic wars, but immediately after 1815 the factory entered a new period of great prosperity certainly until the 1820s, when further decline in business and increasing competition from Staffordshire forced the factory to close in 1833.

Judging by the materials sold at the time of the closure of the factory, the main output of the Herculaneum Pottery was concerned with cream-coloured wares, earthenwares and pearlwares, decorated with a wide variety of printed decoration, both underglaze-blue and in coloured enamels. (The sale indicates that over 700 different prints were used on their wares.)

A limited number of marked wares has enabled a variety of prints to be used to help identify a further range of unmarked wares. All show the rather heavy black prints, some underglaze of a type long associated with a form of jug previously attributed to Liverpool without any substantial evidence.

From about 1800 to 1810 a very fine range of high quality stonewares was produced at the Herculaneum Pottery, many of which bear the impressed mark 'Herculaneum'. The black basaltes made there were at times moulded with well-known groups of classical subjects but they lack the pleasing simplicity of Wedgwood's earlier wares. The stoneware mugs with relief figure subjects, in the John Turner tradition, became a little heavy in appearance due to turned decoration. The buff-coloured earthenware wine-coolers are decorated with vine reliefs and Bacchus heads, almost identical to those produced by John Davenport, but are of a more pleasing cup form than the latter's barrels. Seemingly seeking originality at all costs, the well-shaped coffee-pots of maroon coloured stoneware with applied cream-coloured reliefs are a little too reminiscent of the German imitations of Wedgwood, made by Schiller and Gerbing at Bodenbach, Bohemia.

The City of Liverpool Museum has examples of some very well produced bone-china tewares, some bearing the name 'Herculaneum' impressed. Such wares were decorated in a wide range of designs, including coloured enamel flowers, sepia-toned landscapes, and landscapes with figures in enamel colours, all of good practical form showing originality in shape. The warehouse price for a forty-three piece tea- and coffee-service of 'White China Best' was £1 6s 0d.

(*For colour illustration*, see *pp. 74 and 110*)

Plymouth & Bristol

William Cookworthy, a Plymouth alchemist and Quaker preacher, was very interested in producing a true porcelain and in this connection he made the acquaintance of one Andrew Duché who, as the correspondence of 1745 bears out, claimed to have produced porcelain of the Far Eastern type from clays discovered in America. Research has recently been done into his claims by Graham Hood who is keeper of the collections at Colonial Williamsburg, Virginia, but no evidence has yet been produced by him to support them.

The factory established by Cookworthy and his shareholders in 1768 at Coxside, near Plymouth was moved to Bristol in 1770 where production continued until 1781, when Richard Champion, a shareholder, sold the remaining years of the patented formula to a group of Staffordshire potters, who formed the New Hall porcelain company. It is usual to consider the wares of Plymouth and Bristol together, as those of William Cookworthy and Richard Champion. Champion, who was a Bristol ship-owner and a potter engaged in the manufacture of tin-glazed earthenware, was a partner in the Plymouth New Invented Porcelain Manufactory from the start. He took over control in 1774.

The earliest documentary piece of porcelain known to have been made by this company is in the British Museum, London. It is a small cylindrical mug, decorated in underglaze-blue with the coat-of-arms of the City of Plymouth and the inscription 'Plymouth Manufactory'. It is dated on the base 14th March, 1768. The Plymouth tablewares vary a great deal in quality: the paste was sometimes stained by kiln-smoke as they obviously found it difficult to control accurately the necessary temperature of about 1400 °C, and some over-fired bell-shaped tankards decorated in underglaze-blue have taken on the appearance of a salt-glazed stoneware with grey-black decoration. Their difficulties are also suggested by the lack of flat wares which were very prone to warping.

The tablewares made during the Bristol period (1770–1781) at first tended to continue the Plymouth tradition, but from the time Richard Champion assumed control in 1774, he began to specialise in tea- and coffee-services, modelled in the current classical styles, claiming his wares had 'the strength of

TEAPOT *and* STAND *of hard-paste porcelain, painted in enamel colours. English (Bristol), c.1775; ht. 16.5 cm/6½ in.*

Dresden' coupled with 'elegance perfectly resembling the beautiful manufacture of Sèvres'. A large number of services were especially made to order for his patrons, personal and political friends who included Thomas Pitt, Joseph Harford, Edward Brice and Mrs Edmund Burke. The service made for the latter was a present from Champion's wife, following the successful election of Edmund Burke as the Member of Parliament for Bristol in 1744. In addition Champion produced large quantities of so-called 'cottage-china', decorated with Sèvres-type garlands, festoons, ribbons, laurels and husks. We know little of the artists concerned with these humbler wares, but the work of two of the flower-painters is very distinctive; one painter carelessly scattered small flower-sprays over the entire ground, whilst the other preferred more stylised and carefully arranged floral bouquets. Some rather more ambitious little crimson monochrome harbour-scenes, painted in the Meissen fashion are sometimes seen on Bristol wares accompanied with the crossed-swords mark of the Saxon factory.

The porcelain of Plymouth and Bristol were often marked, first with the alchemists sign for tin (the 2-4 mark) in underglaze-blue, brown or red enamel or gilt. This mark probably continued in use at Bristol until about 1772, when an enamel or underglaze-blue cross, sometimes together with a 'B' was used. Any accompanying numbers refer to the painter or gilder.

(For colour illustration, see p. 119)

New Hall

In 1781, Richard Champion, the proprietor of the Bristol hard-paste porcelain factory, sold the remaining years of his porcelain patent to a group of six Staffordshire potters, who together formed the New Hall China Manufactory.

There was a marked difference in the appearance of the hard-paste porcelain of Cookworthy and Champion's Plymouth and Bristol wares and that produced by the New Hall partners. This was due to the glaze used at the later factory containing a proportion of lead, enabling a lower glaze-firing temperature to be used at a second firing, rather than the more customary hard feldspathic glaze which was usually fired to the same high temperature as the body. This later process resulted in a fairly thick glaze which was often pitted with minute burst bubbles, which tended to reduce the high gloss seen on the earlier wares.

From the start they appear to have concentrated on complete tea-services, including the tea-caddy and spoon-trays, dessert-services and the smaller wares essential for the middle-class dining-table of the late 18th century. The majority of early New Hall teapots were of a globular form, in distinct contrast with the later, and better known, silver shapes. These early teapots can usually be identified by a rather unique handle, made up of two sections, resulting in an upright thumb-rest. An alternative style is very similar to that used at the Bristol factory, and is decorated with a raised husk moulding. A further popular type of handle used on New Hall teapots is today generally referred to as a 'clip' handle, consisting of two separate sections, overlapping to form a less obtrusive, but still practical thumb-rest. This style of handle is rarely seen on wares made after about 1787.

The New Hall factory is particularly associated with teapots which followed silver forms; the lid nestling into a raised circular collar; a simple loop handle sometimes moulded with a fine herring-bone pattern and a straight protruding spout of Chinese form with leaf-moulding on the underside. The later teapots are larger, with swan-neck spouts, simple traditional handles and vase-shaped knobs, with a vertical hole drilled through, to allow for the escape of the steam—a rather impractical idea. The upright walls are either reeded, a combination of facets and flutes, or ogee-curved flutes, again coupled with flat facets.

During the 1790s oval-shaped teapots were introduced, with curved fluted decoration—a style imitated by several other contemporary factories. From about 1800 the well-known boat, or scuttle-shaped pot gained popularity, sometimes with a practical knob in the form of a *fleur-de-lys*. From about 1812 teapot shapes became much simpler and, with the change-over to bone-china, only one form appears to have been made. This was of a rectangular shape with rounded corners a distinctive feature again being the knob which consisted of an inset rectangular pyramid.

In his excellent book *New Hall and Its Imitators* David Holgate explains how the pattern numbers on some New Hall wares can help to decide upon an approximate date. Since the factory closed in 1835, the highest number seen on the later bone-china wares is in the region of 2270. The highest pattern-number recorded on hard-paste porcelain, production of which was stopped in about 1812, appears to be around 1040.

Coalport

Factory site excavations have recently helped to clarify the wares of a factory started by John Rose in Shropshire in about 1797. According to Llewellynn Jewitt's *The Ceramic Art of Great Britain* (first published in London in 1878) John Rose was the son of a farmer and apprenticed to Thomas Turner of the Caughley China Works, which he eventually purchased in 1799. By this time he and his partners were almost certainly producing porcelain at a newly established factory of their own on the banks of the River Severn at Coalport, in Shropshire. There is still some confusion as to which wares were produced by John Rose at Caughley between 1799 and 1814, when the Caughley works was finally closed, and which were produced during the same period at his own Coalport factory. In many instances, wasters found on the Caughley site have enabled a class of wares of the New Hall type to be classified as Caughley/Coalport, whereas those found adjacent to the Coalport site have provided further evidence of the early wares.

A water-colour exhibited in the ceramic gallery of the Victoria and Albert Museum, London shows the interior of Thomas Baxter's London decorating studio at 1 Goldsmith Street, Gough Square. The painting is by Thomas Baxter Junior and dates from 1810. Pinned to a wall in the studio is a list, headed 'Coalport White China', such as Baxter was purchasing for decoration. In the same collection are two beautifully painted plates, unmarked, but of Coalport form, and signed and dated by Baxter (1808 and 1809). The Victoria and Albert Museum collection also includes a rare plate marked 'Coalbrook Dale'. These three plates have one feature in common—six small indentations at regular intervals around the rim, somewhat similar to those sometimes seen on Chinese dishes of the Sung period. Wasters found on the Caughley site have confirmed that this was a comparatively common Caughley/Coalport feature.

Coalport made large numbers of tea- and dinner-services during the pre-1814 period, many decorated with the popular 'Japan' patterns which are more often associated with Derby or Worcester, but in these cases the matching of moulded details on the finished wares with wasters 'in the biscuit' give ample evidence of their origin. The majority of the early Coalport wares are unmarked, but between 1810 and 1825 a so-called 'top-heavy 2' impressed into the reverse of plates, can be taken as a clear indication of Coalport manufacture.

Existing factory pattern books have also confirmed certain indentification of later and more ornate wares, where the enamel patterns help the collector to recognise the rather fussy spouts, handles and knobs of teapots, cup-handles and sucrier handles used from about 1820 onwards.

John Rose took over both the Nantgarw and Swansea porcelain manufactories and in many instances there is a great similarity in the wares of the three concerns.

The pattern numbers used on Coalport can often be a guide to the earlier wares, owing to the method of numbering. The first series started in about 1805. Numbers were used progressively from 1–1000 until about the year 1824; the next series from about 1833–38 used fractions e.g. 2/123, up to 2/999 when a 3/ number was used. This system was continued up to at least 8/number. Later on in the 19th century progressive numbers were used together with self-explanatory and recorded factory-marks.

In the middle of the 19th century Coalport produced some excellent reproductions of Sèvres porcelain, even the mark was at times included.

William Billingsley (Nantgarw & Swansea)

For many years William Billingsley, who was formerly the leading flower-painter of the Derby factory, had cherished the ambition of owning his own porcelain factory where he could produce a porcelain resembling the soft-paste of Sèvres.

After leaving the Derby factory in 1796 Billingsley went to Pinxton where he stayed until 1799, but the Billingsley soft-paste resulted in such a high percentage of faulty wares that he was compelled to move on to various towns in the area, where he worked primarily as an independent decorator. For a short period he was also at the Worcester factory of Barr, Flight and Barr where he carried out further experiments to try and improve the stability of his porcelain body. He was so encouraged with the results it seems, that by November 1813, he had moved to Nantgarw, near Cardiff, where, together with his son-in-law Samuel Walker, he started to produce a soft-paste porcelain which, when successfully fired, was of a most beautiful quality. Financial difficulties, however, necessitated a further move to L. W. Dillwyn's pottery at Swansea where he continued to make a modified and more economic porcelain until 1817 when financial aid enabled him to return to Nantgarw, and there he remained until 1819. It was during the later Nantgarw period that Billingsley produced most of his much sought-after tablewares.

Having produced a frit porcelain nearing the perfection of Sèvres, he was naturally greatly influenced by Sèvres' 18th-century wares and other contemporary French porcelains of the Empire period. The majority of his plates were of French rococo form, with moulded 'C' scrolls forming a six-lobed pattern. This pattern was at one time thought to have been imitated by John Rose, but excavations on the Caughley/Coalport site suggest that Rose was most probably using it prior to Billingsley. The quality of the porcelain of many Billingsley wares is not always seen to advantage, due to the extravagant enamel and gilt decoration added in London where his white-glazed wares were greatly demanded by china dealers and retailers such as Mortlocks of Oxford Street, whose name often accompanies the impressed mark of 'Nant-Garw' over 'CW' (China Works).

Billingsley's style of flower-painting was often used by the London decorators and can at times be identified by an iridescent outline around the edge of the enamel, which is not present on the porcelain decorated in South Wales. Some later Nantgarw porcelain can be identified through the work of the painter Thomas Pardoe (d. 1823) who was engaged by Billingsley's and Walker's financial backer, W. W. Young, to decorate stock left behind in 1819, when he was endeavouring to try and recoup some of his losses. In addition to the customary flowers and birds, Pardoe was a talented painter of gardens and landscapes.

The recipe of the porcelain made during Billingsley's stay at Swansea was changed, bone-ash was added and the translucency took on a so-called 'duck-egg' green, but further modifications involving the use of soaprock resulted in a less pleasing material with a slightly pitted glaze and a brownish translucency. The mark on this paste consists of a single trident or two crossed tridents, impressed into the clay, which is referred to by collectors and dealers as 'trident' paste.

The majority of the wares produced at Swansea were in the French Empire style and included cabaret services, cabinet-cups with matching milk-jugs and sugar-basins. A less appreciated Swansea form is a straight-sided cylindrical mug with a distinctive angular handle.

Longport

Despite the fact that the factory established by John Davenport at Longport, Staffordshire, in 1794, continued in production until 1887, lack of knowledge concerning the productions had, until recently, meant that this very productive concern had been sadly neglected. Owing to the research of Terence A. Lockett, Chairman of the Northern Ceramic Society, this is no longer the case. His book *Davenport Pottery & Porcelain* has helped to fill this gap in our knowledge of these mainly 19th-century wares.

The factory was prosperous from the outset and by 1801 Davenport had also started to manufacture glass. Despite the fact that cream-coloured earthenware would have been considered a little out-dated by the end of the 18th century, the impressed anchor factory-mark is often found on tablewares of this type, with pattern numbers recorded between 59 and 275.

The factory produced wares in all the well-known Staffordshire bodies, including some finely potted tea-services from unglazed cane-coloured stoneware, often with attractively applied blue enamel decoration. Some rather unique wine-coolers with moulded decoration appear to have been a popular form in this same material. One of the most distinctive types of teawares produced during the early years of the 19th century were of an earthenware body, coloured throughout to a salmon-pink and decorated with sepia-toned landscapes or transfer-prints.

In common with the owners of many other Staffordshire concerns, John Davenport who, in about 1815, had taken his cousin James into partnership, made large quantities of pearlware, decorated with underglaze-blue transfer-prints. These were sometimes marked with the impressed anchor, without the accompanying name of 'Davenport'. Lockett notes that on rare occasions use was made of stipple-engraved transfer-prints.

Records indicate that Davenport began to produce wares from the comparatively new body of bone-china as early as about 1805, and if one is to assume that all the early pieces were marked with 'Longport' written in red enamel, they are exceedingly rare. A fine example of this ware is a two-handled covered cup and saucer in the collection of the Victoria and Albert Museum, which is painted with a landscape showing St Paul's cathedral in the far distance. Bone-china tea- and dessert-services were produced in quantity with well-painted flower subjects in the full enamel palette, usually on well-moulded forms of Continental origins.

Davenport's wares of 'Stone China', the tough and thickly potted earthenware body patented earlier by John Turner and the Masons, had a current reputation for being finer in potting and colour than that made by his competitors. This is certainly the case with his range of jugs of the well-known octagonal form, popularised by the Mason factory.

A form of mark used by Davenport between about 1830 and 1860 helps to date precisely some very fine earthenware decorated with delicate multi-coloured prints to 1836, pre-dating the better known prints seen on pot lids by many years.

During the second quarter of the 19th century Davenport produced some beautiful teawares of a quality more usually associated with Spode or John Rose of Coalport, including examples decorated with the so-called Billingsley-type roses.

The production of a dessert-service for King William IV is said to have brought Rockingham to financial ruin, but this was certainly not the case with Davenport, who, in 1830, received an order for a service for the King 'with a red and white rose, shamrock, thistle and leek, tied with the Union Riband', 134 pieces of this service still survive at Buckingham Palace.

(For colour illustration, see overleaf)

Opposite: SUCRIER *and* COVER, BREAKFAST CUP *and* SAUCER, *and* TEAPOT *of hard-paste porcelain, the family crest of a chough is possibly that of Tothill of Peamore, Devon. English (Bristol), c.1776; ht. (teapot) 15 cm/6 in.*

Overleaf: *Group of wares made at John Davenport's factory of Longport, Staffordshire.* CUP *of porcelain with gilt decoration, 1830–37.* MUG *of earthenware with 'bat-printed' decoration, 1815–30.* CUP *of porcelain with enamel decoration, mark in red for 1820–25.* CUP *and* SAUCER *of porcelain, 'Davenport' and registration mark in underglaze-blue, c.1850–55.* TEAPOT *of porcelain with red and puce enamel marks, c.1815.* MILK-JUG *of earthenware with salmon-coloured body, mark 'Davenport' and anchor impressed, c.1805–15; ht. (teapot) 14 cm/5½ in.*

Earthenware & Porcelain

Miles Mason

Overleaf: SAUCER-DISH *and* CREAM-JUG, *porcelain, decorated in enamel colour and gilt. The bat-printed insets represent the Four Seasons. The dish is marked 'N:128' in gold, the jug is impressed 'M. Mason' on foot-rim, 1802–06.* COFFEE-CAN *and* SAUCER *of bone china, with painted medallions in gold border, unmarked, 1805–10. All English (Staffordshire, made by Miles Mason at Lane Delph); dia. (saucer-dish) 20.8 cm/8 in.*

Opposite: *A group of Rockingham teawares, porcelain, showing five of the eight types of handle known to have been used. All pieces, with the exception of the* SUGAR SUCRIER, *bear the red 'Griffin' mark used from 1826 to 1830, the former has the same mark in puce, used from 1830 to 1842. All English (Rockingham).*

Some of the finest Staffordshire wares were those of Miles Mason (1752–1822) and his descendants, who continued the production until 1848. Mason's earlier years were spent in London where he became a prominent member of the Worshipful Company of Glass-Sellers. His venture into the field of porcelain manufacture did not start until 1796, when he entered a partnership with Thomas Wolfe and John Luckcock (or Lucock) to make porcelain at Islington China Works, Liverpool. At the same time he became a partner to George Wolfe who was concerned with an earthenware pottery at Fenton Culvert in Staffordshire. Both these partnerships ended in 1800, shortly before he started to produce both earthenware and porcelain independently at Victoria Works, Lane Delph, where he remained until 1807 when he moved to a larger factory, the Minerva Works, Fenton. These works were eventually taken over by his sons, George and Charles James, in 1813. The Bagnall factory which Miles Mason had also acquired was continued by his son, William.

When the New Hall patent for producing hard-paste porcelain from china-clay and china-stone expired in 1796, the same two materials were used by many potters to produce wares of the New Hall type which was almost identical in body to Far Eastern porcelain, but with a much softer glaze applied at a second kiln-firing at a lower temperature.

In common with other Staffordshire potters Miles Mason produced a wide range of tablewares of this newly available material. He later made bone-china, earthenware and stone-china (Ironstone China).

These materials were used to fashion a wide range of tablewares; in 1804 he was advertising 'British Nankin' wares, similar to the underglaze-blue printed wares coming to England via the vessels of the East India Company. He was in addition making reproductions of these wares to order, either to enlarge or replace breakages of Oriental or Continental services.

Our knowledge concerning the life and wares of Miles Mason is due primarily to the research of Reginald Haggar, President of the Northern Ceramic Circle and widely known to all students of English pottery and porcelain. Mr Haggar informs us that Miles Mason produced 'five basic teapot shapes which were capable of variation by fluting or grooving and/or by changes of handles and spouts. The earliest is a silver shape, oval in plan, straight sided with a flattened shoulder' (English Ceramic Circle Transactions). He also gives detailed descriptions of boat-shaped teapots and of three different ovoid forms with sucriers and creamers *en suite*. The majority of coffee-cans, tea-cups and creamers have a very good aid to easy identification: the handles have a short 'spur' at the top, to serve as a thumb-rest.

Miles Mason used a great variety of patterns applied in almost every manner then known, including underglaze-blue prints, sometimes with additional gilt borders, bat-prints in enamel from stipple-engraved plates, enamel painting in both Chinese and Japanese styles, simple neo-classical border patterns in colour and gilt, New-Hall-type sprigs and border patterns and good quality painting using animals, birds, landscapes, etc.

The name Mason is better known by today's collector's for the large quantities of 'Mason's Ironstone China' produced between 1813, when C. J. Mason took out the necessary patent for a novel type of hard, opaque earthenware, and 1848, when the factory was taken over. This material was used to produce large dinner- and dessert-services.

(For colour illustration, see p. 121)

Spode

Josiah Spode was born in 1733, his father died when he was only six years of age and one year later, it is said, he was working in the 'Potteries'. He was sixteen years old when he was hired by Thomas Whieldon at a sum of 2s 3d to 3s 3d per week. In 1762 Josiah Spode was working at the factory of Turner and Banks in Stoke. By this time he was married and had a son, Josiah Spode II (1754–1827) and by 1770, Josiah I and Tomlinson had taken over the Turner and Banks works and were producing a blue-decorated cream-coloured earthenware of a very high quality. By 1776 Josiah Spode had completed the purchase of the works and had become a master potter.

Whilst his contemporary, Josiah Wedgwood, was influenced by the current taste for the neo-classical, Spode fell under the charm of the Chinese porcelain wares which were coming into England in great quantities via the vessels of the East India Company. His aim was to reproduce these wares in a refined white earthenware, decorated in underglaze-blue transfer-prints. These wares number among the most popular present-day collectors' items ever made by the Spode factory.

In *Blue and White Transfer Ware 1780–1840* A. W. Coysh writes about the original sources of many of the engraved designs used on Spode's tablewares. The names of the patterns were often printed on the reverse side of the pieces, but usually only as subjects, not source. The title 'Chase after a Wolf' for example, has now been identified as one of the Indian Sporting series. The original aquatint engraving was by Thomas Hewitt and was used to illustrate a publication by G. Ormer of New Bond Street, which appeared during 1805 in monthly parts, with text by Captain Thomas Williamson. Each item of the dinner-service was illustrated with a different subject, including 'Death of the Bear', 'Hunting a Buffalo' and many other sadistic titles. These patterns were obviously popular for they were used until after 1847, when the factory was under the sole direction of William Copeland. The same subjects were also used by other Staffordshire potters. Another 'Caramanian' series was based on the engravings used to illustrate a published series of 1801–4, showing 'views in the Ottoman Empire', chiefly in Caramania, a part of Asia Minor. The transfer-printed wares of Spode can often be easily recognised without the aid of a

PLATE *of earthenware, transfer-printed with version of 'Willow' pattern, marked 'Spode' impressed. English (Staffordshire, Spode's factory at Stoke); dia. 23 cm/9 in.*

mark, on account of their superb quality of material and well-applied prints.

Josiah Spode II (1754–1827) is accredited with bone-china, introduced soon after 1796 when he was permitted to mix the ingredients of hard-paste porcelain with calcined bone (approximately 25% china-clay, 25% china stone and 50% bone ash) to produce a fine white translucent material, which has remained the pattern for all English china to this day. Bone-china was used by Spode to produce a wide range of tea- and dessert-services which had a great deal in common with Mason's wares. Spode china, like that of late Caughley and Coalport, was sometimes painted with attractive landscapes in monochrome enamel. Knowledge of the exact form of the handles used by Spode is a great aid to identification of the earlier pieces which often had only a pattern number, up until about 1810, from which time this number was usually accompanied with the word 'Spode'.

From 1805 Spode was producing fine dinner- and dessert-services from 'Stone China', or 'New Stone', a patent he is thought to have purchased from W. and J. Turner.

(For colour illustration, see p. 133)

Minton

Prior to establishing his own pottery at Stoke-upon-Trent in 1793, Thomas Minton, who was born and educated in Shrewsbury, was apprenticed as an engraver to Thomas Turner at the Caughley factory. For a time he was working as an engraver of copper-plates in London, where he reputedly did work for Spode, Adam and Wedgwood. He returned to Staffordshire in about 1788 to 1789, continuing as a master-engraver until 1793.

His early, unmarked wares were mostly decorated with underglaze-blue transfer-prints on good quality pearlware. One of Minton's earliest engravings is thought to be a form of the so-called Willow Pattern, a design suggested by Chinese export porcelain and executed by Minton whilst at the Caughley factory. Another popular design attributed to Minton is seen on Staffordshire blue-and-white transfer wares, this is The Buffalo Pattern, which according to Jewitt, was engraved for Spode. Other potters also used this same pattern.

Within a short time of establishing his own pottery, Minton was sending pottery to warehouses in London and Bath, and selling wares to Chamberlain of Worcester and to Wedgwood. Until 1797 Minton produced only white and cream-coloured earthenware and blue-printed wares. He then introduced porcelain into his range, and in common with several contemporary potters, he took advantage of the recently expired patent of New Hall to make a comparable hard-paste porcelain, which, due to the addition of bone-ash, was a considerably whiter body. Several Minton patterns on these wares are so like those of New Hall that sure attribution cannot be made on the study of the decoration alone. The much lower range of pattern numbers are often a good guide. For example, Minton's pattern number 18 matches the New Hall pattern number 415. Less confusion arises when the number is accompanied with Sèvres-type crossed Ss with 'M', used from about 1805 to 1816. Minton used two very distinctive types of handle on his New Hall fashioned teapots.

Thomas Minton (d. 1836) halted the production of porcelain between 1816 and 1824. The greater proportion of his earlier wares were unmarked and it is only during recent years, since the factory has made its early pattern books available, that it is possible to name with certainty Minton pieces which for many years have been vaguely attributed to Stafford-shire. Many of the tea-cups recognised in this way have a common feature in the design of the handle which is usually a supported ring-type, where many other potters use an oval. Some early New Hall tea-wares also use the same ring handle.

The entire success of the firm of Minton, who are now part of the Doulton group, seems to have been due to the fact that, in order to maintain a very high standard, they hired the best labour available. Some of their finest early-19th-century painting was the work of Joseph Bancroft, George Hancock and Thomas Steel, all of whom had previously worked as fruit- and flower-painters at the Derby factory.

From about 1822 the majority of Minton's blue-and-white transfer-printed wares were marked with a cartouche, which gave the title to the pattern, and the initial 'M': this letter was replaced with 'M and B' between about 1834 and 1841, when John Boyle was taken into partnership. The term 'M and Co.' was then used until 1873, although 'M and H' (for Minton and Hollins) was occasionally used from about 1845 to 1868. From 1873 'S' was added to 'Minton'.

Year-marks are particularly useful for more exact dating and between 1842 and 1942 a device was impressed into the clay to signify the year. This system was terminated in 1942 with an impressed 'V', for Victory, anticipating a successful end for Britain in World War II.

(For colour illustration, see p. 131)

SALT of earthenware with inlaid clay decoration in imitation of French 'Henri II' ware. English (Staffordshire, Minton's factory at Stoke), c.1870; lgth. (approximately) 12.5 cm/5 in.

Swinton & Rockingham

The factory known today as Rockingham, at Swinton, Yorkshire, was initially established in 1745 by Edward Butler who, in 1759, was paying an annual rental of £11 to the Marquis of Rockingham. When Butler died in 1763 the pottery was taken over by William Malpas and William Fenney who were partners until the works were taken over by 'Bingley, Wood and Co.' in 1778. John Brameld, who also worked at the pottery, later became a partner and from 1785 until 1806, the factory was run in association with the Leeds Pottery of Hartley, Greens and Co., known at Swinton as Greens, Bingley and Co.

John Brameld and his two sons William and Thomas took over the lease of the pottery independently in 1806 and by 1819, when the father died, the factory had grown to the extent that they were employing about 300 workers, but a decline in trade and bad debts forced them into bankruptcy in 1826. They were still able to continue in a more limited fashion due to the financial assistance they received from the Earl Fitzwilliam whose crest was used as a factory-mark. It was at this time that the name Rockingham Works was adopted (the Marquis of Rockingham was a kinsman of the Earl Fitzwilliam).

Prior to the Bramelds taking over in 1806, the wares produced were similar to those being made in other Staffordshire potteries at the same period: first the coarse domestic necessities from local clays, and by 1770 the more refined tablewares and household requirements, including creamwares decorated in the typical Leeds styles, Whieldon-type glazed earthenware and marbled wares. During the Greens, Bingley and Co. period, their price list was an exact duplicate of that used at the Leeds branch and included 'Earthenware, Cream, Coloured or Queens, Nankeen Blue, Tortoise Shell, Fine Egyptian Black, Brown China, etc.'.

Over recent years more attention has been paid to the high quality Rockingham porcelain produced between 1826 and 1842, when, once again because of bankruptcy, the factory was forced finally to close.

For many years a wide range of porcelains, often decorated in revived rococo style have, without any good reason, been wrongly attributed to Rockingham. Many lavishly decorated dinner- and dessert-services were produced at Rockingham, together with more modestly decorated tea-, coffee- and breakfast-services. The latter often included egg-cups

PLATE *of bone china, enamel and gilt decoration, marked with griffin from crest of Earl Fitzwilliam and 'Royal Rockingham Works, Brameld'. Pattern plate for dessert service for King William IV. English (Swinton), 1830; dia. 24 cm/9⅜ in.*

and stands, honey-pot with stand, butter-tub, covered muffin-dish, tray and toast-rack. On tea-services the griffin-mark was usually only applied to the underside of saucers, red enamel being used from 1826 to 1830, and puce from 1831 to 1842. Pattern numbers are often a good guide and at times are certain evidence of a piece of Rockingham-type porcelain being made elsewhere. Progressive numbers, in gold or an enamel colour, were used at Rockingham and range from about 400 up to 1565; higher numbers must be attributed to other factories. Fraction numbers were used in the lower range with 2/ approximately 1 to 100, no higher. Numbers in these ranges can often be seen on teawares, where the shape of the cup-handle is again a great aid, one particular handle in the form of a horse's hoof was entirely original. The dinner- and dessert-service were also numbered in a separate range and wares have been recognised as Rockingham with numbers from 417 up to 875. A form of inferior decoration not usually associated with this Yorkshire factory, is the technique of using transfer-prints to give guide lines to enable unskilled decorators to apply the enamel colours.

(For colour illustration, see p. 122)

Staffordshire

The history of the ADAMS family of potters is very involved. According to Llewellynn Jewitt, writing in 1878, the business was started originally in Stoke by William Adams in about 1769 and traded under his name until about 1829 when it became William Adams and Sons. The business was moved to Tunstall in 1834. The wares made prior to 1800 are difficult to identify as they had much in common with contemporary pottery in the same area. But from 1800, when the concern was under the direction of Benjamin Adams, some very fine blue-printed pearlwares often marked 'B Adams', were produced often with pierced borders.

During the early 19th century the Adams factory was producing a good range of blue Jasperwares in the Wedgwood manner. From soon after the middle of the 19th century their principal trade was with the countries of both North and South America, to where they exported large quantities of tea- and table-services made in White Granite (or Ironstone China).

The firm of SAMUEL ALCOCK AND CO. established in about 1828 at Burslem, is better known for its decorative wares, often in classical styles, and its Parian Ware figures, but it also produced some very finely modelled Parian Ware jugs, a wide range of blue-printed earthenwares and some very high quality bone-china. Alcock's Hill Top Pottery was taken over in 1860 by SIR JAMES DUKE AND NEPHEWS, who for three years continued the tradition of Alcocks and produced some excellent earthenware services from both white and cream-coloured earthenware and bone-china, but unfortunately most of these wares were unmarked.

The firm of JOHN AND EDWARD BADDELEY was producing earthenware at Shelton from 1786 until 1806. They made a wide variety of tablewares, often enamelled in red and black on a creamy-coloured earthenware. A favourite pattern depicts a very stylised lion (or Dog of Fo) in a centre panel with a foliated background. The wares were usually marked 'I E B' or 'I E B/W'.

Today it is appreciated that many potters other than WILLIAM PRATT of Lane Delph made wares from about 1780 which were decorated in the limited range of high temperature colours available at that time. But the term 'Prattware' is once again an example of the name of the man best associated with a type being used to indicate a particular technique. (This is also the case with Whieldon and Astbury.) One potter who certainly made Prattware was RICHARD BARKER who was working at Lane End between about 1784 and 1808, but since Barker was a fairly common name among potters, the impressed mark of 'Barker', seen on black basaltes tablewares and pearlware moulded teapots with well-modelled figures of swans as knobs, could be the work of other potters of the same name.

A Staffordshire potter whose work is deserving of more attention is CHARLES BOURNE who started to manufacture good quality bone-china tablewares at the Foley pottery in 1807, continuing until 1830. His wares are equal in quality to those of Spode, Coalport, Davenport and other major potters of that period. His work can usually be identified by the pattern numbers, which were progressive and written under the initials C B for Charles Bourne.

The Newport Pottery of Burslem was taken over by MESSRS CORK AND EDGE in 1846, continuing under different partners until 1903 when it was taken over by S. W. Dean. According to Jewitt their ordinary earthenware, which they introduced in the early years involved a process of inlaying patterns of different colours in the ground body. These were intended for the cheaper markets, but were produced in good taste.

Three of these designs, two teapots and a ewer, were shown at the Great Exhibition of 1851.

The name DOULTON is commonly associated with that factory's 19th-century production of both utilitarian and ornamental salt-glazed stoneware, made at Lambeth, London but, in 1877, a further production was started in Staffordshire for fine earthenware and porcelains, the bulk of which was made for export to the United States of America. Among the talented artists whose names are sometimes seen as painted signatures are: Percy Curnock, who specialised in floral and landscape painting; David Dewsberry, a flower-painter; Fred Hancock, a painter of fish and game subjects; Edward Raby, a flower-painter previously employed at Worcester; George White, a figure-painter, and many others who are listed with their dates in Desmond Eyles's *Royal Doulton 1815-1965*.

During his comparatively short stay at Lane End, between 1802 and 1808, THOMAS HARLEY manufactured a wide range of earthenware table-pieces,

Staffordshire

often of very distinctive forms. A good example of work is the teapot in the Victoria and Albert Museum, London, with the name 'Harley' impressed, of diamond-shape with short flattened corners and a well-moulded swan to form a good practical knob. The decoration is a *Chinoiserie* print, washed over with enamel colours. Other less decorative wares were made in a similar form, but with spiral fluting of the Worcester/Caughley type of about 1790.

Some exceptionally fine teawares are often found with the mark 'H and S' within a crowned wreath, or in a rectangular tablet surmounted by a winged bird. These are the marks used by the Lane End factory of HILDITCH AND SON, between 1822 and 1830. Their wares have been compared with those of Josiah Spode or Thomas Minton, but this is rather an exaggeration. The decoration, which consists primarily of underglaze-blue, is inclined to become very blurred. The later wares of HILDITCH AND HOPWOOD are hard to identify because they are unmarked. This factory exhibited at the 1851 Exhibition, where its display included a dessert-service decorated in the Renaissance style in gold, with landscape and figure

vignettes and tea-services which 'were remarkable for their excellent body, the design and execution of the painted decoration, the high class of the ground colours, and the massiveness of the gilding' (Jewitt).

SAMUEL HOLLINS was potting at Shelton from about 1784 to 1813, and he was also a partner in the New Hall company. His work was very much influenced by the wares of Josiah Wedgwood but were inclined to be too heavily decorated. Hollins made many tablewares including teawares and mugs, all from high-fired stonewares of various colours, including buff, red, green, maroon, and black basalt. His wares were usually marked 'S Hollins' or 'Hollins' impressed into the clay.

The Burslem concern of LAKIN AND POOLE is discussed very fully by Jewitt. The partnership was active from about 1792 to 1795. Their various billheadings described themselves and their wares: 'Manufacturers of Staffordshire Earthenware, Table Services Enamelled or Painted with Arms', and 'Burnished gold got up as in London', 'Blue Painted Table Services, etc., . . . Coloured in all its various Branches', 'Table Service Enamelled with Arms,

SUCRIER, COVER *and* PLATE *of stone-china, decorated in enamel colours, marked 'Turner's Patent' over 'N6'. English (Staffordshire, Turner's factory at Lane End), 1800–03; ht. (sucrier) 14.5 cm/5¾ in.*

Staffordshire

Crests, Cyphers, etc., etc.' Dated invoices give some idea of the large range of wares: cream-colour, blue-printed, fawn-colour, black, stone, and other wares, oval concave dishes of various sizes, flatt plates, soups, twifflers, muffins, tureens compots, sauce-boats and stands, root dishes, cover dishes, sallads, bakers, dessert-services of various patterns, ewers and basins, cups and saucers, bowls, cream-jugs, teapots, choco-lates, flower-horns, flower-pots, jugs, sugar-boxes, double-handled coffee-cups, salad dishes, sauce boats, gravy pots, baskets and stands, black teapots, etc., etc., and a host of more practical kitchen wares.

Another name well known to collectors and stu-dents of Staffordshire pottery is that of MAYER. The name occurs quite frequently. It was Elijah Mayer who first established a pottery at Cobden Works, Hanley, in about 1790. In 1805 the name was changed to Elijah Mayer and Son, continuing until 1834. Of Mayer, Jewitt says: 'Elijah Mayer was a potter of considerable eminence, and produced an extensive variety of goods. His Egyptian black, or basaltes ware, was, in quality of body, nearly equal to that of Wedgwood, and the ornamentation sharp and well defined, in this he produced teapots, cream ewers, bowls, and other articles'. The Mayers also produced a wide variety of tablewares in cream-coloured earthenware, cane-ware and drab stone-ware.

Another Staffordshire potter who found it worth-while to produce the type of wares being popularised by Josiah Wedgwood was HUMPHREY PALMER, who started a business at Church Works, Hanley in about 1760. Most of his early productions were decorative rather than practical, consisting of black basalt, cream-coloured and agate-ware vases, seals, and cameos, sometimes modelled by J. Voyez.

When Palmer's business failed in 1778, it was taken over by JAMES NEALE, his London agent, who had apparently been a partner from about 1769. The works continued under Neale until about 1784 when Robert Wilson took over the factory, continuing until 1818, although during the later years the con-cern was run by his son and grandsons. Neale con-tinued the reproduction of Wedgwood-type decor-ative wares, but in addition made many cream-coloured tablewares of excellent quality, still very much in the Wedgwood styles, and equal to, if not at times even superior to, those of Josiah. It must be noted that unlike many other Wedgwood imitators, Neale obviously had sufficient confidence in the quality of his wares to apply his own factory-marks. The creamwares made by ROBERT WILSON were also of good quality, with elaborately perforated and painted decoration.

The name one comes across again and again in connection with the wares of the 19th-century Staffordshire potteries is Ridgway. The founders JOB AND GEORGE RIDGWAY started their production at the Bell Works, Shelton, in about 1793. The Bell Works, and another pottery at Cauldon Place, con-tinued to be run by various relations and partners until the Cauldon Place works were taken over in 1862 by Brown-Westhead, Moore and Co. (This name is constantly recurring in the Patent Office Register of Designs Class IV.) The Bell Works was vacated in 1848, and the business was continued at the Church Works, Hanley.

Geoffrey Godden has recently made the task of recognising unmarked Ridgway porcelain wares a lot easier for the collector by publishing many designs from the factory pattern-books. The Ridgways' main productions were of stone-china, but the porcelain tablewares are also of a very high quality, and apart from the published decorative designs, they appear to have used many distinctive handles to their coffee- and tea-cups. Tureens were made with hand-les in the form of eagles, decorated with either Wedgwood-type reliefs or painted decoration. Their dessert-plates with twin side-handles are a surprising-ly early form, used by them from about 1815, but more common during the 1840s elsewhere. A further good clue to plates revealed by the pattern-books is the use of a small moulded bunch of grapes with accompanying vine-leaves, used at intervals on the rims of plates. Ridgway porcelain dessert-services of about 1835 have a great deal in common with con-temporary Spode, showing similar coloured grounds, flower-painting and heavy gilding.

(For colour illustration, see p. 85)

AMERICA
Pottery & Porcelain

The study of American pottery has until recently been a rather neglected field of research, but today that gap is being filled by highly qualified American researchers, who, in many instances, are carrying out excavations on known early pottery sites and studying previously overlooked documentary records.

In her booklet *Early New England Pottery* (published by Old Sturbridge Village, Mass.) Lura Woodside Watkins points out that, out of a total of 700 New England potters, over 300 were plying their skill prior to 1800 in the making of 'redware' or 'brownware'. Their wares were primarily for cooking or storage purposes but they were also capable of producing many more refined wares for use at the dining-table. These wares were usually decorated with contrasting coloured clay slips. The most common were plates or platters, and bowls were made in varying sizes, some small enough for drinking tea, others for more general kitchen use. Pitchers or jugs were also produced in a wide range of sizes, sometimes left in the simple clay colours, but often attractively decorated with brushed or 'splashed' slip.

The New England porringer took the form of a large shallow cup with a single handle, from which the diner would eat his porridge, soup or stew with a pewter spoon. Drinking mugs were made from about 1700 to 1840 for a variety of purposes; the tall cylindrical form most probably for ale or cider. Later in the century mugs were made in a more attractive barrel-like form.

It was during the middle of the 18th century that American potters became increasingly aware of the health hazards to both themselves and the users of heavily lead-glazed earthenwares and in consequence turned their attention to the manufacture of salt-glazed stoneware. The texture of this material made it very unsuitable for the table, as it was a body more akin to the early German ware, rather than the finer white salt-glaze of mid-18th-century Staffordshire. By the time good stonewares of a more refined type were being produced, the mass of exported white earthenwares from the English potteries of Staffordshire were readily available at very low costs, which the American potter could not match.

The first claims concerning the manufacture of porcelain in America were made as early as about 1739, when the Governor of Georgia wrote: 'Andrew Duché is the potter at Savannah who goes on very well there is one of the most industrious in the Town and has made several Experiments which seem to look like the making of China'. This son of a Huguenot potter, was born in Philadelphia, and was apparently successful in his experiments and in a report made in 1741 by William Stephens, Secretary of the Colony, his wares were described as 'translucent'. Duché was invited to England to show his work to the trustees of the Colony. Much research had been made regarding Duché's porcelain, but no further knowledge concerning its actual production has been discovered, although in *A History of American Art Porcelain* by Marvin D. Schwartz and Richard Wolfe, mention is made of a blue-and-white bowl as being a likely experimental piece of this early American potter's work.

There were doubtless other potters engaged in similar experimental work, but knowledge concerning them and their wares is very small. None-the-less Josiah Wedgwood, who was engaged in exporting his own wares to the Colonies, was a little perturbed in 1765, when he mentioned a new pottery set up in South Carolina, where they seemed to have all the necessary materials, which were 'equal, if not superior to our own for carrying on that manufacture'. It has been suggested that Wedgwood was referring to the

Opposite: PLATE, SMALL SOUP-TUREEN *and* STAND *of bone china, painted in enamel colours and gilt. The plate was painted by A. Gregory in 1890, the tureen and stand, painted in the Sèvres style, are dated 1911. All English (Staffordshire, Mintons).*

Overleaf top: BOWL *of redware with a dark brown glaze. Manganese, used in varying proportions to create tan, brown or black, was an inexpensive and common glaze. American, 18th century; dia. 35 cm/14 in.*

Overleaf bottom: DISH *of redware with slip decoration and lead glaze. The* CUP *was used to pour the slip onto the object being decorated. Both American, 18th century; dia. (dish) 15 cm/6 in.*

Overleaf: *A group of Spode.* TEAPOT, SUGAR BOWL *and* CREAMER *in black basaltes, c.1810.* TEAPOT *of creamware with a 'Rockingham' glaze, c.1830. Small* JUG *of stoneware, c.1820. Large* JUG *of redware with encaustic decoration, c.1820.* CUSTARD-CUP *and* COVER, *made in imitation of Wedgwood jasperware, c.1810.* MUSTARD-POT *of creamware, c.1820. Each object is impressed with the name Spode.*

Opposite: PITCHER *of earthenware, decorated with gothic panels in relief under dark brown so-called 'Rockingham' glaze. American (American Pottery Company), 1838-45.* PITCHER *of lead-glazed creamware, with underglaze-black transfer-printed portrait of William Henry Harrison, log cabin and legend 'The Ohio Farmer' and American eagle below. American (American Pottery Company), 1840; ht. (earthenware pitcher) 22.6 cm/9 in.*

English potter John Bartlam who advertised in 1770 that 'A China Manufactory and Pottery is soon to be opened in this town . . . by Messrs Bartlam and Company, the proper hands etc., for carrying it having lately arrived from England . . .'

By 1771, it seems, the Pottery and China Manufactory in Old Church Street was active in the manufacture of Queen's Ware as it was advertising in the South Carolina Gazette for finer clays, possibly with the intention of producing porcelain, but again no documentary wares relating to this manufacture have been discovered.

The high taxation on imports, which eventually resulted in war with Britain, prompted further endeavours to produce more of the necessities and luxuries demanded by the Colonials. By 1770 Gousse Bonnin and George Morris were advertising their Philadelphia New China Ware and stated that they had 'proved to a certainty that the clays of America are as productive of good porcelain as any heretofore manufactured at the famous factory in Box (Bow) near London . . .'

Following excavations on the site of the factory it has now been possible to identify a limited number of Bonnin and Morris porcelains made for the American table. Examples are on exhibition in The Brooklyn Museum, New York, and the Philadelphia Museum of Art.

One example, a shell centrepiece, has a great deal in common with Bow and is decorated in underglaze-blue. Baskets are more in the style of early Derby, with pierced interlocking circles seen on the early

Japanese wares of Arita. The sauce-boats show many similarities to those of the Worcester factory.

Knowledge concerning American porcelain manufacture in the years following the Revolution and the early 19th century is very scanty and confined primarily to documents rather than authenticated examples. But pottery and creamware were apparently being produced by several potters in the Philadelphia and Trenton areas during the early years of the 19th century. There is, for example, only one single soft-paste vase which is attributed to the New York physician, Dr Henry Mead. Another manufacturer of that period was Abraham Miller, who was producing 'porcelain and white ware' in Philadelphia in about 1824. In 1826 The Jersey Porcelain and Earthenware Company was manufacturing 'the best China from American materials', but the wares of these and other factories of that period probably had so much in common with contemporary French porcelain that they continue to be wrongly attributed. It is, for example, very difficult to distinguish between the hard-paste porcelain made by William Ellis Tucker of Philadelphia and Paris porcelains of the same period.

BUTTER CROCK *with blue cobalt decoration. American (Pennsylvania), c.1840; ht. 16.5 cm/6½ in.*

DISH *of earthenware with calligraphic slip decoration typical of certain New English potters. American (Eastern Massachusetts), 2nd half of 18th c.; dia 22.8 cm/9 in.*

Tucker started his porcelain production in about 1826, using clays from Pennsylvania and New Jersey. The factory continued with various partners until 1838. Thomas Hulme became a partner in 1828 and Alexander Hemphill in 1831. Today we are mostly familiar with their jugs and pitchers, but tea-sets and dinner-services were also produced in forms which had much in common with Staffordshire earthenwares, although the flower-painting and landscapes in sepia monochrome with tastefully applied gilding were more in the Continental taste. Many of these fine examples of early-19th-century American porcelain can be firmly attributed to Tucker and his partners by the factory pattern books which are now in the Philadelphia Museum.

There is little doubt that many Continental manufacturers moved to the United States of America during the middle decades of the 19th century. Smith, Fife and Company were obviously of British stock, whereas Kurlbaum and Schwartz would almost certainly have acquired their knowledge of the trade from Europe. The American porcelains were made in the so-called Empire styles over a far longer period than in England and the revived rococo taste was not popular in the United States until nearer the middle of the 19th century.

It was in the early 1850s that Charles Cartlidge who was the American agent for the English pottery of Ridgway, began to manufacture bone-china tablewares at Greenpoint, New York, continuing until 1856. During the third quarter of the 19th century some highly decorative teawares were produced at the Union Porcelain Works at Greenpoint, New York, from the designs of Karl Müller. The painted decoration has a lot in common with that seen on the hard-paste porcelains made by Jacob Petit at Fontainebleau in France, but the use of human and animal heads and figures as knobs, handles and feet was entirely original and not altogether pleasing.

Although many fine decorative wares and portrait busts were produced in glazed or biscuit Parian ware bodies in the United States, there were very few attempts made during the 19th century to compete with the English bone-china tablewares which were being made by so many Staffordshire factories—a technique the American manufacturer was unable to match.

(For colour illustration, see pp. 143 and 144)

CANADA
Pottery & Porcelain

Canada continued to produce brown earthenwares and stonewares much later than independent North America and as late as 1880 all the finer tablewares of earthenware and porcelain were being imported. This was due principally to lack of raw materials and intense competition from the mass-produced English wares which were being made so cheaply that even tariffs provided no safeguards.

It was not until 1876 that Canadian potters judged their wares to be of a high enough standard to compete with foreign manufacturers at the American Centennial Exhibition held in Philadelphia. The only Canadian concern making 'white granite ware' at that period was the St Johns Stone Chinaware Company which won an international award for its tablewares. This company was established in 1873 and continued to flourish for twenty-five years, at the peak of its prosperity 400 hands were employed. Its whitewares were of the popular Staffordshire types of hard opaque earthenwares such as ironstone, white granite and stone china. Many of these Canadian tablewares were moulded in the same decorative forms as the imported English wares, which is not really surprising, for at least half the Canadian potters had previously been employed in English potteries. The tablewares were only modestly decorated with broad bands of enamel colours, lined with black or gold, although in 1888 the company was advertising that it was prepared to decorate wares to the order of individual customers or commercial companies, such as hotels, steamships lines or railways. In her outstanding book *Nineteenth Century Pottery and Porcelain in Canada* Elizabeth Collard stresses the fine wares of 'St Johns blue', a stone china coloured throughout and decorated with applied reliefs in white, which was described in 1879 in the Montreal Gazette as being a new style of dinner- and teaware. This factory did little to encourage competition for as late as 1931, the National Development Bureau in Ottawa reported that there was no production of white tableware of any kind in the country.

From at least 1840 coarser earthenwares were being produced in large quantities in the St Johns area of Quebec Province by the Farrar family. (This region was referred to as Canada East prior to the Confederation of 1867.) The Farrar's finer wares were similar to the so-called brown-glazed Rockingham wares made at the pottery of Christopher Webber Fenton of Bennington, Vermont. The material, also known as 'Flint Enamelled Ware', was covered with a rather crude form of the variegated glazes used during the 18th century by such Staffordshire potters as Thomas Whieldon.

These Rockingham wares were popular with both the English and French Canadians, and although the majority of the pieces can hardly be considered refined tablewares, teapots feature in almost all the advertisements. Towards the end of the 1870s Elijah Bowler of the St Johns Rockingham and Yellow Ware Manufactory, St Johns, P.Q. was offering 'CANE, ROCKINGHAM AND MAJOLICA WARE, Teapots, Milk Pans, Lip Bowls... Round and Oval Dishes etc.'

Another successful potter producing similar wares was Charles E. Pearson of Iberville, P.Q. who exhibited at the Montreal Dominion exhibition of 1880 'a capital display of the Rockingham and yellow ware teapots, vases, dishes . . .'

Glossary

AGATE WARE: earthenware made by blending various coloured clays in order to imitate agate stone; a similar effect can be obtained with surface clay slip. This ware can be found either with a salt-glaze or a lead-glaze, or occasionally in the biscuit.

BASALTES: the name given by Josiah Wedgwood to the hard black stoneware he perfected in 1767.

BISCUIT: ceramic body fired only once, without the addition of glaze.

BODY: name to describe the composite material used for the production of a particular type of ceramic.

BONE-ASH: calcined animal bones, rich in lime and phosphoric acid, used as an ingredient in many forms of artificial porcelains.

BONE-CHINA: hard-paste porcelain modified with addition of up to 40% bone ash. Standard English porcelain since 1800.

Camaieu, en: decoration painted in various tones of a single colour (monochrome).

CHINA: name given in 18th century England to many kinds of white porcelain, especially with blue painting in the Chinese style. Came to denote translucent porcelain in 19th century. Now often has restricted meaning of bone china.

CHINA-CLAY: white refactory clay formed over a very long period from decomposed granite (known originally in China as kaolin).

CHINA-STONE: fusible stone which, when fired at about 1350°C together with china-clay, forms the hard, white, translucent material of hard-paste porcelain; it is known as *petuntse*.

Chinoiserie: generic term for Chinese ornamental motifs, particularly for those executed by European craftsmen with rather distant knowledge of Oriental art.

CRAZING: minute surface cracks in the glaze caused by the glaze shrinking at a different rate to the body during cooling.

CREAMWARE: cream-coloured earthenware covered with a pale yellowish lead-glaze. Perfected by Josiah Wedgwood in about 1760, it was soon imitated by many other English and continental potters. Also known as Queen's ware after Wedgwood made a service in the material for Queen Charlotte.

DELFTWARE: tin-glazed earthenware made at Delft in Holland; however, the term was often used to describe English wares that in many cases pre-date the Dutch ones.

Deutsche Blumen: naturalistically painted German flowers used on Meissen porcelain from about 1740 and imitated on the wares of several English factories.

DRESDEN CHINA: the name often wrongly given to porcelain made at Meissen. (In the 19th century there were several minor establishments in the city of Dresden producing poor quality porcelain.)

EARTHENWARE: low-fired pottery that is not vitrified; it is normally glazed in order to render it waterproof.

ENAMEL COLOURS: opaque or translucent vitreous pigments fused to the surface of the glaze or the ceramic body at a temperature not exceeding 800°C.

FAIENCE: the term for French tin-glazed earthenware, made using a technique similar to that of Faenza in Italy. (*see fayence.*)

Famille rose: Chinese porcelain that includes in the decoration the various tones of pink to a deep crimson derived from chloride of gold. This colour was used by German enamellers from about 1680.

Famille verte: the palette of Chinese colours used from the reign of the Emporer K'ang Hsi, in which various green tones predominate. It was also copied in Europe.

Fayence: the German equivalent of faience.

FELDSPATHIC GLAZE: glaze rich in feldspar (alumino silicates) that is used on hard-paste porcelain and fired at the same time as the body.

FERRUGINOUS: describing a body or glaze that is rich in iron; this results in a buff to brownish-red colour or, when fired under special conditions, to a 'celadon'.

FINIAL: ornament finishing off the apex of lids etc.

FLINT ENAMEL WARE: American pottery glazed by process using powdered metal oxides sprinkled on unfired Rockingham glaze (see Rockingham glaze).

FLUTING: ornamentation with shallow parallel grooves of semi-circular cross-section, usually vertical, sometimes oblique or curved.

FOOT-RIM: bottom edge of cup, mug etc. as distinct from footring.

FOOTRING: protective rim in variety of shapes and sizes made separately and attached to base of cups, mugs etc.

FRIT: powdered form of the ingredients of glass, used in soft-paste porcelain as an alternative to china-stone in hard-paste.

GILDING: the application of various forms of gold to the surface of ceramic wares. Early gilding consisted of ground gold-leaf or gold powder with honey as a medium, which was applied in liquid form and then fired to the glazed ware. From the late 18th century the honey gilding was replaced by an amalgam of mercury and then similarly fired. After the firing, the gilding was burnished to give a high sheen.

GLAZE: covering of vitreous substance over a body to give a glossy coating that is impervious to liquids. The glaze on hard-paste porcelain is usually feldspathic; the glassy glaze applied to other porcelain bodies in a thin layer of glass made from frit.

GLOST KILN: kiln used to fuse the glaze to ceramic ware.

HARD-PASTE PORCELAIN: the type of porcelain first introduced by the Chinese in about AD 850 and made from china-clay and china-stone, two varying forms of decomposed granite.

Hausmalerei: Independent decoration of faience and porcelain by *Hausmaler* (home painters) in Germany, Austria and Bohemia from late 17th century onwards.

HIGH-TEMPERATURE COLOURS: colours applied to a body with the glaze and fired at high temperatures. Originally the only ones that could be used as underglaze colours on hard-paste porcelain were cobalt (giving blue) and copper (giving a dull red). These two colours, together with antimony, manganese, and iron were used to decorate tin-glazed wares and were applied to the powdery glaze prior to the glost firing.

JASPER WARE: hard, fine-grained stoneware, sometimes slightly translucent. Introduced by Josiah Wedgwood in about 1774. It is best known in the popular blue-and-white form but it could be tinted to a variety of colours with the use of metallic oxides.

KAKIEMON: a 17th-century Japanese potter's family who specialized in an asymmetrical style of enamel decoration holding a subtle balance between areas of white and those decorated with fine drawing.

LEAD-GLAZE: transparent glaze containing lead oxide. Such glazes were originally applied in a dry powdered form, but later the ingredients were suspended in water into which the ware was dipped.

LUSTRE DECORATION: metallic colours fused to the glaze of wares in a reduction kiln.

Maiolica: the term applied to Italian tin-glazed earthenwares. English potters in the 19th century adopted the name 'majolica' for relief-decorated pottery covered in coloured glazes and today in America 'majolica' is used as a synonym for 'maiolica'.

MOULDING: the shaping of clay with the use of prepared moulds.

MUFFLE KILN: the low-firing kiln (about 800°C) used for applying enamel colours to ceramics.

OXIDIZING KILN: kiln into which air is freely admitted, the kiln atmosphere creating colours different from the wares or decoration.

PARIAN WARE: white ceramic body introduced in Staffordshire in about 1840, and becoming very popular in American potteries especially in Bennington, Vermont.

REDUCTION KILN: kiln to which the supply of air is restricted, thus creating a smoky atmosphere to achieve certain effects and colours on the ceramics being fired.

ROCKINGHAM GLAZE: Brown glaze applied to English earthenware made at the Rockingham factory. In America Rockingham ware has a yellow earthenware body covered with a mottled brown glaze.

SALT-GLAZE: glaze used on stoneware, made by throwing salt into the kiln at the peak firing temperature.

SLIP: clay watered down to a creamy consistency.

SLIP-CASTING: the forming of clay wares by pouring slip into hollow plaster of Paris moulds. The plaster absorbs the water and in so doing builds up a layer of clay onto the inside wall of the mould, any surplus slip is then poured off and the remaining cast can be removed from the mould.

SOFT-PASTE PORCELAIN: artificial porcelain made from various white-firing clays and the ingredients of glass, bone-ash, or steatite, etc.

SPRIGGING: the application of separately-moulded decoration to the surface of wares, as on salt-glazed stonewares or 'Astbury'-type pottery.

STONEWARE: high fired pottery that contains sufficient natural fluxes for it to vitrify between 1200°C and 1400°C; it is completely impervious to liquids.

THROWING: the process of forming a hollow circular shape from clay by hand with the use of a fast-turning potter's wheel.

TIN-GLAZE: lead-glaze (translucent) made white and opaque by the addition of tin oxide.

TRANSFER-PRINTING: the transferring of a design engraved on a copper-plate or wood-block by means of a thin tissue paper or slab of gelatine onto the surface of the body, or onto the glaze of a ceramic or enamel ware.

WASTERS: faulty wares, usually discarded during manufacture and often good evidence of types of manufacture carried out at old potteries.

Further Reading

GENERAL

CAIGER-SMITH A. *Tin-Glaze Pottery*. London and New York, 1973.

CHARLESTON J. (ed.) *World Ceramics*. London and New York, 1968.

COLLARD E. *19th Century Pottery and Porcelain in Canada*. Montreal, 1967.

CUSHION J. *Pocket-Book of German Ceramic Marks*. London, 1961.

CUSHION J. *Pocket-Book of French & Italian Ceramic Marks*. London, 1965.

CUSHION J. *Collector's Guide to Pottery & Porcelain*. London, 1972.

CUSHION J. *English China Collecting for Amateurs*. London, 1967.

CUSHION J. (new Edn) *Pocket-Book of British Ceramic Marks*. London, 1976.

CUSHION J. *Porcelain*. London, 1973.

GODDEN G. *Illustrated Encyclopaedia of British Pottery and Porcelain*. London and New York, 1966.

HONEY W. B. *English Ceramic Art* (2 Vols). London, 1952.

JEWITT L. *Ceramic Art in Great Britain* (2 Vols). London and New York, 1972 (reprint of 1878).

PHILLIPS P. (ed.) *The Collector's Encyclopaedia of Antiques*. London and New York, 1973.

SAVAGE & NEWMAN. *An Illustrated Dictionary of Ceramics*. London, 1974.

CONTINENTAL

CHARLES R. *Continental Porcelain*. London, 1964.

CUSHION J. *Continental China Collecting for Amateurs*. London 1970 and New York, 1971.

CUSHION J. *Continental Porcelain*. London, 1974.

DUCRET S. *German Porcelain and Faience*. London, 1962.

FROTHINGHAM A. W. *Lustreware of Spain*. New York, 1951.

HONEY W. B. *Dresden China*. London, 1954.

HONEY W. B. *French Porcelain of the 18th century* (2nd Ed.). London, 1972.

LANE A. *French Faience*. London, 1948.

LANE A. *Italian Porcelain*. London, 1954.

ENGLISH POTTERY

COYSH A. W. *Blue-Printed Earthenware 1800-1850*. Newton Abbot, 1972.

EAGLESTONE & LOCKETT. *The Rockingham Pottery*. Newton Abbot, 1970.

GARNER & ARCHER. *English Delftware* (2nd Ed.). London, 1972.

KELLY A. *The Story of Wedgwood*. London, 1962.

LAWRENCE H. *Yorkshire Pots and Potteries*. Newton Abbot, 1974.

LOCKETT T. A. *Davenport Pottery and Porcelain*. Newton Abbot and Vermont, 1972.

RICE D. G. *Rockingham Pottery and Porcelain*. London and New York, 1971.

SMITH A. *Liverpool Herculaneum Pottery*. London, 1970.

TOWNER D. *The Leeds Pottery*. London, 1963.

TOWNER D. *English Cream Coloured Earthenware*. London, 1967.

WAKEFIELD H. *Victorian Pottery*. London, 1962.

WHITER L. *Spode*. London and New York, 1970.

ENGLISH PORCELAIN

CUSHION J. *English Porcelain*. London, 1974.

GODDEN G. *Victorian Porcelain*. London and New York, 1961.

GODDEN G. *Caughley & Worcester Porcelains 1775-1800*. London and New York, 1969.

GODDEN G. *Lowestoft Porcelains*. London and New York, 1969.

GODDEN G. *Coalport & Coalbrookdale Porcelain*. London and New York, 1970.

GODDEN, G. *Ridgway Porcelain*. London, 1972.

HOLGATE D. *New Hall and its Imitators*. London, 1971.

LOCKETT T. A. *Davenport Pottery and Porcelain*. Newton Abbot, 1972.

RICE D. G. *Rockingham Pottery and Porcelain*. London, 1971.

SANDON H. *Worcester Porcelain*. London 1969 and New York, 1970

WATNEY B. *Longton Hall Porcelain*. London, 1957.

WATNEY B. *English Blue and White Porcelain of the 18th Century*. London, 1963.

WHITER L. *Spode*. London and New York, 1970.

SHREWSBURY ART GALLERY. *Caughley Porcelains* (Exhn). 1972.

AMERICAN POTTERY AND PORCELAIN

BARBER E. A. *The Pottery and Porcelain of the United States*. (2nd ed.). New York and London, 1902.

BARRET R. C. *Bennington Pottery and Porcelain: A Guide to Identification*. New York, 1958.

BIVENS J., JR. *The Moravian Potters in North Carolina*. Chapel Hill, 1972.

HENSKE L. *American Art Pottery*. Camden and New York, 1970.

HENSKE L. *American Art Pottery*. Camden and New York, 1970

HOOD G. *Bonnin and Morris of Philadelphia, the First American Porcelain Factory, 1770-1772*. Chapel Hill, 1972.

The Pottery and Porcelain Collector's Handbook. New York, 1971.

RAMSAY J. *American Potters and Pottery*. Boston, 1939; 2nd ed., New York, 1947.

SCHWARTZ M. D. & WOLFE R. *A History of American Art Porcelain*. New York, 1967.

SPARGO J. *Early American Pottery and China*. New York 1926; repr., 1948.

TUCKER CHINA 1825-38 (Exhn). *Philadelphia Museum of Art,* 1957.

WATKINS L. W. *Early New England Potters and their Wares*. Cambridge, Mass. 1950, repr. Hamden, Conn., 1969.

Picture Acknowledgements

Permission to reproduce photographs has kindly been given by the following; for easy reference page numbers have been given in italics.

Colour

1. Tin-glazed earthenware bowl. Spanish (Manises, Valencia), early 15th century. Courtesy of the Hispanic Society of America, New York.

2. Group of 18th century Italian porcelain. (Doccia, Capodimonte and Cozzi). The National Museum of Wales, Cardiff.

11. Hard-paste porcelain cup and saucer. Italian (Doccia), late 18th century. The Victoria and Albert Museum, London.

12. Group of German salt-glazed stoneware drinking vessels of 16th, 17th and 18th centuries. Private Collection.

13. Tin-glazed earthenware tankard. German (Nuremberg), late 17th century. The Victoria and Albert Museum, London.

14. Hard-paste porcelain tea service. German (Meissen), mid 18th century. Private Collection.

23. Hard-paste porcelain centre-piece. German (Meissen), mid-18th century. The Victoria and Albert Museum, London.

24. Hard-paste porcelain plate. German (Nymphenberg), late 18th century. The Antique Porcelain Company Limited, London, New York and Zurich.

25. Hard-paste porcelain coffee-service. Austrian (Vienna), early 19th century. Private Collection.

26. Tin-glazed earthenware tureen and stand. Dutch, (Delft), De Porcelyne Byl factory, mid 18th century. The Campbell Museum, Camden, New Jersey.

35. Hard-paste porcelain chocolate jug and teapot. Dutch, (Oude Loosdrecht), late 18th century. The Rijksmuseum, Amsterdam.

36. Hard-paste porcelain coffee-service. Danish, (Royal Copenhagen factory), late 18th century. The Royal Copenhagen Porcelain Manufactory Limited, Copenhagen.

37. Tin-glazed earthenware tureen. Norwegian, (Herreboe), mid 18th century. The Campbell Museum, Camden, New Jersey.

38. Tin-glazed earthenware tureen. Swedish, (Rörstrand), mid 18th century. The Campbell Museum, Camden, New Jersey.

47. Hard-paste porcelain teapot, cup and saucer and jug. Swiss, (Zurich), late 18th century. The Victoria and Albert Museum, London.

48. Lead-glazed earthenware dish. French, (Palissy), late 16th century. The Victoria and Albert Museum, London.

49. Tin-glazed earthenware jug and cover. French, (Rouen), late 18th century. The Victoria and Albert Museum, London.

50. Tin-glazed earthenware tureen and stand. French, (Strasbourg), mid-18th century. The Campbell

Museum, Camden, New Jersey.

59. Soft-paste porcelain tureen and cover. French, (Saint-Cloud), mid-18th century. The Victoria and Albert Museum, London.

60. Soft-paste porcelain cup and saucer, coffee cup and saucer and milk jug. French, (Chantilly and Mennecy), 18th century. Reproduced by permission of the Syndics of the Fitzwilliam Museum, Cambridge.

61. Soft-paste porcelain milk jug, tray, cup and saucer. French, (Vincennes and Sèvres), 18th century. The National Trust, James A. de Rothschild Collection, Waddesdon Manor, Aylesbury.

62. Soft-paste porcelain covered bowl and stand and one saucepan. French, (Sèvres), 18th century. Reproduced by permission of the Trustees of the Wallace Collection, London.

71. Group of 18th and 19th century veilleuses. Collection of Harold Newman, New Orleans, Louisiana.

72. Lead-glazed earthenware dish and posset pot. City Museum and Art Gallery, Stoke-on-Trent.

73. Tin-glazed earthenware toy tea service. Reproduced by permission of the Syndics of the Fitzwilliam Museum, Cambridge.

74. Selection of lead-glazed earthenware. Mann Scharf and Lloyd Bleier Collection, Los Angeles, California.

83. (top and bottom) A group of Wedgwood stoneware and cream-coloured earthenware. Mann Scharf and Lloyd Bleier Collection, Los Angeles, California.

84. A group of 18th and 19th century Yorkshire pottery. Leeds Art Galleries, Temple Newsam House. The coffee pot is illustrated by courtesy of the W.A.H. Harding Trust.

85. Lead-glazed earthenware tureen and stand. The Campbell Museum, Camden, New Jersey.

86. A group of soft-paste Chelsea porcelain. Winifred Williams, London.

95. A group of soft-paste Bow porcelain. Gilbert Bradley Collection.

96. A selection of Lowestoft soft-paste porcelain. English, late 18th century. Norfolk Museums Service (Norwich Castle Museum).

97. A group of Pinxton soft-paste porcelain. The City of Sheffield Museum, Weston Park, Sheffield.

98. Part of a soft-paste porcelain tea service. The Dyson Perrins Museum, Worcester.

107. Soapstone porcelain ice-pail, cover and liner. The Dyson Perrins Museum, Worcester.

108. (top and bottom) Bone china tea-cup and saucer, cabinet cup, cover and stand. English, (Worcester), mid-19th century. The Dyson Perrins Museum, Worcester.

109. A collection of Caughley porcelain. Private Collection.

110. A selection of soft-paste Liverpool porcelain. Gilbert Bradley Collection.

119. Hard-paste porcelain sucrier and cover, breakfast cup and saucer and teapot. English, (Bristol), late 18th century. City of Bristol Museum and Art Gallery. The sucrier is part of the McGregor Duncan Collection of Bristol porcelain.

120. A group of Davenport wares. Terence A. Locket.

121. Porcelain saucer-dish and cream-jug and bone china coffee-can and saucer. English, (Staffordshire), early 19th century. The Dorothy and Reginald Haggar Collection.

122. A group of porcelain Rockingham teawares. English, early 19th century. E.M. Eaglestone.

131. Bone china plate, soup-tureen and stand. Royal Doulton Tableware Limited, Stoke-on-Trent, Staffordshire.

132. (top and bottom) Redware bowl, dish and cup. American, 18th century. The American Museum in Britain, Claverton Manor, Bath. Photograph supplied by the Cooper-Bridgeman Library, London.

133. A group of spode. English, early 19th century. Private Collection.

134. Earthenware and creamware pitchers. American, (American Pottery Company), early 19th century. Collection of the Newark Museum, Newark, New Jersey, photo Armen.

143. Soft-paste porcelain sweetmeat stand. American, (Bonnin and Morris), late 18th century. The Smithsonian Institution, Washington, D.C.

144. Porcelain jug. American, (Tucker), early 19th century. The American Museum in Britain, Claverton Manor, Bath. Photograph supplied by the Cooper-Bridgman Library, London.

The following photographers were specially commissioned to take colour photographs for this book:

Derek Balmer, Bristol, 119.
John Beckerley, Hanley Swan, 98, 107, 108.
C. Cannings, London, 11, 48.
A.C. Cooper Limited, London, 12, 13, 14, 23, 25, 47, 49, 59, 61, 62, 71, 86, 95, 110, 122.
Gordon Elliott, 121.
Pat and Carl Jameson, Shrewsbury, 109.
West Park Studios, Leeds, 84, 97.

Monochrome

19. Soft-paste porcelain plate. Crown copyright, Victoria and Albert Museum, London.

20 Earthenware ewer. Crown copyright, Victoria and Albert Museum, London.

27. Soft-paste porcelain ewer. Crown copyright, Victoria and Albert Museum, London.

28. Soft-paste porcelain sugar bowl with cover, hard-paste porcelain plate and teapot. Victoria and Albert Museum, London.

43. Hard-paste porcelain coffee, tea and chocolate service. Crown copyright, Victoria and Albert Museum, London.

44. Hard-paste porcelain coffee-pot. Crown copyright, Victoria and Albert Museum, London.

58. Tazza, tin-glazed earthenware. Crown copyright, Victoria and Albert Museum, London.

64. Tin-glazed earthenware tureen and cover. Crown copyright, Victoria and Albert Museum, London.

66. Tin-glazed earthenware plate. Crown copyright, Victoria and Albert Museum, London.

67. Tin-glazed earthenware ice-pail. Crown copyright, Victoria and Albert Museum, London.

68. Soft-paste porcelain teapot. Crown copyright, Victoria and Albert Museum, London.

69. Soft-paste porcelain ice-pail. Crown copyright, Victoria and Albert Museum, London.

77. Hard-paste porcelain tea-caddies. Crown copyright, Victoria and Albert Museum, London.

79. Earthenware cup. City of Manchester Art Galleries, Thomas Greg Collection.

80. Salt-glazed stoneware jug or mug. Crown copyright, Victoria and Albert Museum, London.

89. Earthenware dish. Crown copyright, Victoria and Albert Museum, London.

90. Earthenware sauce-boat. Crown copyright, Victoria and Albert Museum, London.

102. Soft-paste porcelain soup tureen, cover and stand. Crown copyright, Victoria and Albert Museum, London.

104. Porcelain jug and cover. Crown copyright, Victoria and Albert Museum, London.

111. Soapstone porcelain spoon-tray. English, Crown copyright, Victoria and Albert Museum, London.

112. Porcelain leaf-shaped dishes. Crown copyright, Victoria and Albert Museum, London.

114. Hard-paste porcelain teapot and stand. Crown copyright, Victoria and Albert Museum, London.

124. Earthenware plate. Crown copyright, Victoria and Albert Museum, London.

125. Earthenware salt-cellar. Crown copyright, Victoria and Albert Museum, London.

126. Bone china plate. Crown copyright, Victoria and Albert Museum, London.

128. Stone china sucrier, cover and plate. City of Stoke-on-Trent Museum and Art Gallery.

135. Salt-glazed stoneware butter crock. The Smithsonian Institution, Washington, D.C.

136. Slip-decorated earthenware dish. The Smithsonian Institution, Washington, D.C.

236. Teawarmer (Philadelphia, Pennsylvania). Bequest of Bertha L. Landis. Philadelphia Museum of Art.

Endpapers: Jug, English, early 19th century. Arthur Hurst Bequest, Victoria and Albert Museum, London.

Opposite: SWEETMEAT-STAND of soft-paste porcelain, painted in underglaze-blue, unmarked. American (Bonnin & Morris, Philadelphia), 1770-72; ht. 14 cm/5½ in.

Overleaf: JUG painted with polychrome flowers and gilt. The initials 'ES' painted in gilt under the spout are believed to be those of the original owner Elizabeth Slater. American (Tucker Factory), 1828.

Part 2
An Identification Guide

Cups

The single most important characteristic of a cup is its handle, or lack of one. The transition from Chinese tea-bowls to handled cups spanned many years; early St. Cloud cups usually had handles yet tea-bowls were made as late as 1820 by English potters. A handle provides a very good identification point: look at its shape, and the way it is attached top and bottom. This is the weakest part, so check carefully for repairs.

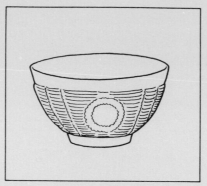

Finely moulded teabowl, English, Longton Hall, c.1755.

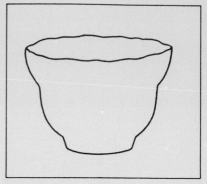

Hard-paste porcelain teabowl, English, Bristol, 1775.

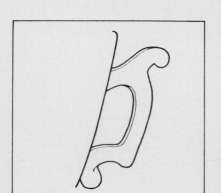

Porcelain cup handle, English, Chelsea, c.1749-52.

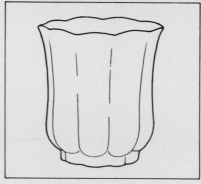

Porcelain cup, underglaze-blue decoration, English, Chelsea, c.1750.

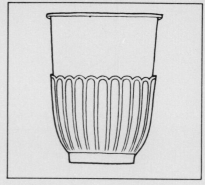

Handleless porcelain cup, Austrian, Vienna, c.1730–35.

Porcelain, unmarked, attributed to London, c.1750.

Early porcelain miniature cup, English, Bow, c.1752, incised 'R'.

Bone porcelain, applied prunus decoration, English, Bow, c.1754.

Porcelain, English, Bow, 1762. Note heart-shaped terminal.

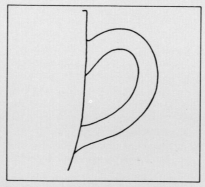

Porcelain handle, floral decoration, English, Bow, c.1762.

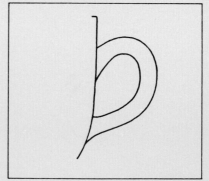

Bow loop handles vary according to date. Here, c.1765-68.

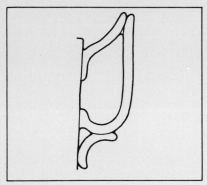

Characteristic handle, English, Derby, *c*.1830.

Fluted, hard-paste porcelain, English, New Hall, 1790–1803.

Simple cup, often decorated with cornflower sprigs. English, Pinxton.

Porcelain, handle fashioned after Sèvres, English, Pinxton, 1796–99.

Large early paste teacup, 4 in. diameter, English, Pinxton, 1796–99.

Circular cup, decagonal foot-rim, 'A' marked, London (?), *c*.1750.

Fluted walls, 'A' marked, London (?), 1750.

Porcelain, underglaze-blue decoration, English, Longton Hall, *c*.1756.

Porcelain, reeded decoration, English, Longton Hall, *c*.1755.

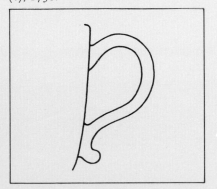

Simple handle, similar to Lowestoft, English, Longton Hall, *c*.1758.

This handle appears in many sizes, English, Longton Hall, *c*.1755.

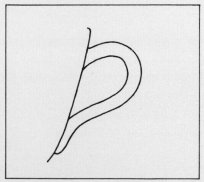

Simple loop handle, English, Longton Hall, *c*.1755–58.

Cups

'Liverpool' is used to describe a group of small potteries, some as yet not fully documented, working in and around that city. The early cups were considerably influenced by Worcester designs and decorations, and Liverpool production had no reputation until after the mid-18th century. It was imported into the United States in large quantities and almost never bares a factory mark. Typical 'Liverpool' porcelain is greyish, the handles of cups are skimpy and the foot-rims rather undercut.

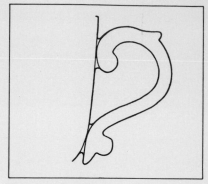

Early porcelain handle, Chaffers, English, Liverpool, c.1755.

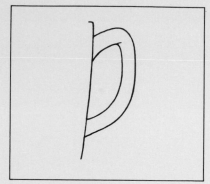

Porcelain handle, type attributed to Ball, c.1755–69.

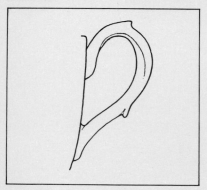

Porcelain cup handle, English, (Wolfe) Liverpool, 1795–1800.

Porcelain, Reid, Liverpool, c.1755 –61.

Worcester's early period produced cups and saucers of a sharp-edged crispness; perhaps this was due to the soap-stone in the porcelain body, enabling it to be worked quite thinly. Misshapen pieces are rare. The later Davis & Flight period has, in common with Caughley, fluted shapes and plain forms as dictated by the neo-classical style. Excavations at the factory have now made the dating of Worcester pieces a lot easier.

Hard paste porcelain, rare handle, English, New Hall, c.1790.

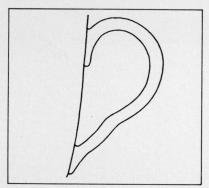

Porcelain handle, English, Worcester, 1780–85.

Porcelain, spiral fluting, English, Worcester, 1783–93.

Fluted, typical handle, English, Caughley, c.1785.

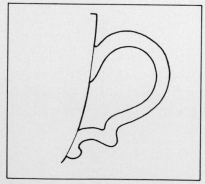

Typical handle, English, Caughley, c.1785–95.

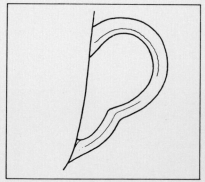

Typical handle, English, Caughley, 1780–85.

From 1781 to *c*.1814 New Hall made only a modified type of hard-paste porcelain. The production of hard-paste seems to have stopped when their pattern numbers had reached about 1046. Ridgway cups, on the other hand, reflect the new, more elaborate designs of the early Victorian period. Their cups and handles have only recently been identified from factory pattern books, and are both unusual and well-made. Unmarked Ridgway was also imported into the United States until the 1860s in substantial quantities.

New Hall cup with common Staffordshire handle, *c*.1820.

One of at least eight handles used by Rockingham, English, *c*.1830–42.

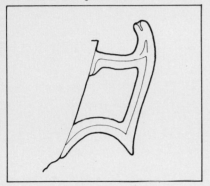

Porcelain handle used by J. & W. Ridgway, England, *c*.1810.

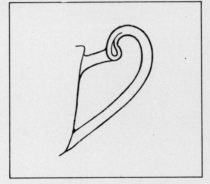

Porcelain handle used by A. J. & W. Ridgway, England, *c*.1820.

Type of handle used by J. Ridgway, England, *c*.1835.

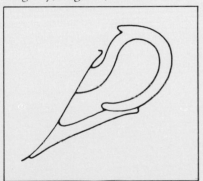

Type of handle used on tea-cups by J. Ridgway, England, *c*.1840–45.

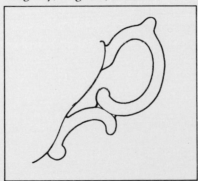

Typical handle, English, J. Ridgway, *c*.1840.

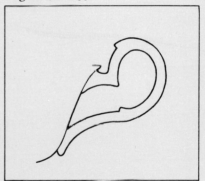

Typical bone china handle, English, J. Ridgway, *c*.1845–50.

Early simple form of porcelain cup, English, Plymouth, 1768–70.

Hard-paste porcelain, English, Plymouth or Bristol, *c*.1770.

Outline of porcelain custard cup, English, Minton, *c*.1830.

Cups

Not all Davenport wares are marked but, in his book *Davenport Pottery and Porcelain*, T. A. Lockett suggests the following pattern numbers and dates: 300-500, *c.*1810-20; 500-800, *c.*1820-30; 800-1200, *c.*1830-40; 1200-2000, *c.*1840-50; 2000-3000, *c.*1850-65. Davenport earthenware often had 'country' blue printed transfer patterns, but the porcelain was more sophisticated, especially after the Derby factory closed in 1848, and many craftsmen moved to Davenport, influencing shapes and decoration.

Porcelain cup and saucer, English, Davenport, 1815-20.

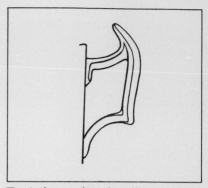

Typical porcelain handle, English, Davenport, *c.*1815-25.

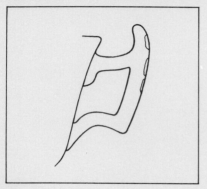

Porcelain handle, English, Davenport, 1820-25.

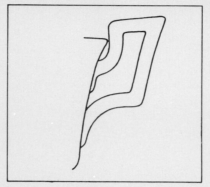

Porcelain handle, English, Davenport, mark of 1820.

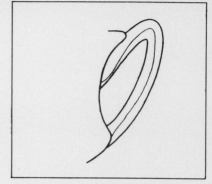

Handle of richly decorated porcelain cup, English, Davenport, *c.*1820.

Porcelain handle, English, Davenport, printed mark of *c.*1830.

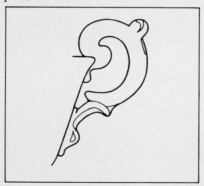

Porcelain handle, English, Davenport, printed mark of *c.*1840.

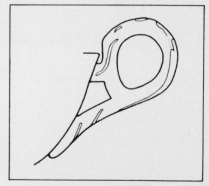

Porcelain handle, English, Davenport, printed mark of 1840-45.

Rather vulnerable porcelain handle, English, Davenport, 1840-45.

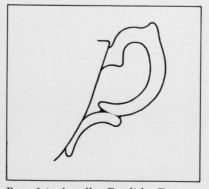

Porcelain handle, English, Davenport, printed mark of *c.*1845.

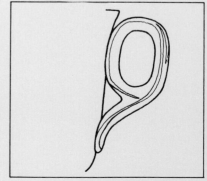

Porcelain handle, English, Davenport, *c.*1850-55.

Porcelain, underglaze-blue decoration, English, Lowestoft, *c.*1765.

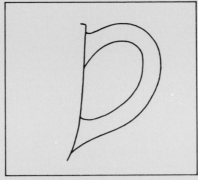

Porcelain handle, *chinoiserie* decoration, English, Lowestoft, *c.*1775–78.

Porcelain, reeded decoration, English, Lowestoft, *c.* 1768.

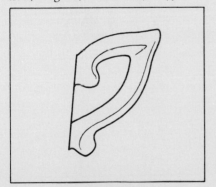

Porcelain handle, *chinoiserie* decoration, English, Lowestoft, *c.*1790.

The porcelain body of the early (Duesbury) period of Derby was a fine ivory white with a waxy surface; this contrasts with the poor quality porcelain produced in the later Bloor period. Coffee-cups of the early period were especially original in design, for instance the small bell-shaped cups with handles shaped like a pixie's ear (3rd row, left). These cups were often painted with flower-sprays.

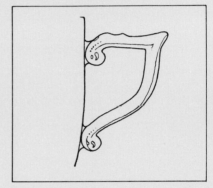

Early type of porcelain handle, English, Derby, *c.*1760.

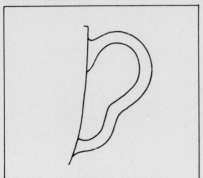

Rather cumbersome form of porcelain handle, English, Derby, *c.*1755.

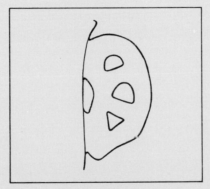

Unique handle, English, Derby, *c.*1760.

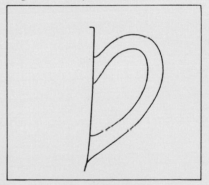

Handle used on cups with *chinoiserie* decoration, English, Derby.

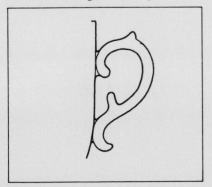

Handle of blue and white porcelain coffee cup, English, Derby, *c.*1770.

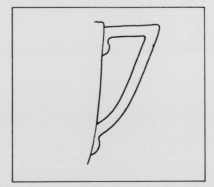

Porcelain handle, English, Derby, 1785-90.

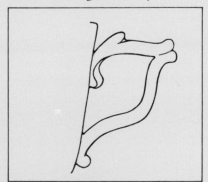

Easily identified 'pinched' two-piece handle, English, Derby, *c.*1810.

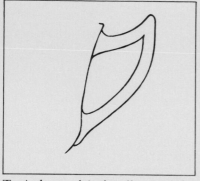

Typical porcelain handle, English, John Rose, Coalport, *c*.1812.

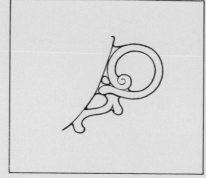

Typical porcelain handle, English, John Rose, Coalport, *c*.1820–25.

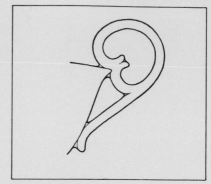

Typical porcelain handle, English, Coalport, *c*.1836–40.

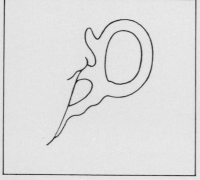

Typical porcelain handle, English, John Rose, Coalport, *c*.1845.

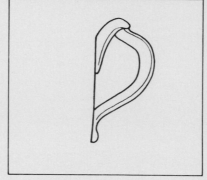

Typical porcelain handle, English, New Hall, *c*.1800.

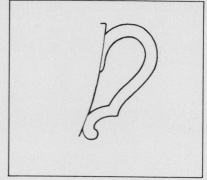

Porcelain handle, Bute pattern, English, Spode, *c*.1800.

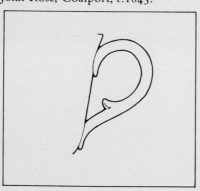

Porcelain handle, referred to as the 'porringer', English, Spode, *c*.1810.

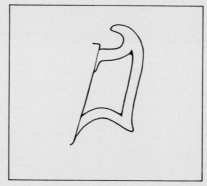

'London' shape handle, similar to others but more upright.

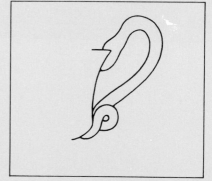

Handle used on Etruscan patterned cups, English, Spode, 1816–*c*.25.

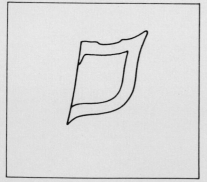

Handle used on cups of Dresden shape. English, Spode, *c*.1820.

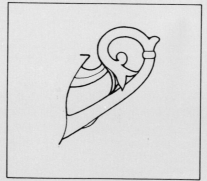

Intricate handles typical of bell-shaped cups, English, Spode, *c*.1820.

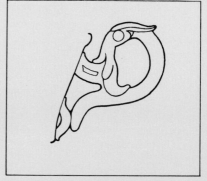

Handle used on gadrooned edged cups. English, Spode, *c*.1820.

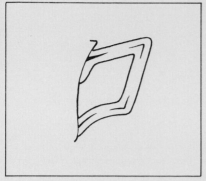

Type of handle used on octagonal cups. English, Spode, c.1829.

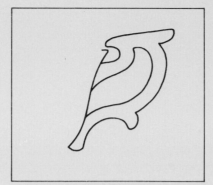

Type of handle popular during the Victorian period, English, Spode.

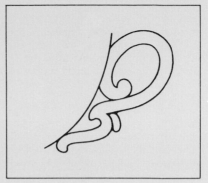

Handle exclusive to Spode porcelain, c.1827.

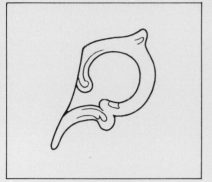

Late type of handle used by Copeland & Garrett, England, 1833-47.

Interest has been growing in the Staffordshire firm of Hilditch & Son (1822-30). The drawn handles appear on marked pieces. Later, under the management of Hilditch & Hopwood, no mark was used. Unfortunately we have no documentary evidence to help distinguish their production from the many mid-Victorian potteries making richly decorated and gilded tablewares.

Note the Minton mug handle (bottom, right) and *see* main text.

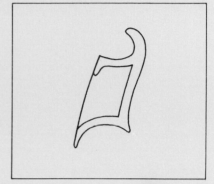

Bone-china handle, English, Hilditch, c.1825: compare with Spode.

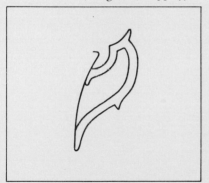

Rarer type of porcelain handle appearing on marked examples.

Typical bone china handle, English, Hilditch, c.1825.

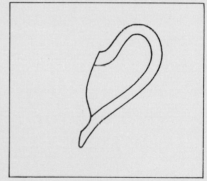

Simple bone china handle, English, Hilditch.

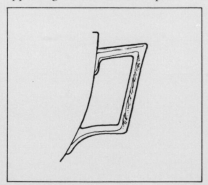

Typical porcelain handle, English, Minton, 1800-05.

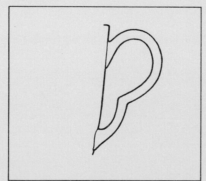

Early handle, usually on printed earthenware. English, Minton.

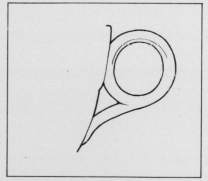

Popular 'ring' porcelain handle, English, Minton, c.1800. (*See* p.125.)

Cups

The early American potter was limited in his choice of forms by the fact that his products were made for hard use; sturdy forms took precedence over ornate, slender shapes. In the materials of redware, stoneware and yellow-ware the New England potters mainly produced simple cups like the one on this row, but more delicate ware was made later in the 19th century in Belleek porcelain and Parian. Fine ironstone in beautifully simple but elegant shapes, often decorated with transfer-printing is characteristic of the Onondago pottery. Almost all early American pottery was made in small workshops and may vary from piece to piece. Glazes are simple—lead-glaze (clear and coloured), salt-glaze and slip with sgraffitto decoration. Earthenware chips easily and early examples with unbroken rims are rare.

Redware, American, Pennsylvania and New England, 19th century.

Earthenware, painting by Young, England, Swansea, c.1803.

Handle of adjacent cup.

Earthenware teacup by Enoch Wood, England, Burslem, Staffs., c.1825.

Stoneware loving cup, English, Nottingham, c.1740.

Salt-glazed stoneware loving cup, English, Nottingham, c.1740.

Porcelain, gold striping, American, Bennington, Vermont, 1850-58.

Belleek porcelain, fluted, American, Trenton (New Jersey), c.1879.

Porcelain, American, (Bennington), Vermont. c.1850.

Redware, common form, American, Virginia, 19th century.

Coffee came into general use in Europe as a popular drink around 1650, tea' a little later. Cups were also used for chocolate, custard, syllabub, punch, etc., and strict rules about shapes, covers, and handles were usually ignored. French and Italian handles are often quite distinctive and were usually marked. Soft-paste and hard-paste porcelain were used, as well as the heavier maiolica body, and the Meissen factory remained an important influence.

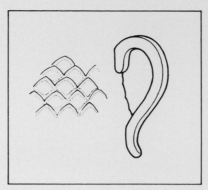

Detail, and typical handle of custard cup. French, St. Cloud, c.1730.

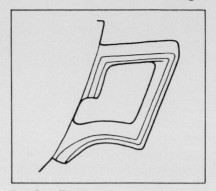

Cup handle, French, (Clignacourt), Paris, c.1800.

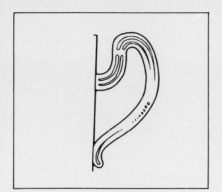

Porcelain handle, Belgian, Tournai, c.1760.

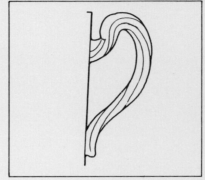

Porcelain handle, Belgian, Tournai, late 18th century.

Porcelain, Belgian, Tournai, 1775. Decorated at the Hague.

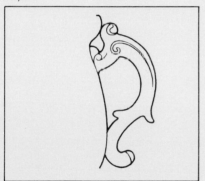

Handle of small covered pot, German, Meissen, 1730–40.

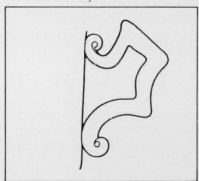

Handle of small bowl, Austrian, Vienna, c.1725.

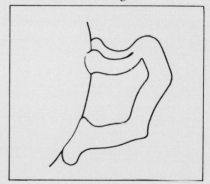

Handle of small bowl, Austrian, Vienna, c.1725.

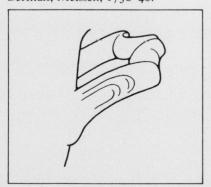

Handle of small bowl, Austrian, Vienna, c.1730.

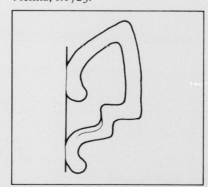

Porcelain handle made during the State Period. Vienna, 1744-84.

Porcelain ice-cream cup, Switzerland, Marieberg, 1766–69.

Cups

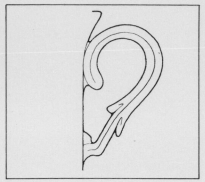

Porcelain handle, Austrian, Vienna, 1760–70.

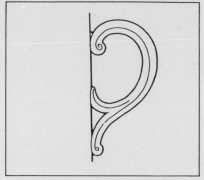

Porcelain handle, French, Sèvres, mark of 1774.

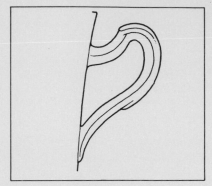

Graceful handle, French, Vincennes, c.1750.

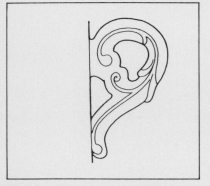

Detail of Sèvres two-handled porcelain cup, date letter of 1758.

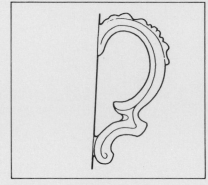

Porcelain handle, French, Sèvres, c.1780.

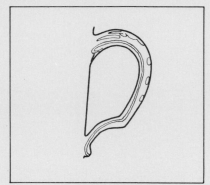

Late form of porcelain handle, French, Sèvres, 1799.

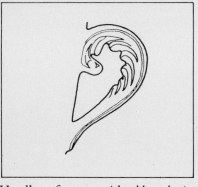

Handle of cup with *bleu lapis* ground, French, Vincennes, 1753.

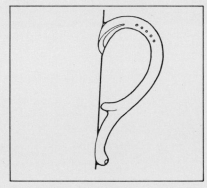

Cup handle, French (La Courtille) Paris, early 19th century.

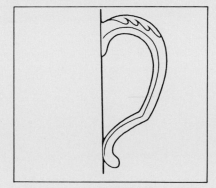

Early shape continued into First Republic. French, Sèvres, c.1800.

Hard-paste porcelain handle, French, Sèvres, 1822.

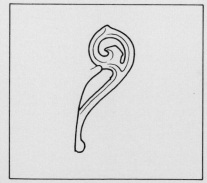

Cup handle, Rue de la Roquette, French, Paris, c.1830.

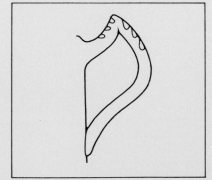

Porcelain handle, French, Sceaux, c.1770.

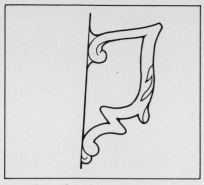

Handle of gilt decorated cup, Italian, Capodimonte, 1745–50.

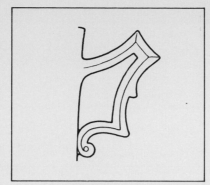

Handle of cup, early neo-classical style, Italian, Capodimonte, c.1745.

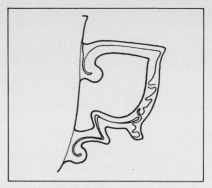

Cup handle, gilt decoration, Italian, Capodimonte, c.1750.

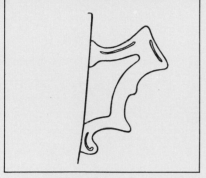

Cup handle, severe neo-classical style, Buen Retiro, Spain, c.1780.

Hard paste porcelain custard cup, Italian, Cozzi, Venice, c.1770.

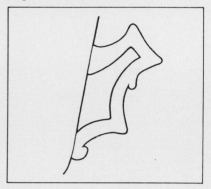

Porcelain handle, Doccia, c.1760: similar style used by Capodimonte.

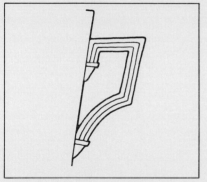

Typical, classical porcelain handle, Italian, Doccia, late 18th century.

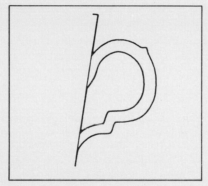

Typical simple porcelain handle, Italian, Doccia, c.1760.

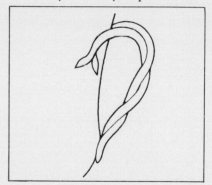

Doccia handle, relief decoration, often mistaken for Capodimonte.

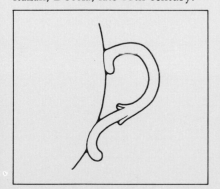

Porcelain handle, Italian, Cozzi, Venice, c.1770.

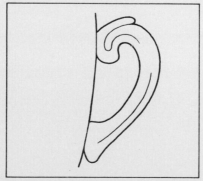

Heavily produced porcelain handle, Italian, Le Nove, late 18th century.

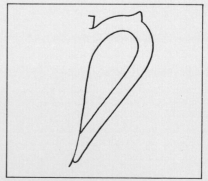

Porcelain handle, Italian, Le Nove, late 18th century.

Cups

German porcelain, especially Meissen, set European styles for most of the 18th and early 19th centuries. Early baroque shapes have scroll handles and moulded decoration. Later, rococo handles full of whorls and asymmetrical curves were set on simple cups. By the 1750s, almost all German factories used a distinctive mark, and identification is much easier, except for copies or deliberate fakes. Meissen in particular was imitated all over Europe.

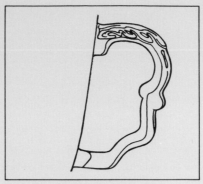

Handle from two-handled cup, German, Meissen, c.1731.

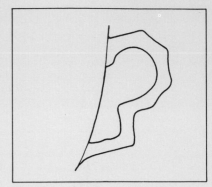

Porcelain handle, early Böttger period, German, Meissen, c.1710–20.

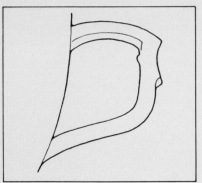

Graceful porcelain handle, German, Nymphenburg, c.1765.

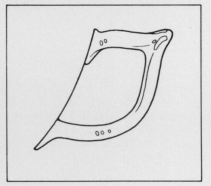

Simple porcelain handle, German, Fürstenberg, c.1755.

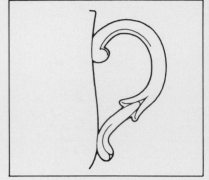

Porcelain handle, German, Nymphenburg, 1755–65.

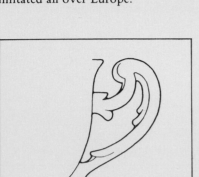

Porcelain handle, German, Royal, Berlin, c.1770.

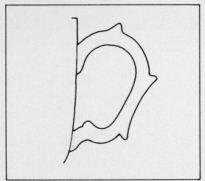

Porcelain handle, German, Berlin, c.1765, 'sceptre' mark.

Porcelain handle, Gotzkowsky period, German, Berlin, 1761–63.

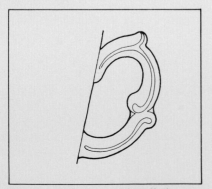

Pattern used on two-handled porcelain cup, Berlin, c.1770.

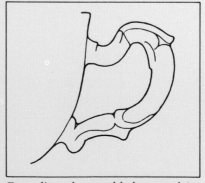

Complicated moulded porcelain handle, German, Würzburg, c.1775.

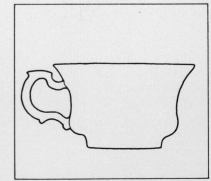

Porcelain cup with handle similar to that alongside.

Cabinet-cups, chocolate-cups and caudle-cups all have similar shapes; most are two-handled, some lidded, others not. Chamberlain's order book refers to Caudle-cups with covers, suggesting that chocolate-cups were without. Note the functional aspect of the large, open handles on Pinxton cups and the oversized ones on Chamberlain's, also the 'O'-shaped knobs for easy lifting. On the whole they were made for display, not use.

Porcelain cabinet- or caudle-cup and cover, English, Bow, c.1762.

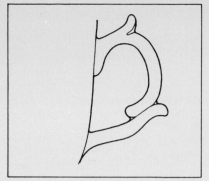

One of two handles, porcelain cabinet-cup, English, Derby, c.1775.

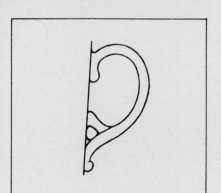

Handle of porcelain cabinet-cup, English, Derby, c.1790.

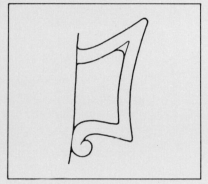

Handle of porcelain cabinet-cup, English, Derby, c.1775.

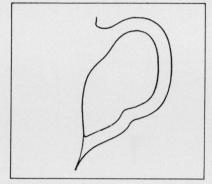

Handle of porcelain cabinet-cup, English, Derby, c.1775.

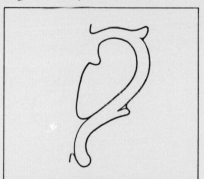

Handle of porcelain cabinet-cup, English, Derby, c.1775.

Cabinet-cup, typical yellow ground, English, Pinxton, c.1800.

Soft-paste porcelain cabinet-cup English, Pinxton, c.1800.

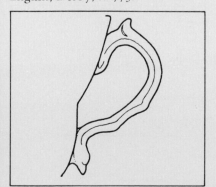

One of two handles of chocolate-cup, English, Worcester, c.1775–80.

Cabinet-cup and saucer, Worcester (Chamberlain), c.1811.

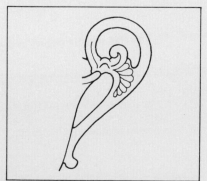

Detail of handle, Worcester (Chamberlain), c.1811.

Soapstone porcelain chocolate-cup, English, Caughley, *c.*1790-95.

Knob of chocolate-cup cover, English, Caughley, *c.*1785.

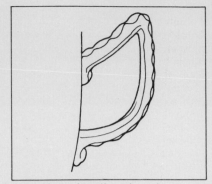

One of two handles, chocolate-cup, English, Caughley, *c.*1785.

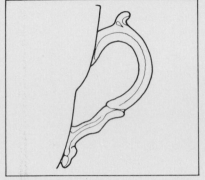

One of two handles, chocolate-cup, English, Caughley, *c.*1790.

Covered cup for caudle or chocolate, English, Davenport, *c.*1805.

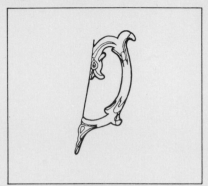

Handle of chocolate cup, English, Spode, *c.*1815.

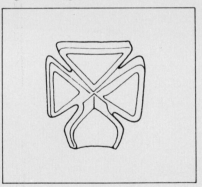

Detail of knob of cover, chocolate cup, English, Spode, *c.*1833-47.

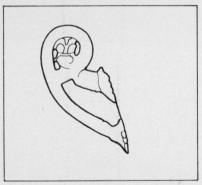

One of two handles, chocolate cup, Copeland & Garrett, Spode, 1833.

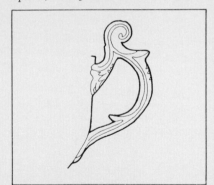

Single handle of large cabinet-cup, English, J. & W. Ridgway, *c.*1815.

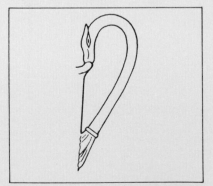

Porcelain handle of cabinet-cup, English, J. & W. Ridgway, *c.*1820.

Rare type of covered chocolate-cup, English, New Hall, *c.*1795-1800.

Rare type of covered chocolate pot, English, New Hall, *c.*1787-90.

Plates & dishes

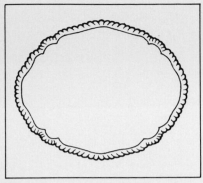

Outline of rare dish, transfer-printed decoration, English Bow, c.1763.

Plates are one of the favourite hunting grounds for collectors. They were made in comparatively large quantities and provide a wonderful surface for decoration as elaborate or simple as required, and generally suffer less damage than hollow-ware pieces. There are many features in plate production which will help to narrow the field (see main text) but dessert dishes are more elaborate, and therefore often easier to identify.

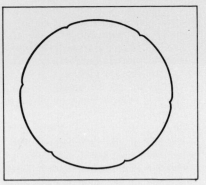

Porcelain plate, type recently identified as Coalport, English, c.1805–10.

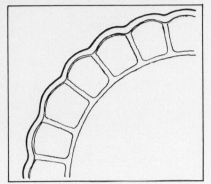

Moulded border of rare plate, English, Caughley, c.1775–85.

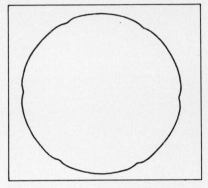

Porcelain plate, English, Rockingham, c.1830. Similar to Coalport.

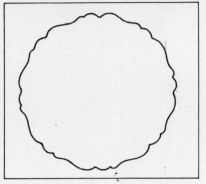

Bone china plate, English J. Ridgway, c.1840.

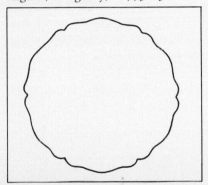

Bone china plate, J. & W. Ridgway, c.1815–20.

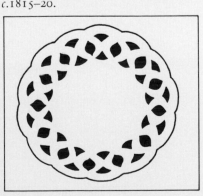

Porcelain basket, pierced decoration, English, Bow, c.1753.

Detail of porcelain plate, Sèvres style, English, Derby, c.1840.

161

Plates & dishes

Most major English porcelain fact-ories made a wide range of dessert dishes, some in elaborate relief and highly decorated. Outlines, mould-ed border decorations and handles are a great aid to identification. Worcester made very attractive diamond shapes as early as 1765, often with pierced rims and elabo-rate 'Japan' patterns. Caughley des-sert services might have had 16 dishes in 4 patterns. Rare New Hall examples in hard-paste porcelain have simple, shell-like moulded forms, a dark-blue border edged with gold and sometimes pierced rims.

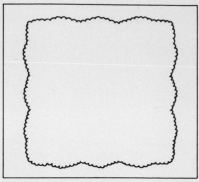

Porcelain dessert dish, English, Worcester, c.1820.

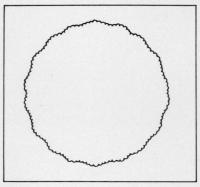

Porcelain dessert dish, English, Worcester, c.1820.

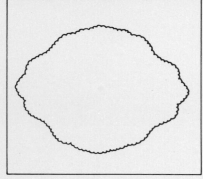

Porcelain dessert dish, English, Worcester, c.1820.

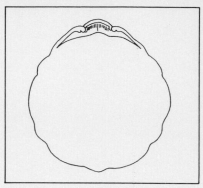

Outline of porcelain dessert dish, English, Worcester, 1807-13.

Detail of handle of dessert dish, English, Worcester, c.1820.

Detail of moulded border of porce-lain plate, English, Derby, c.1860.

Dessert-dish, relief moulded decor-ation, c.1820, marked 'New Hall'.

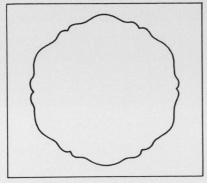

Creamware, transfer-printed decoration, English, Cockpit Hill, Derby.

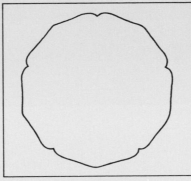

Outline of soft-paste porcelain plate, English, Chelsea, *c.*1755.

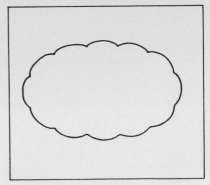

Outline of soft-paste porcelain dish, English, Derby, *c.*1770.

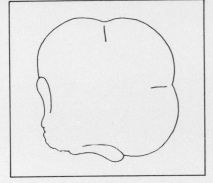

Outline of shell-shaped dish, English, New Hall, 1782-87.

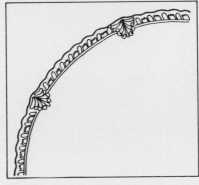

Border of porcelain dessert plate, English, Rockingham, 1826-30.

Border of porcelain dessert plate, English, Rockingham, 1830-42.

Porcelain dessert dish, pierced border, English, New Hall, *c.*1782.

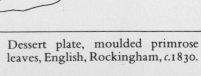

Fluted plate, Belleek ware, American, Trenton (New Jersey) *c.*1880.

Dessert plate, moulded primrose leaves, English, Rockingham, *c.*1830.

Plates & dishes

The porcelain dessert wares of Minton's factory were similar to the contemporary wares of Spode, due mainly to Minton's early connection with Spode. Pattern books kept by both concerns are very helpful. Pierced and moulded decoration is also characteristic of Coalport to 1850. From then onwards, wares were lightly decorated and use made of pleasant green- and rose-coloured grounds in the 'French' taste.

Section of porcelain plate, relief moulded, English, Minton, c.1840.

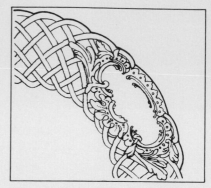

Section of porcelain plate, pierced decoration, English, Minton, c.1846.

Decoration on dessert service, English, Davenport, c.1830.

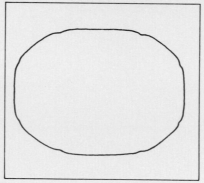

Plate, blue printed American (Bennett Pottery Co.) Baltimore, c.1826.

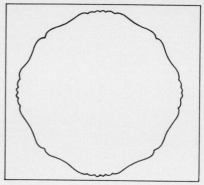

Outline of porcelain dessert dish, English, Derby, c.1860.

Ironstone china dessert dish, English, Mason, c.1813–20.

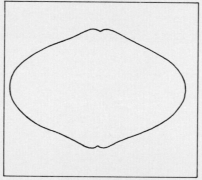

Dessert dish, 'bat' printed, English, Masons, early 19th century.

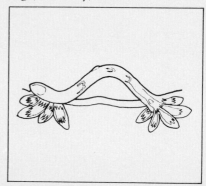

Twig-like porcelain handle on dish, Welsh, Swansea, c.1815.

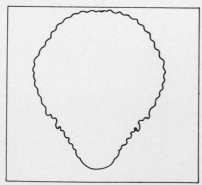

Popular type of porcelain dessert dish, English, Coalport, 1820–30.

Handle of 'Union' dessert service showing emblems.

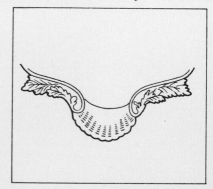

Detail of porcelain dessert dish, English, Coalport, c.1820–25.

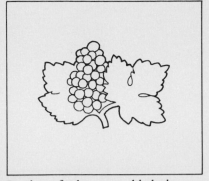

Border of plate, moulded decoration, English, Coalport, *c.*1825.

Outline of dessert dish, English,
Coalport, *c.*1825, impressed anchor.

Detail of handle of dessert dish
shown alongside, English, Coalport.

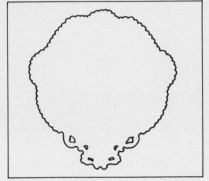

Outline of dessert dish, English,
Coalport, *c.*1826–27.

Detail of handle of dessert dish
shown alongside, English, Coalport.

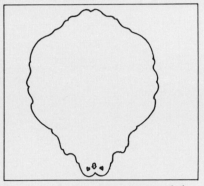

Outline of porcelain dessert dish,
English, Coalport, *c.*1835–40.

Ridgway was particularly prolific
in new designs and decoration for
the export trade. Prior to about
1830, the dessert services were unmarked apart from pattern numbers.
The earliest pattern books are not
as yet known, but Geoffrey Godden
notes that the earliest available
pattern numbers, 562 to 1216, date
from 1810. Unusual handles and
moulded decoration are good indications of Ridgway both in porcelain and stone china.

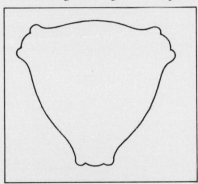

Outline of early porcelain dessert
dish, English, Ridgway, *c.*1810.

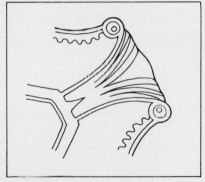

Moulded corner of dessert dish
shown alongside, Ridgway, *c.*1810.

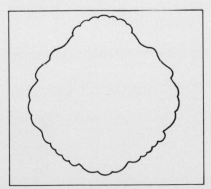

Shell-shaped dessert dish, J & W
Ridgway, *c.*1825.

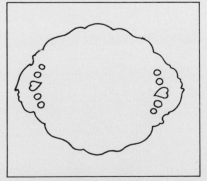

Outline of dessert dish, note pierced
holes, English, J. Ridgway, *c.*1841.

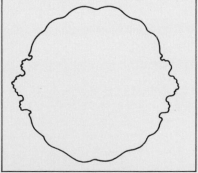

Porcelain dish from tea service,
English, J. Ridgway, *c.*1850.

Plates & dishes

Ridgway's pattern numbers on dessert wares of the 1840s cover about 8241 to 9014, progressive numbering was used on both dessert and dinner services. Teawares were given fractions e.g. 2/768 to such high numbers as 2/9546. Twin side-handles were used on dessert-plates as early as 1815. Another pointer is the moulded bunches of grapes at intervals on the rims. Ridgway and Spode dessert services c.1835 have similar coloured grounds, flower-painting and heavy gilding.

Handle of bone-china dessert dish, English, J & W Ridgway, c.1850.

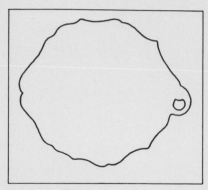

Outline of porcelain dessert dish, English, J. & W. Ridgway, c.1825.

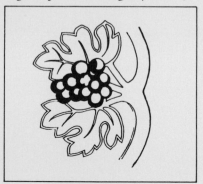

Detail of porcelain dessert dish, English, J. & W. Ridgway, c.1825.

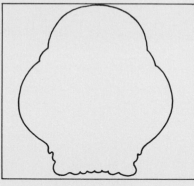

Popular handle used on dessert wares, J. & W. Ridgway, c.1821.

Pierced section of porcelain dessert plate, English, Ridgway, c.1850.

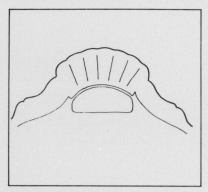

Another typical vine moulded decoration, English, Ridgway, c.1815.

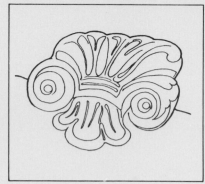

Outline of shell-shaped porcelain dish, English, Rockingham, 1830-42.

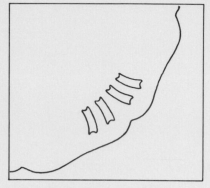

Detail of elaborate handle of dish shown alongside.

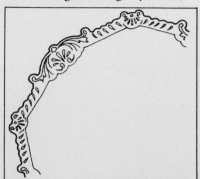

Border on octagonal comport, English, Rockingham, c.1826.

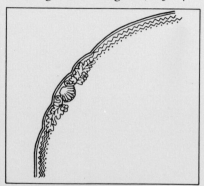

Border of circular dessert plate, English, Rockingham, 1826-30.

Section of border of dessert plate, English, Rockingham, c.1830-37.

Dessert dish, painted by Hadley, English, Coalport, *c*.1826.

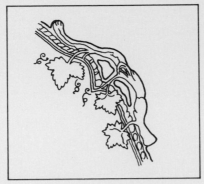

Detail of dessert dish, Grainger, Lee & Co., English, Worcester, *c*.1815.

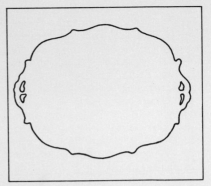

Type of porcelain dessert dish, Grainger, Lee & Co., 1815–25.

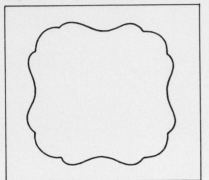

Type of soapstone porcelain dish, English, Caughley, 1785–95.

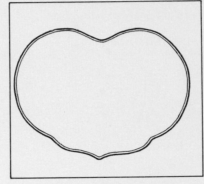

Outline of typical porcelain dessert dish, English, Caughley, *c*.1785–95.

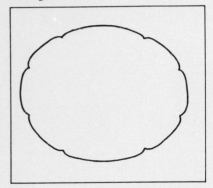

Outline of porcelain dessert dish, miniature service, Caughley, *c*.1780.

Caughley is one of the confusing factories and hard to distinguish from Worcester and Coalport. Again, look for the details of moulded decoration.

For many years Spode specialised in richly decorated dessert wares, of earthenware, bone china or stone china. Not all are marked, but most at least made use of a particular pattern number which can be used as an indication of date. Porcelain closely followed the French *Empire* style, and unusual plates indicate a departure from the traditional circ-

ular and oval shapes. Flower, fruit and bird motifs abound on rich ground colours. Gilding was profuse, stippled or solid gold grounds, reminiscent of Sèvres, were frequently used. The pattern books of the time suggest the following dates: 565 or lower, 1799; 565-1056, 1804; 1057-3692, 1806; 3693-4167, 1822; 4168-4517, 1825; 4518-5057, 1827; 5058-5446, 1831; 5447-5766, 1833; 5767 and higher, 1836.

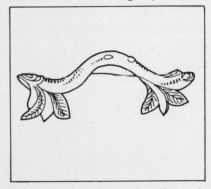

Popular type of twig-handle used on comports, *c*.1800–20.

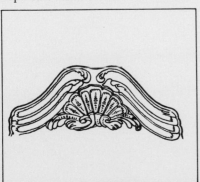

Detail of porcelain footed comport, English, Spode, 1800–20.

Detail of porcelain tray, English, Spode, 1800–20.

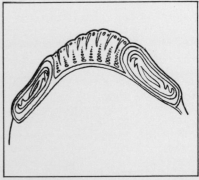

Handle of shell-shaped dish, English, Spode, early 19th century.

Plates & dishes

The ground colours of 18th-century Sèvres plates and dishes were excessively brilliant, broken up by the softening effect of gilding applied in many styles e.g. 'pebbling' and 'Partridge eye'. Tournai plates in general were imitative of Meissen and Sèvres but shapes were more distinctive. Plates divided into four rim panels by spiral ribbing are typical, occurring with or without basketwork. More original still is the close spiral reeding of the rim and shoulder (top centre).

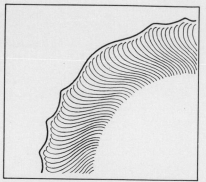

Border pattern on plate, soft-paste porcelain, Belgian, Tournai, c.1760.

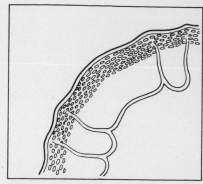

Plate border with basket-work pattern, Belgian, Tournai, c.1780.

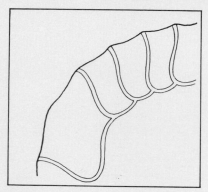

Tournai plate border of spirally curved ribbing, late 18th century.

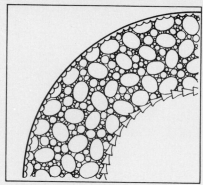

Caillouté (pebbled) diaper of gilding on saucer, French, Sèvres, 1758.

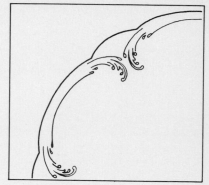

Common moulded border, French, Sèvres, 1768.

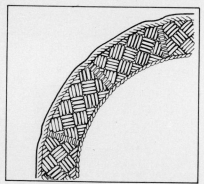

Example of typical basket-work pattern, German, Meissen, c.1735.

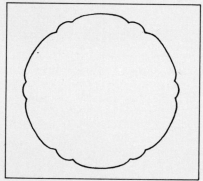

Shape of hard-paste porcelain plate, Niderviller, France, c.1795.

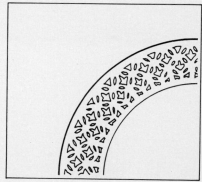

Pierced plate of hard-paste porcelain, French, Sèvres, 1866-76.

Almost all early American pottery was utilitarian, made for kitchen and farm use. Fine tableware was imported. The potters of Pennsylvania, New York and south western Connecticut made redware plates and dishes by rolling out sheets of clay like dough and draping them over moulds, whereas potters of Massachusetts, Rhode Island and New Hampshire 'threw' dishes on the wheel. Both methods resulted in the characteristic pan-shape, sometimes decorated with calligraphic slip or an all-over glaze in black, green or brown. Salt-glazed stoneware often had cobalt-blue free-hand painting. As refined clays developed, lighter and finer yellow-wares, white-wares and ironstone wares were made in considerable quantity. 19th-century American pottery is often un-marked, and attribution is a matter of history, traditions and subtle characteristics of shape and glaze.

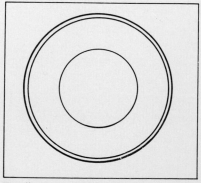

Earthenware dish, slip decoration, east Massachusetts late 18th c.

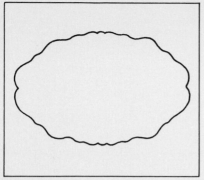

Earthenware dish, probably F. & R. Pratt, Fenton, England, *c.*1820–30.

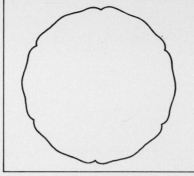

Earthenware plate, high temperature colours, Welsh, Swansea, *c.*1790.

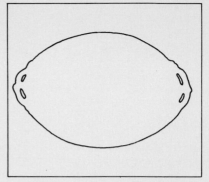

Earthenware dessert dish, English Copeland & Garrett, 1833–47.

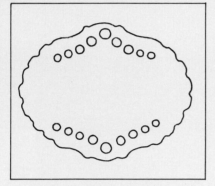

Earthenware plate, English, probably R. Stevenson, 1810–25.

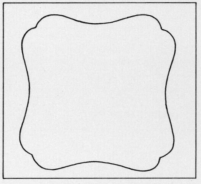

Cane-coloured earthenware dish, English, Rockingham, *c.*1806–25.

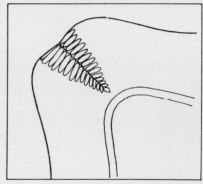

Underside of dish shown alongside, impressed 'BRAMELD'.

Handle of stone china dessert dish, English, J. & W. Ridgway, *c.*1820.

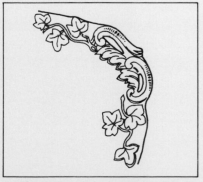

Earthenware dish, English, Copeland & Garrett, *c.*1833–47.

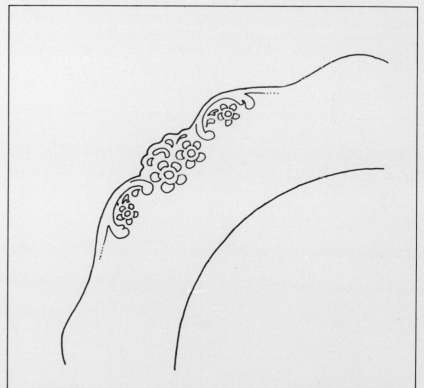

Pierced earthenware dish, English, W. Ridgway, Hanley, *c.*1830–35.

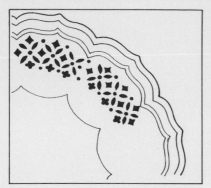

Pierced decoration on earthenware plate, English, Melbourne, *c*.1770.

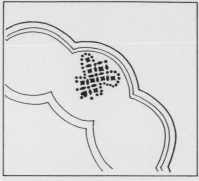

Enamel decoration on creamware dish, English, Melbourne, *c*.1770.

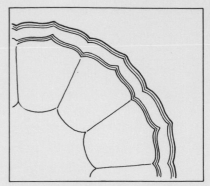

Moulded earthenware plate, English, Melbourne, *c*.1770.

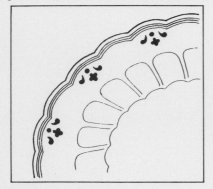

Border on oval dish, enamel, decoration, English, Melbourne, *c*.1770.

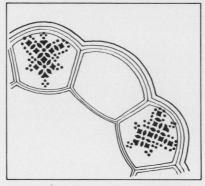

Moulded plate, gilt decoration, English, Melbourne.

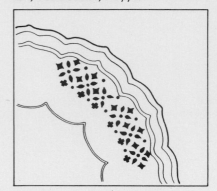

Earthenware, English, Melbourne. Previously thought to be Leeds.

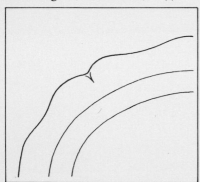

'Oval Royal Dish', earthenware, English, Leeds Pattern Book, *c*.1785.

Stand of creamware basket, English, Whitehead, Hanley, *c*.1798.

'Round Royal Pierced Desert Plate', English, Leeds Pattern Book, *c*.1785.

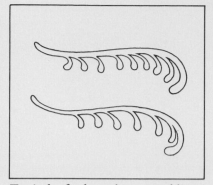

Typical feather-edge moulding, English, Leeds, *c.*1775.

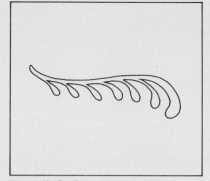

Typical feather-edge border, Bacchus, English, Fenton.

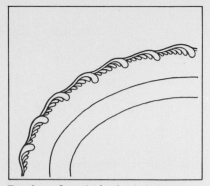

Border of oval 'feather' dish, English, Leeds Pattern Book, No. 19.

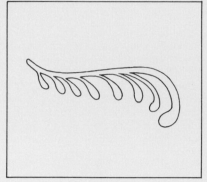

Typical feather-edge, English, Rothwell, Leeds, *c.*1765–75.

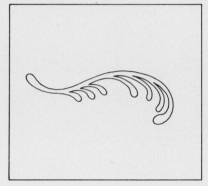

Typical feather-edge used on creamware, English, Wedgwood, *c.*1770.

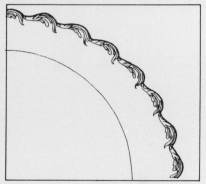

Typical 'cock's tail' border (Towner), English, Melbourne, *c.*1770.

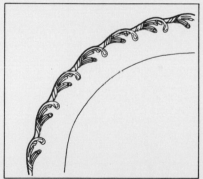

Another variation of 'cock's tail' border, English, Melbourne.

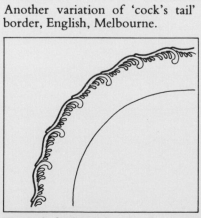

Typical feather-edge border used on creamware, Melbourne, *c.*1770.

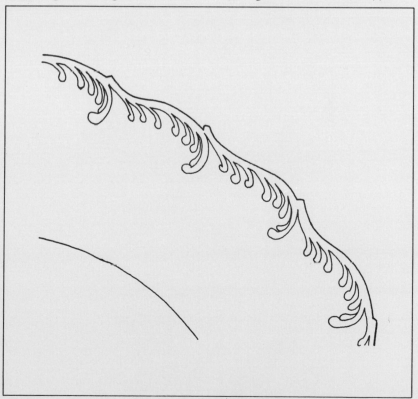

Feather-edge border on circular plate. English, Wedgwood, *c.*1780.

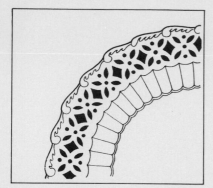

'Round Feather Pierced Desert Plate', English, Leeds Pattern Book.

'Round Feather Pierced Desert Dish', English, Leeds Pattern Book.

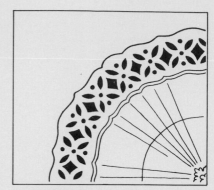

'Royal deep Pierced Desert Plate', English, Leeds Pattern Book.

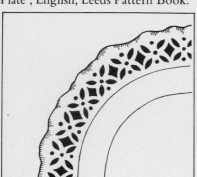

'Shell Edge Pierced Desert Plate', English, Leeds Pattern Book.

'Queen's Pierced Desert Plate', English, Leeds Pattern Book.

Creamware was one of the most popular earthenware bodies ever made. It could be potted almost as finely as porcelain, yet was easy and cheap to make. A simple but shining glaze was often left plain with moulded and pierced decoration. The finest came from England, but it was also made in Europe and America. John Davenport's production of creamware was low, probably because, when he started his factory in Staffordshire, around 1793, it was no longer as fashionable as before.

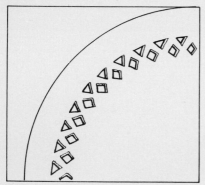

Early creamware plate, pierced border, English, Davenport, *c.*1800.

Creamware dessert dish, English, Davenport, *c.*1800.

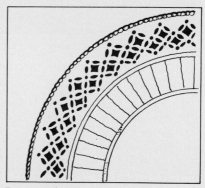

Dessert plate by J. & C. Whitehead of Hanley, England, *c.*1798.

Spode's earthenware plates up to 1800 are rarely marked. The period favoured oriental designs and these were used and improved by Spode. Transfer-printing was also used to good effect, Josiah Spode I doing much to improve the method and thereby the quality.

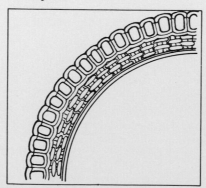

Creamware pierced decoration, English, Spode II, early 19th century.

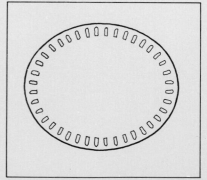

Moulded dish with pierced border, Spode I, late 18th century.

172

The detail of the fine dish shown on this page is an outstanding example of the newly identified Melbourne creamware.

Dessert dish. Decoration in relief by Lakin, Stoke, England, *c*.1815.

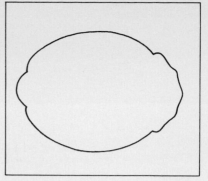

Cream-coloured earthenware dessert dish, English, Davenport, *c*.1800.

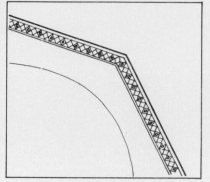

Octagonal creamware plate, moulded border, English, Melbourne.

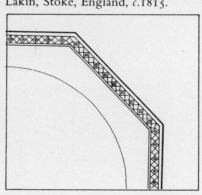

Creamware dish, purple enamel decoration, Melbourne, *c*.1770.

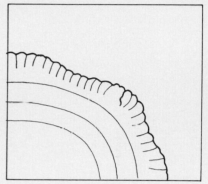

Cream-coloured dish, English, Dunderland & Co., Castleford, Yorks.

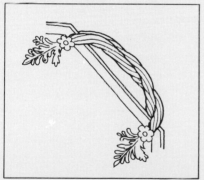

Detail of typical terminals used on cake-baskets, English, Melbourne.

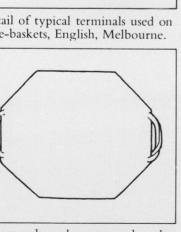

Cream-coloured octagonal cake dish, English, Melbourne, *c*.1770.

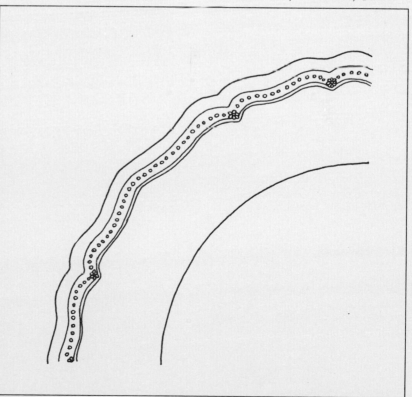

Plate border, earthenware, English, Clementson & Reed, Hanley, *c*.1832.

Section of moulded earthenware plate, green-glazed, Spode, *c*.1810.

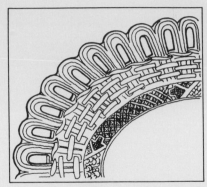

Moulded earthenware dish, printed decoration, English, Turner, *c*.1800.

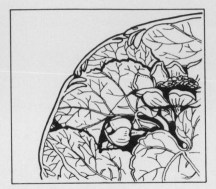

Moulded earthenware plate, *c*.1870. Impressed 'J. ADAMS & CO.'

Porcelain spoon tray, English, Caughley, *c*.1780.

Moulded earthenware plate, green-glazed, English, Davenport, *c*.1850.

Earthenware dish, pierced border, English, Meigh, Old Hall, *c*.1805.

Porcelain spoon tray, 'Davis & Flight' English, Worcester, 1776–93.

Hard paste porcelain spoon tray, English, New Hall, *c*.1782–87.

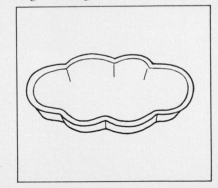

Spoon tray, English, (Gilbody), Liverpool, *c*.1755.

During the 18th century, shiploads of earthenware (especially creamware) plates were imported into the United States from England. Although Wedgwood had a certain snob appeal, there is little evidence to show that American buyers differentiated between factories. Certainly some queensware was made in America. The examples (illustrated here) show a plate found in Maryland and a mould from which it could have been made.

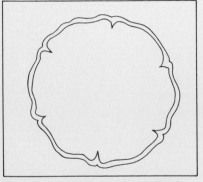

Queen's ware-type plate, (Bethabara), North Carolina, *c*.1780.

Plaster mould for Queen's ware plate, Salem, N. Carolina, *c*. 1790.

Leaf dishes or pickle trays were made by a number of English factories but luckily the shapes do vary. The glaze was usually dark green, Leeds in particular having a rich, glassy surface. Worcester made a wide range of shapes for many years, varying in size from about 3 to 13 inches. The smaller versions usually have very detailed modelled veining on the underside which shows great care in craftsmanship (see following page).

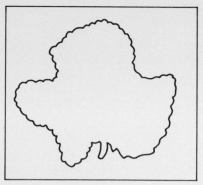

Leaf-shaped porcelain pickle tray, English, Bow, *c.*1756.

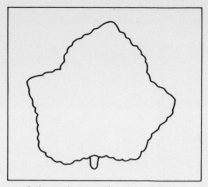

Leaf-shaped porcelain pickle tray, English, Bow, *c.*1756.

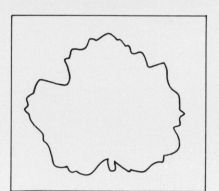

Small leaf-shaped porcelain pickle tray, English, Bow, *c.*1749–50.

Small porcelain pickle tray, English, Bow, *c.*1756.

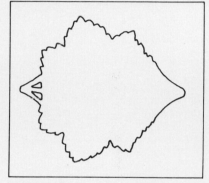

Outline of porcelain pickle dish, English, Derby, *c.*1775–85.

Leaf-shaped porcelain stand, English, Longton Hall, *c.*1752.

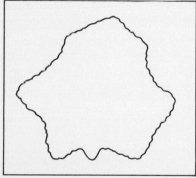

Outline of leaf-shaped porcelain dish, English, Worcester, *c.*1775–85.

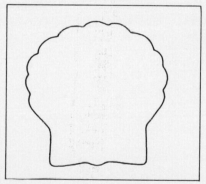

Porcelain pickle tray, W. Reid, English, Liverpool or Shelton, *c.*1760.

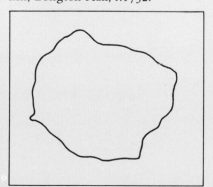

Porcelain pickle tray, W. Reid, English, Liverpool or Shelton, *c.*1760.

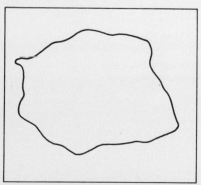

Porcelain pickle dish, W. Reid, English, Liverpool or Shelton, *c.*1760.

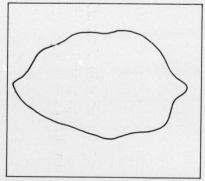

Porcelain pickle dish, W. Reid, English, Liverpool or Shelton, *c.*1760.

Creamware 'Pickle Leaf', English, Leeds Pattern Book, No. 11, *c.*1790.

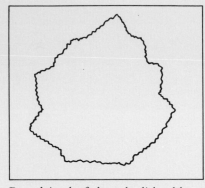

Porcelain leaf-shaped dish, blue-printed, English, Caughley, *c.*1780.

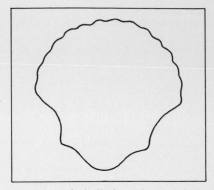

Outline of shell-shaped porcelain dish, English, Caughley, 1785–95.

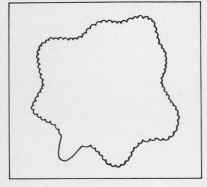

Type of hard-paste pickle tray, English, New Hall, *c.*1782–87.

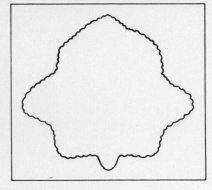

Leaf-shaped porcelain dish, blue-printed, English, Caughley, *c.*1785.

Creamware 'Escollop Shell'; Leeds, length 4 in.–9 in.

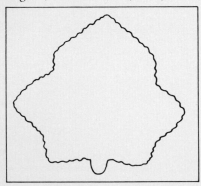

Leaf-shaped porcelain dish, blue-printed, English, Caughley, *c.*1780.

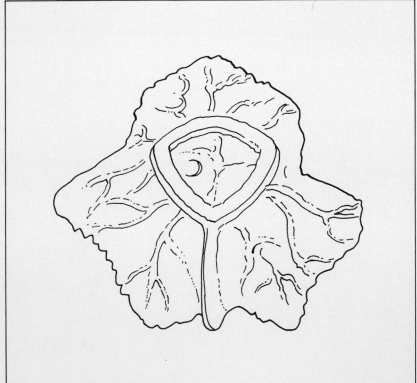

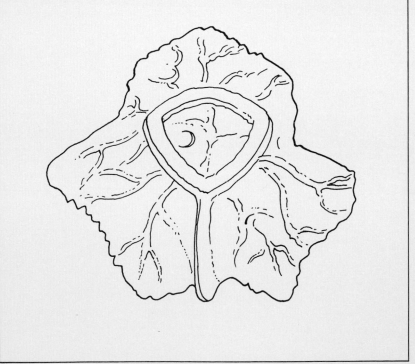

Early stand for finger bowl, blue decoration, English, Bow, *c.*1752.

Underside of porcelain pickle tray, English, Worcester, *c.*1768.

Mugs, jugs, tankards & pitchers

Another overlap in shape and use occurs with coffee cups, mugs and tankards. In general, a one-handled, straight-sided, low shape is a coffee cup, taller, it becomes a mug or tankard. All were made in everything from rough salt-glaze to the finest egg-shell thin porcelain. They make a delightful collector's item. Bow made some of the prettiest, and the heart-shaped handle terminal on bell-shaped mugs is unique.

Porcelain coffee-can, blue decoration, English, Bow, c.1753.

Porcelain coffee-can from set of six, English, Pinxton, 1800.

Porcelain mug, 'heart-shaped' terminal, English, Bow, c.1755.

Late Bow porcelain mug, transfer-printed decoration, c.1760.

Porcelain tankard, 'powder-blue' decoration, English, Bow, c.1762.

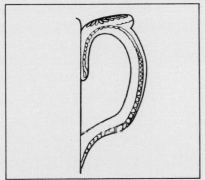

Handle of early minton porcelain mug, English, c.1800–05.

Hard-paste porcelain coffee-can, English, Champion, Bristol, c.1775.

Hard-paste porcelain coffee-can, English, New Hall, 1795–1805.

Longton Hall wares vary a great deal. The early mugs in salt-glazed stoneware or thickly potted porcelain, often have bands of deep Littler Blue. Later examples are better made, but had weak handles and rather uninspired painting. Pinxton had simple shapes, often decorated in brown and purple. The Liverpool factories made a great many mugs of varying quality, mostly with a curved body, but the straight-sided coffee-cups made by Gilbody can be identified by their unusual decoration (*see* main text).

Porcelain mug, English, Longton Hall, c.1758. Note handle shape.

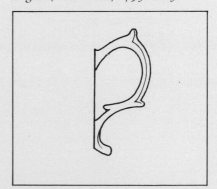

Late form of porcelain handle, English, Lowestoft, c.1795–99.

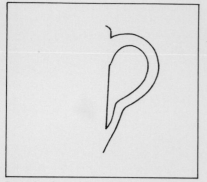

Detail of popular porcelain handle shape, English, Pinxton, *c.*1800.

Porcelain mug, grey-black painting, yellow ground, Pinxton, *c.*1800.

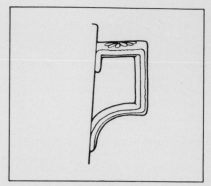

Handle of mug, early pattern number, English, Minton, *c.*1800.

Chaffers & Christian of Liverpool produced a characteristic bell-shaped mug, but mugs came from all the Liverpool factories: the cylindrical variety usually have flat, unglazed bases. Rounded mugs, like silver pitchers without the spout, were often decorated in delicate flower sprays. There was a vogue, especially in Europe, for moulded figures, animals and natural shapes. Coffee-cans almost always are simple and cylindrical even if they had elaborate handles.

Mug, early form, attributed to Billingsley.

Mug, late form, English, Pinxton, 1803-13.

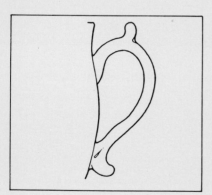

Handle, English (Chaffers), Liverpool, *c.*1755.

Early bone porcelain mug, English, Chaffers, Liverpool, *c.*1755.

Soapstone porcelain mug, English, Chaffers, Liverpool, *c.*1756.

Porcelain mug, English, Gilbody, Liverpool, *c.*1754-60.

Mug of salt-glazed stoneware form, porcelain, Gilbody, Liverpool.

Mug of salt-glazed stoneware form, porcelain, Gilbody, *c.*1754-60.

Prior to the excavations on the Worcester and Caughley sites, there was a great deal of confusion over their wares due to what at first appeared to be identical under-glaze blue transfer-prints on both types. There are, in fact, slight differences.

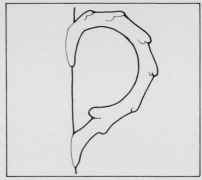

Porcelain mug, English, Caughley, c.1790. Note slight thumb-rest.

Typical handle, porcelain, normally unmarked, English, Coalport, c.1825.

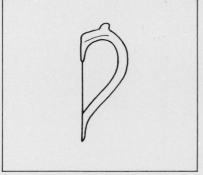

Typical porcelain handle, English, Masons, c.1800.

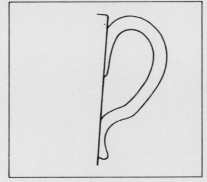

Porcelain mug handle, English, Davenport, c.1870.

Late Davenport porcelain mug, mark of c.1850–60.

Experimental porcelain mug, Welsh, Swansea, c.1796.

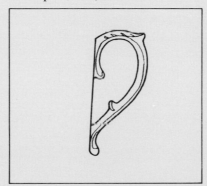

Porcelain mug handle, English, Grainger, Worcester, c.1846.

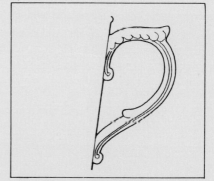

Porcelain mug handle, attributed to Worcester, c.1870.

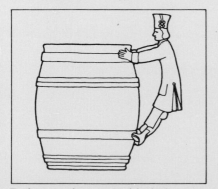

Early porcelain mug, black decoration, Austrian, Vienna, c.1725.

Typical handle on jug, English, Lowestoft, c.1769.

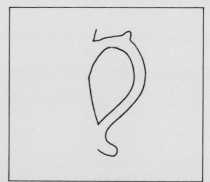

Porcelain jug handle, enamel decoration, English, Lowestoft, c.1780.

Early bone porcelain coffee-can, English, Chaffers, Liverpool, c.1755.

Porcelain coffee-can, English, Gilbody, Liverpool, 1754–60.

Porcelain mug, enamel decoration, Gilbody, Liverpool, 1754–60.

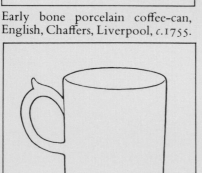

Porcelain mug, underglaze-blue decoration, Gilbody, Liverpool.

Porcelain coffee-can, English, Gilbody, Liverpool, c.1754–60.

Porcelain coffee-can, fluted sides, Gilbody, Liverpool, c.1754–60.

Early American redware and stoneware mugs resembled earlier European forms, especially from Germany. Straight-sided mugs were in vogue by 1700, and widespread by 1720, sometimes with bands of toolings and simple clear or coloured glazes. The Bell family (Pennsylvania, c.1833-99) made plain redware often glazed only inside. Moulded brownwares with the popular Rockingham glaze (see p. 182) were made at Bennington and Illinois from the 1850s in scenic patterns.

Salt-glazed stoneware mug, English, Francis Place, Yorkshire, c.1680.

Salt-glazed stoneware mug, English, Francis Place, Yorkshire, c.1680.

Redware mug, corrugated, American, Mid-west, 19th century.

Stoneware mug, common form, American, Massachusetts, 19th c.

'Majolica' earthenware mug, American, Pennsylvania, c.1879.

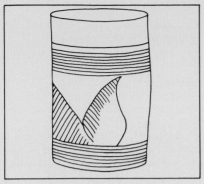

Salt-glazed stoneware tavern tankard. English, Staffordshire, c.1710.

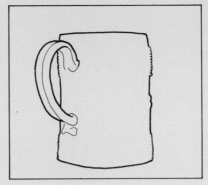

Red stoneware mug, English, probably Elers, Staffs., late 17th century.

Red stoneware mug, English, probably Elers, Staffs., late 17th century.

Salt-glazed stoneware jug, English, Nottingham or Derby, 1850s.

Stoneware jug, English, Nottingham or Derby, early 18th century.

Red earthenware tankard, white slip edge, English, Pomona, 1724.

A jug has a small mouth which can be closed by a stopper, a pitcher has a wide mouth shaped into a pouring spout. Both were very popular utensils in America until the early 19th century, and pitchers were as simple as possible. A distinct Connecticut form reflects German and Dutch influence, with a rounded body slanting inwards towards an elongated neck, almost at an angle. Usually a wide handle describes a generous curve. Northern New England pitchers have rather long handles set at a slight curve from the body. Later, every kind of ornamentation was used, restrained and wild, from the classic round shapes to the 'news and views' wares, moulded in the form of prominent political figures.

Stoneware Rockingham, ironstone or simple kitchen red- and yellow-ware give the collector plenty of variety. Look for comfortable handles, well made, and well balanced. There is little elaborate painted decoration until 1880, mostly moulding, transfer-printing and multi-coloured glazes.

Redware pitcher, corrugated, American, Pennsylvania, early 19th c.

Stoneware pitcher, corrugated, American, Mid-west, 19th century.

Redware pitcher, American, Pennsylvania, 19th century.

Redware pitcher, common form, American, New England, 19th c.

Redware pitcher, common form, American, New England, 19th c.

Stoneware pitcher, common form, American, 19th century.

Rockingham Pitcher, American, Bennington (Vermont) 1844–47.

Rockingham glaze was first produced in Swinton, Yorkshire, better known today for its bone-china, made from 1826 to 1842. In America, 'Rockingham' became a generic term for a brown 'tortoise-shell' glaze used for much domestic pottery, made in every major factory. The hound handle is a unique American design; details can identify the factory. Bennington's hound has a long, flattened nose resting on its paws, with an arched neck so the finger can fit underneath.

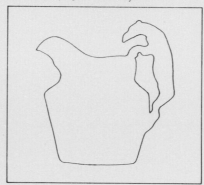

Rockingham pitcher, hound-handle, American, East Liverpool, c.1850.

Rockingham pitcher, hound-handle, American, Bennington, 1852–67.

Small salt-glazed stoneware jug, English, Nottingham, 1703.

Salt-glazed stoneware mug, English, Nottingham, 1730–70.

Salt-glazed stoneware jug, English, Nottingham, late 17th century.

Salt-glazed stoneware, English, Nottingham, c.1730.

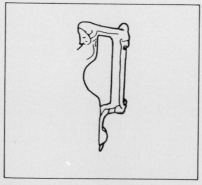

Stoneware jug handle, 'smear-glaze', English, Meigh, 1842.

Cane-coloured stoneware jug, English, Davenport, Longport, c.1800.

Porcelain was a new material in the mid 18th century and although plate making was fairly simple, hollow wares such as jugs were clearly more difficult. Longton Hall shapes are somehow not quite satisfactory. Other English factories were more adept and the new material was used with restraint and balance. English and Continental porcelain jugs sometimes had a lid, especially smaller sizes made and decorated to match tea- and coffee-sets and used for milk and cream.

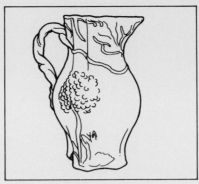

Porcelain moulded plant decoration, English, Longton Hall, 1755.

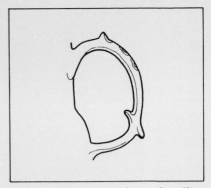

Characteristic porcelain handle, English, Longton Hall.

Jug with typical handle, English, Longton Hall, c.1758.

Soft-paste porcelain jug, English, Longton Hall, c.1755.

Porcelain jug, enamel decoration, English, Gilbody, Liverpool, c.1754.

Porcelain jug, French sprig decoration, English, Caughley, c.1785–95.

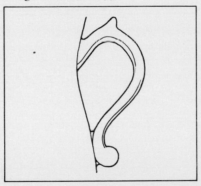

Common Worcester handle. *See* p.185 (top right).

Corrugated porcelain cream or milk jug, characteristic New Hall handle.

Corrugated cream- or milk-jug, popular handle, English, New Hall.

Porcelain cream jug, typical handle, English, New Hall, c.1800.

Parian porcelain pitcher, American, Bennington, Vermont, 1855.

In Philadelphia, William Ellis Tucker and partners produced a range of porcelain in the Empire style, with many classic, elegant pitchers. Use of moulded natural forms branches, acorns, etc., is more typical of Baltimore pottery and appears on handles and knobs. American stoneware remained simple, but English decorations were more ambitious. Jugs, mugs and pitchers had tooling, incised patterns, and enamel flowers over the brown Nottingham salt-glaze.

Hard-paste porcelain jug or pitcher. moulded hunting scene, 1835.

Small porcelain jug, known as 'Walker' shape, American, c. 1835.

Porcelain pitcher, enamel decoration, American, Tucker, 1834.

Small hard-paste porcelain pitcher, enamel and gilt decoration, 1835.

Large hard-paste porcelain pitcher, painted American eagle, 1835.

Hard-paste porcelain pitcher, fluted sides, American, Tucker.

Porcelain pitcher, painted colours, reeded band at base, 1835.

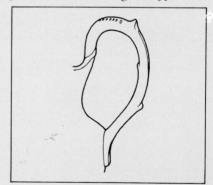

Detail of handle, porcelain pitcher, American, Tucker, c. 1835.

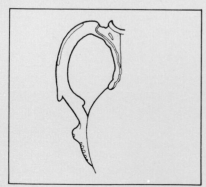

Detail of handle, porcelain pitcher, American, Tucker, 1834.

Many pitchers were made in the United States of Parian ware. A hard, unglazed porcelain, it was developed first in Staffordshire, England, in 1842 and introduced into America by Christopher Fenton, and eventually made at the New England Pottery Company, the New York City Pottery among others. By the 1890s, factories were marking their wares and identification becomes much easier. European influence was strong, but some Parian designs are American in origin like the corn-husk.

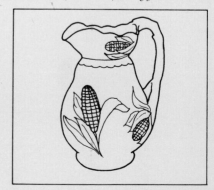

Parian, corn-husk pattern, American, New England, c. 1860.

Mask-head spouts are indicative of two English factories in particular, Caughley and Worcester, although others made similar types. Details of the mask can help in identification—a pleasant-looking old gentleman on Worcester contrasts with the rather stern-looking Caughley. American mask-head jugs are usually in stoneware. Masks were also made all over the Continent on crude Bellarmines, or expressively in the finest porcelain.

Parian, mask lip, American (Fenton), Bennington, Vermont, 1852.

Soapstone porcelain mask jug, English, Worcester, 1757.

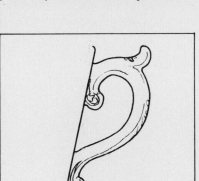

Porcelain milk jug handle, English, Caughley, c.1785-95.

'Cabbage-leaf' jug, mask-head, English, Caughley, c.1785.

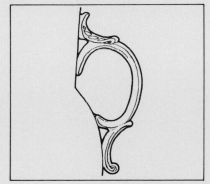

Porcelain handle on cabbage-leaf jug, English, Caughley, c.1785.

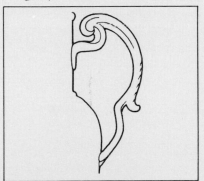

Soapstone porcelain handle, English, Caughley or Coalport, c.1796.

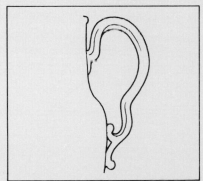

Porcelain jug handle, English, Caughley or Coalport, 1796.

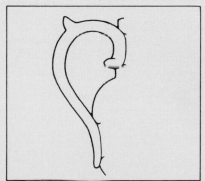

Porcelain jug handle, English, Rose, Coalport, c.1810.

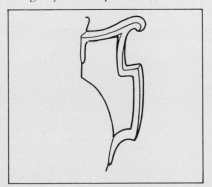

Porcelain handle, attached with imitation rivets, English, Coalport.

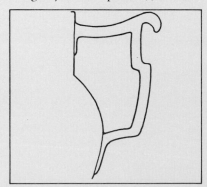

Jug handle, English, Coalport (Anstice, Horton & Rose) c.1810.

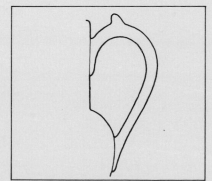

Jug handle, English, Coalport, (Anstice, Horton & Rose) c.1810.

Mugs, jugs, tankards & pitchers

Pinxton porcelain is only rarely marked and the pattern numbers which do at times appear cannot be compared with the factories pattern book, which as yet has not been located. The script letter 'P' is frequently seen together with a pattern number and an occasional impressed letter. It is important to recognise the unusual Pinxton handle, which was, as far as present research can tell, made only in that factory.

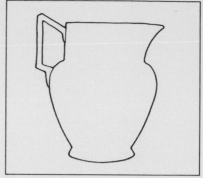

Porcelain jug with unique handle, English, Pinxton, c.1800.

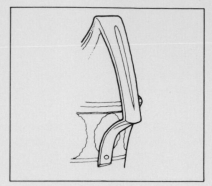

Unusual form of jug handle, attributed to Pinxton, c.1800.

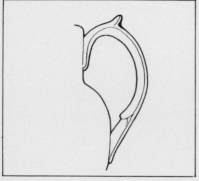

Porcelain jug handle, Sèvres-type mark, English, Minton, c.1810.

Bone china milk jug, English, Masons, early 19th century.

Porcelain cream-jug, American, Bennington, Vermont, c.1850.

Hard-paste porcelain hot water jug, English, New Hall, c.1782-87.

Large porcelain jug, enamel landscape, English, New Hall, c.1790.

Hard-paste porcelain water jug, English, New Hall, c.1810.

Porcelain cream jug, faceted sides, English, New Hall, c.1782.

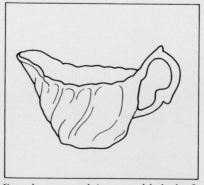

Popular porcelain moulded leaf creamer, English, New Hall, c.1782.

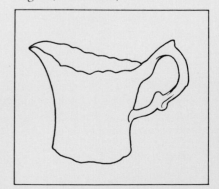

Hard-paste porcelain creamer, English, New Hall, c.1782-87.

Another warning about marks: small teawares with an underglaze blue 'A' for many years have been the subject of controversy. Once thought to be Italian they were probably made at Vauxhall, London.

Note the similarity and the difference between the bell-shapes of Liverpool and Bow.

The two American examples made of porcelain (top) and Parian (bottom) were made at Bennington and are typical shapes for small milk or cream jugs from this area.

'A' marked porcelain cream jug, English, London, c.1750.

'A' marked cream jug, probably Vauxhall, London, c.1750.

Small porcelain cream jug, English, Bow, c.1753.

Porcelain cream jug, typical wide pouring spout, English, Bow, c.1753.

Late porcelain leaf-shaped cream boat, English, Bow, 1763.

Porcelain creamer, American, Bennington, Vermont, c.1850.

Rare cream jug, English, Derby. Similar to Worcester.

Very rare creamer, early Planché period, incised 'D.1750'.

Creamer, earthenware, American, Jersey City Pottery, c.1828.

Porcelain creamer, English, (Reid), Liverpool or Shelton, c.1760.

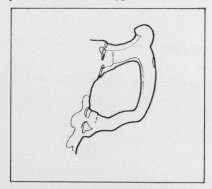

Porcelain cream jug handle, English, (Reid), Liverpool or Shelton.

Porcelain cream jug, English, Pennington, Liverpool, *c.*1775.

More typical English shapes, easily confused. It was common practice for many years to attribute any inferior Worcester porcelains of the 1776–1793 period to Caughley. Excavations have proved otherwise. Compare the two examples on this page. The Worcester handle (top, right) is more forward bending with a knuckle joint. In the later Worcester example (2nd row, centre), the handle is more rectangular and upright.

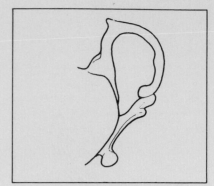

Porcelain cream-boat handle, English, Worcester, 1775–80.

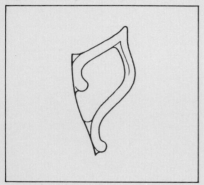

Typical porcelain handle, English, Worcester, *c.*1760.

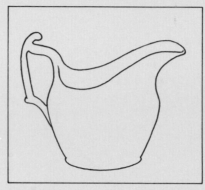

Hard-paste porcelain cream jug, English, Worcester, *c.*1800.

Porcelain creamer similar to earlier Chelsea wares, English, Caughley.

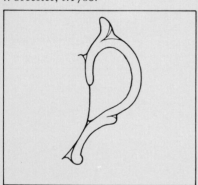

Porcelain cream-boat handle, English, Caughley, *c.*1775–80.

On the Lowestoft creamers, note the characteristic handle and raised lip and the one (bottom centre) which could easily be mistaken for Lowestoft. On the Minton creamer handle (bottom right) notice the rather slight concave curve. The Pinxton jugs on the facing page are more examples of that special, angled Pinxton handle. See page 186.

Common type of creamer, English, Lowestoft.

Porcelain cream jug, heavily potted, English, Longton Hall, *c.*1754.

Porcelain, English, Longton Hall, *c.*1756.

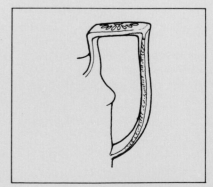

Creamer handle, English, Minton, 1800–05.

Porcelain cream jug, English, Pinxton, *c*.1800, impressed 'H'.

Typical cream jug, classical handle, English, Pinxton, *c*.1800.

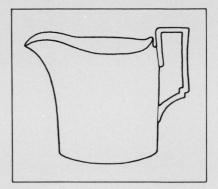

Porcelain cream jug, classical handle, English, Pinxton, impressed 'J'.

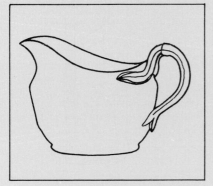

Porcelain cream jug, note slip type handle, English, Davenport, *c*.1810.

Porcelain cream or milk jug, English. Davenport, *c*.1820-25.

Porcelain creamer, English, Davenport, mark for *c*.1815-25.

The wares made by John Rose's factory at Caughley and the nearby factory of Anstice, Horton & Rose which ceased in 1814 are almost identical. There are slight differences, however. The bottom row indicates the similarities between Ridgway and New Hall creamers and milk jugs of the same period. This kind of experience in judging proportion and balance helps identify unknown pieces. The expert clue of spout and the ease of grasping the handle are good 'tactile' hints.

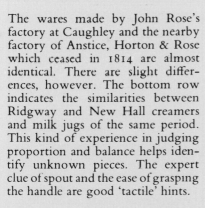

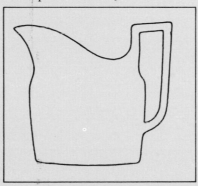

Creamer with spiral fluting, English, (Anstice, Horton & Rose), Coalport.

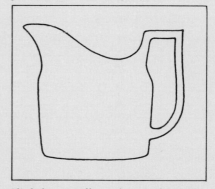

Slightly smaller than adjoining creamer, (John Rose), Coalport.

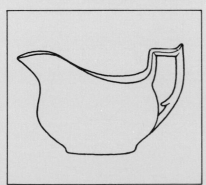

Porcelain creamer, English, J. & W. Ridgway, Cauldon Place, *c*.1815.

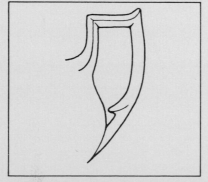

Detail of typical porcelain creamer handle, English, J. & W. Ridgway.

Bone-china creamer, English, New Hall, *c*.1814-31.

Mugs, jugs, tankards & pitchers

Rockingham in Swinton, Yorkshire, is known best for its fine production of bone-china but also produced all the other popular types of earthenware and stoneware. Cane-coloured wares were among the finest productions. Cockpit Hill made elaborate, elegant creamers (2nd row, centre) and ample jugs as in 3rd row, (centre). Church Gresley was a another small, unknown factory making popular cane-coloured pottery. The last shapes show how simple, round forms were used all over Europe.

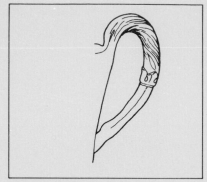

Mug handle shaped like hoof. English, Rockingham, c.1806.

Cane-coloured mug, English, Rockingham, c.1815, marked 'BRAMELD'.

Earthenware jug printed decoration, English, Rockingham, c.1820.

Form of creamware jug, English, Cockpit Hill, c.1770.

Stoneware jug handle, English, attributed to Church Gresley.

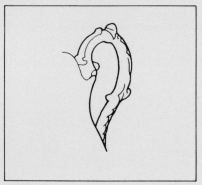

Earthenware jug handle, English, Copeland & Garrett, 1833–47.

Creamware jug, Holdship print, English, Cockpit Hill, Derby.

Hard-paste porcelain creamer, English, New Hall, c.1782–87.

Earthenware jug, fluted sides, English Minton, 1830.

Soft-paste porcelain jug, early form, form, Italian, Naples, c.1800–06.

White stoneware cream jug, English, Turner, Lane End, 1780–1800.

The handles on this page are all in the rococo style (Louis Quinze) (1714-74) which predominated in scrolls, shells, etc., and asymmetrical poise by nervous vitality of line and sensuous feeling for the material. This style was admirably suited to the crisp hard-paste porcelain of Meissen and diffused through other factories in Germany to Italy and France.

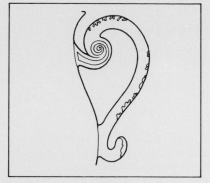

Porcelain jug handle, German, Meissen, 1735-40.

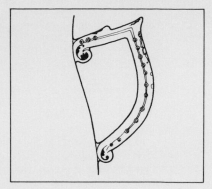

Porcelain jug, Du Paquier period, Austrian, Vienna, 1719-44.

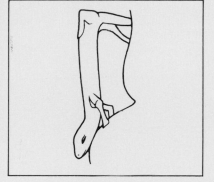

Porcelain jug handle in the form of a lizard, Austrian, Vienna, c.1730.

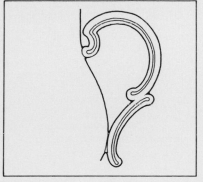

Rare porcelain jug handle, German, Ottweiler, c.1740.

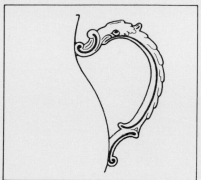

Ornate porcelain jug handle, German, Ludwigsburg, c.1765.

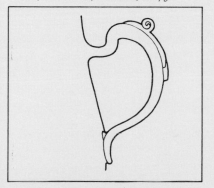

Porcelain jug handle by N. F. Hewelcke, Italian, Venice, c.1760.

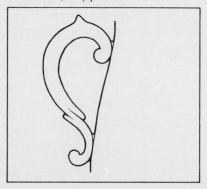

Porcelain jug handle, Italian Doccia, c.1780.

Small porcelain jug, Swiss, Zurich, 1765-75.

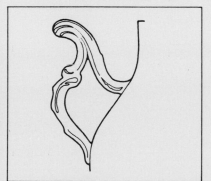

Detail of unusual type of porcelain jug handle, Swiss, Zurich, c.1770.

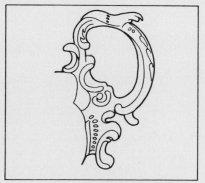

Jug handle, French, Paris. Sometimes mistaken for Rockingham.

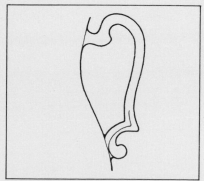

Soft-paste porcelain jug handle, Italian, Capodimonte, 1755-59.

Mugs, jugs, tankards & pitchers

These salt-glazed stoneware jugs were made in various parts of Germany from the 14th century onwards. Relief moulding is a common characteristic. These solid, sturdy shapes influenced country pottery until the 20th century, particularly in America where German and Moravian potters worked in small settlements recreating traditional decorations and shapes. The return of gothic fashion from the 1850s and later in America meant that many 'mediaeval' jugs are actually Victorian copies.

Jacobakanne, salt-glazed stoneware, German, Siegburg, *c.*1400.

Schnelle, pewter mounted, German, Siegburg type, mid-16th century.

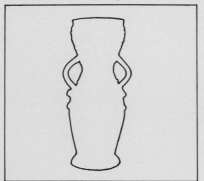

Trichterbecher, German, Dreihausen, 16th century.

Schnabelkanne, stoneware, German, Siegburg, late 16th century.

Dark brown stoneware jug, German, Raeren, 16th century.

Stoneware jug, Jan Emens Mennicken, German, Raeren, 1576.

Detail of *Bartmannskrug* German, characteristic of Cologne.

Stoneware, type made at Westerwald, Germany, *c.*1600.

Humpen, dark brown stoneware, German, Kreussen, 17th century.

Stoneware bottle, German, Muskau, Upper Lusatia, 17th century.

Stoneware jug, German, Bunzlau, Silesia, late 18th century.

Early form of soft-paste porcelain, English, Bow, *c.*1753.

Basic forms are globular, pear-shaped, cylindrical. Both Bow and Lowestoft made large numbers of teapots with simple Chinese-type loop handles and straight spouts. Typical Lowestoft pots of the mid-18th century had asymmetrical flower or fruit knobs which gave way to buttons, fire-cones or figural knobs later on. These natural forms were also used by the Baltimore potters in America towards the end of the 19th century. The Derby knobs are quite distinctive.

Miniature porcelain teapot, English, Caughley, *c.*1780-90.

Detail of open flower porcelain knob, English, Lowestoft, *c.*1770.

Porcelain teapot from miniature service, English, Bow, *c.*1760.

Porcelain teapot, open flower knob, English, Lowestoft, *c.*1770.

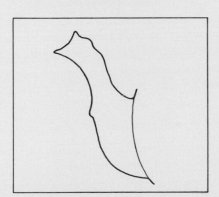

Typical porcelain spout, English, Derby, *c.*1775.

Typical porcelain teapot shape, English, Derby, *c.*1775.

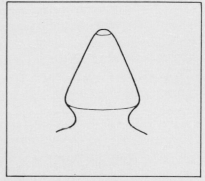

Distinctive porcelain knob, English, Derby, *c.*1775.

Soft-paste porcelain barrel-shaped teapot, English, Lowestoft, *c.*1768.

Porcelain, *chinoiserie* decoration, English, Liverpool, *c.*1775.

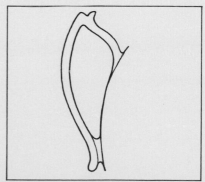

Porcelain handle, English, Derby, *c.*1775.

Teapots

Liverpool pots like these were exported in very large quantities to America and are now generally evaluated as poor to adequate copies of the fine and more valuable Worcester porcelain. Notice particularly the mis-matched handle (2nd row, left), far too fussy, and the better balance of the teapot (3rd row, left).

Hexagonal teapot, English, Liverpool (W. Reid), c.1760.

Porcelain, English, Liverpool, c.1754-61.

Porcelain, ill-matched handle, by Ball, English, Liverpool, c.1755-69.

Porcelain, W. Reid, English, Liverpool, c. 1755-61.

Porcelain, manufacturer undetermined, English, Liverpool, c.1770.

Porcelain, English, probably Chaffers, Liverpool, c.1760.

By the late 18th and early 19th centuries. Worcester teapots begin to show the change to more elaborate shapes. The c.1810 pot is in the newly fashionable boat-shape with exaggerated lip, somewhat skimpy handle and strange, flammiform knob. This later Worcester ware was less well designed than the early Dr. Wall period.

Porcelain, 'Davis & Flight' period, English, Worcester, c.1780.

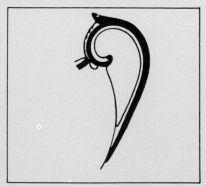

Handle of adjacent teapot.

Porcelain, 'Flight, Barr & Barr' period, English, Worcester, c.1807.

Detail of knob of same teapot.

Soft-paste porcelain, 'A' marked.

Similar porcelain teapot, 'A' marked.

For 'A' mark wares, *see* page 187. Teapots were the pride and joy of almost every English factory, and were made in every material, style and decoration. By the 1900s, whole new wealth of 'modern' shapes came into use—Masons used the boat shape (bottom, centre) but less exaggerated and somehow more pleasing than the Worcester example, (opposite bottom, centre).

Porcelain teapot, by Turner of Caughley, English, *c.*1785-90.

Typical Chantilly-type spray decoration, English, Caughley, *c.*1785.

Soapstone porcelain, fluted spout, English, Caughley, *c.*1785-95.

Rare porcelain teapot, 'cherry' knob, English, Longton Hall, *c.*1758.

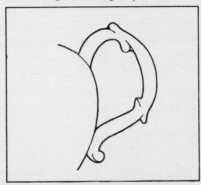

Glassy soft-paste porcelain, moulded decoration, English, Longton Hall.

Porcelain, English, Davenport, mark for *c.*1815-25.

Typical porcelain handle, English, Spode, early 19th century.

Typical porcelain teapot, English, Masons, early 19th century.

Porcelain, sometimes, decorated with 'bat' printing, English, Masons.

Teapots

William Billingsley's transfer from Derby to Pinxton meant that many styles and shapes were copied,—the Derby use of flowers and leaves in relief was not. Pinxton took the squarish Derby handle (bottom, right) and indeed, the whole pot (3rd row, left and centre) but developed a much squarer sharply angled version. Compare Clignacourt and Doccia handles, pp 155 & 157.

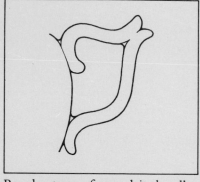

Popular type of porcelain handle, English, Derby, c.1775.

Porcelain teapot, English, Derby, c.1800. Note small pad feet.

Boat-shaped teapot, typical cornflower decoration, English Pinxton.

Porcelain, yellow ground, classical type handle, English, Pinxton.

Porcelain, yellow ground with view of a stately home, English, Pinxton.

Soft-paste porcelain, distinctive handle, English, Pinxton, c.1800.

Globular-shaped, cornflower sprig decoration, English, Pinxton, c.1800.

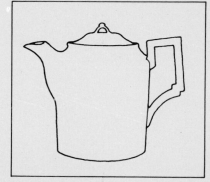

Porcelain, oval form, classical style, typical handle, English, Pinxton.

Soapstone porcelain, probably Christian, English, Liverpool, c.1770.

Outline of porcelain teapot, yellow ground, English, Derby, c.1782.

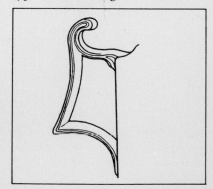

Handle of marked porcelain teapot, English, Derby, c.1782-1800.

Porcelain, one of five basic shapes, English, Masons, early 19th century.

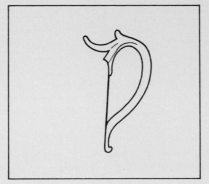

Typical porcelain handle, English, Masons.

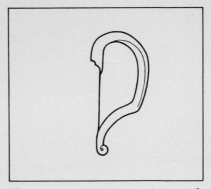

Characteristic handle consisting of two curves, English, Masons.

At this period Mason made only five basic teapots and the double curved handle (top, right) was often used. Notice the unique feature of imitation rivets at top of spout on the John Rose (Coalport) pot (3rd row, centre). The earlier factory of Anstice, Horton and Rose also produced many similar varieties of teapot as illustrated. Study the features of each drawing, for example, the fluting arrangement on spouts in order to be able to tell them apart.

Porcelain teapot, English, (John Rose), Coalport, c.1805-10.

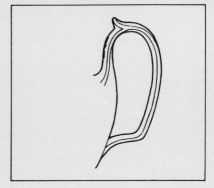

Typical porcelain handle, English, (John Rose), Coalport, 1805-10.

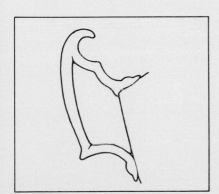

Porcelain handle, attached with imitation rivets, English, Coalport.

Porcelain, very characteristic handle, English, Coalport, c.1810.

Porcelain, typical ribbed type knob, English, Coalport, c.1805-10.

Porcelain, ring handle, English, (John Rose), Coalport, c.1805-10.

Detail of fluting on spout, porcelain, English, (John Rose), Coalport.

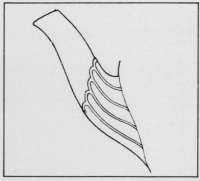

Detail of fluting on spout, English, Anstice, Horton & Rose, c.1800.

Teapots

To distinguish Plymouth china from Bristol is not easy: the paste and glaze were similar although Bristol's is perhaps 'cleaner' with a cold white sheen. Simple mid-18th century shapes were used except for the occasional flower knob and their shapes seem to have been inspired by Worcester and Sèvres as regards useful wares. A double-curved profile was favoured for handles which were often longitudinally ribbed and pots often had a wide curve at the base.

Type of hard-paste teapot, English, Plymouth, c.1770.

Hard-paste porcelain, flower knob after Worcester, English, Plymouth.

Porcelain, underglaze-blue decoration, English, Plymouth, 1770.

Distinctive shape of porcelain teapot, English, Plymouth, c.1768-70.

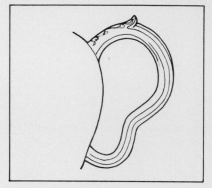

Typical 'ear' shaped handle, hard-paste, porcelain, English, Bristol.

Boat-shaped hard-paste porcelain, English, (Chamberlain), Worcester.

Hard-paste porcelain, oval 'silver-shape'. English, New Hall, c.1795.

Rockingham, 'Rebecca at the Well', American, Pa., c.1850.

Porcelain, sunken lid, faceted sides, English, New Hall, c.1782-87.

Hard-paste porcelain, English, New Hall, c.1782-87. Note handle.

Early porcelain teapot, 'corrugated' moulding, English, New Hall.

Recent research by David Holgate has enabled collectors to sort out the genuine New Hall shapes and patterns from those of the many imitators who were also allowed the unrestricted use of hard-paste porcelain materials in England from 1796 onwards. Compare the boat-shaped pot with Masons and Worcester (pp. 194 & 195). Many of New Hall shapes followed silver forms with details often picked out in gilding.

Porcelain, *chinoiserie* decoration, English, New Hall.

Hard-paste porcelain, English, New Hall, 1782-87

Boat-shaped, hard-paste porcelain, English, New Hall, *c.*1795-1812.

Hard-paste porcelain, note ogee-waisted form, English, New Hall.

Porcelain, moulded with curved fluting, English, New Hall, *c.*1787.

Hard-paste porcelain, rare *fleur-de-lys* knob, English, New Hall, *c.*1795.

Porcelain, 'vase shaped' knob with steam hole, English, New Hall, 1798.

Porcelain, handle with connecting strut, English, New Hall, *c.*1805.

Porcelain, silver-shaped, English, New Hall, late 18th century.

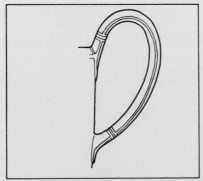

Handle on silver shaped pot picked out in gilt, English, New Hall.

Typical porcelain knob picked out in gilt, also used on matching wares.

Typical teapot, English, (John Rose), Coalport, early 19th century.

Porcelain, revived rococo type, English, Coalport, early Victorian.

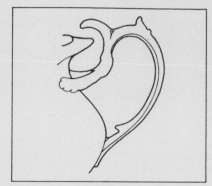

Detail of handle of adjacent teapot.

Porcelain, 'stumpy' knob, English, (Anstice, Horton & Rose), Coalport.

Porcelain, English, (Anstice, Horton & Rose), Coalport.

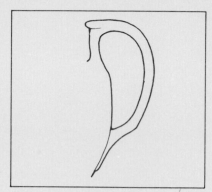

Detail of porcelain handle, English, (Anstice, Horton & Rose), Coalport.

Typical porcelain teapot, English, Anstice, early 19th century.

Dark blue grounds, medallions of flowers, Chinese landscapes and gilding are all very characteristic forms of decoration used on Minton teapots. One common form of spout often found is the forward-looking variety (bottom, centre) usually balanced by an upright handle. Later Minton teapots favoured a more elaborate style of handle and spout, curving rather than angular as the examples (facing page, top) show.

Porcelain, English, Minton, *c*.1812. Marked with pattern number.

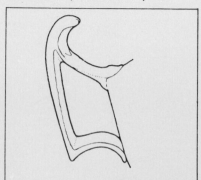

Detail of porcelain handle, English, Minton, *c*.1812-14.

Early shape of porcelain teapot, English, Minton.

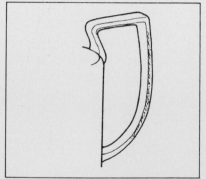

Detail of handle on adjacent porcelain teapot, *c*.1800-05.

Porcelain, pine-cone knob, English, Minton, *c.*1830.

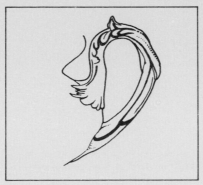

Detail of handle of adjacent teapot, often 'bat' printed.

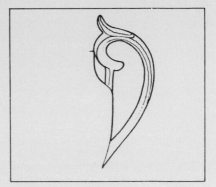

Detail of porcelain handle, English, Minton, *c.*1805-10.

Teapot, English, Minton, *c.*1805-10. Similar type produced by Spode.

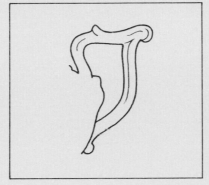

Porcelain teapot handle, English, Minton, *c.*1830.

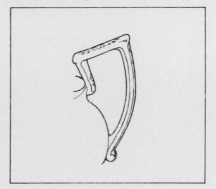

Handle of teapot from tea warmer, English, Minton, *c.*1830.

The most famous American Porcelain works of the 19th century was that of William Ellis Tucker in Philadelphia who made many fine tablewares in porcelain, often with painted and gilt decoration. The adjacent teapot is part of a tea warmer set (see page 229).

Porcelain spout, English, Minton, *c.*1830.

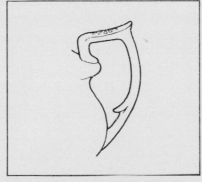

Typical porcelain handle, English, Minton, *c.*1812-15.

Porcelain, American, (Tucker), Philadelphia, *c.*1826.

Porcelain teapot, English, Ridgway, *c.*1815.

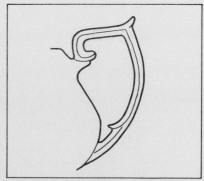

Detail of porcelain handle, English, Ridgway, *c.*1810.

Teapots

Several US potteries made teapots in Balleek porcelain, influenced by the productions at the Balleek works in Ireland. This fragile, egg-shell porcelain was well-suited to teapots and some charming styles were produced from it. Ott & Brewer of Philadelphia, among others such as Knowles Taylor & Knowles, were producing a high-quality Balleek type porcelain from 1882 onwards. They were all competing with English imports, and Ridgways were both elaborate, ornamented and unmarked.

Belleek porcelain, American, Trenton, new Jersey, c.1882.

Porcelain teapot, 'London' shape, English, Ridgway, c.1815-20.

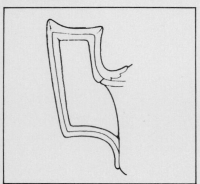

Handle of ornamented porcelain pot, English, Ridgway, c.1820.

Porcelain teapot, usually richly decorated, English, Ridgway, c.1820.

Porcelain teapot, often mistaken for Rockingham. English, Ridgway.

Certain features of Rockingham and Ridgway teapots have distinct similarities. Compare on this page the shapes of handles and spouts (2nd and 3rd rows) of teapots produced at the same period. Rockingham's revived rococo styles especially have been the object of much confusion. Handles are a good aid to identification: the factory seems to have used a distinctive variety of eight shapes.

Porcelain teapot, common shape, English, Rockingham, 1826-30.

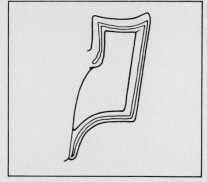

Porcelain handle, English, Rockingham, 1826-30.

Porcelain, English, Rockingham, c.1830-42.

Distinctive porcelain knob, English, Rockingham, 1830-42.

Bone china teapot, 'inset pyramid' knob, English New Hall, 1815-31.

Teapots became increasingly popular in America from 1880s onwards and were made in all kinds of pottery, and in many unusual shapes, not too far removed from the Staffordshire pots made as horses, camels etc. Sometimes a native American animal took pride of place as can be seen from the squirrel knob on this page.

Porcelain, painted with enamel landscape, American, (Tucker).

Porcelain, gold striping, American, New England, 1850-58.

White earthenware, American, Jersey City Pottery, c.1828.

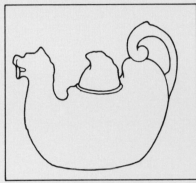

Porcelain, American, (Morris & Willmore), New Jersey, c.1895.

Tcapot with squirrel finial, American, Bennington, Vermont, 1847.

The early wares made by Bell at the Pomona Potworks, Staffs., appear to have been of the local red earthenware, with a rich lead-glaze which did so much to improve the appearance of his large range of tablewares. He seems to have been the first English potter to inlay bands of 'agate' to his wares. Other Staffordshire potters made interesting shapes in black basaltes and stone-china.

Red earthenware, English, Bell, Pomona, c.1724-44.

Red earthenware, vertical fluting by hand, English, Pomona.

Black basaltes, English, Turner, Lane End, 1780-1800.

White stoneware, lined blue enamel, English, c.1780-1800.

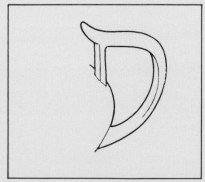

Stone china handle, English, Spode, c.1806-10.

Teapots

Redware forms made in the United States in the 18th century were mostly globular with slightly domed covers that rest over rims and little thin handles like those of a porringer. The globular black pot has persisted in almost identical form to the present day. Thomas Crafts of Whately made them in the 1820s; he turned the rounded bodies but cast the handles, noses and covers.

Redware, American, Strasburg, Virginia, 19th century.

Redware, American, (Thomas Crafts) Whately, Mass., c.1825.

Creamware teapot previously attributed to Leeds, c.1765.

English, Yorkshire, obviously made at factory other than Leeds.

The teapots below show clearly the main features of Melbourne teapots: two basic shapes, globular and cylindrical. Handles were either of plaited-strap or twisted rope. Most knobs were in the form of a convolvulus flower. All these features are also characteristic of Leeds but one of the greatest aids to identification of Melbourne creamwares is the similarity of the various forms of moulded terminals used at the join of the handle to the body (*see* also p. 217).

English, Creamware, identified as Melbourne by terminals, c.1770.

English, Creamware, identified as Melbourne, by terminals, c.1770.

English, Melbourne, c.1770. Previously thought to be Leeds.

Leeds-type creamware, now known to be Melbourne, c.1770.

Creamware teapot, green striped decoration, English, Melbourne.

Creamware, plain surface, enamel decoration, English, Melbourne.

The early forms of cream-coloured earthenware became available in England in about 1720 when potters started to use Devon ball-clays which had the effect of producing a near-white body, along with calcined flints from Dorset. Fired to a higher temperature, these materials were being used for salt-glazed stoneware.

Creamware was immediately adapted for use in almost every pottery in England. Leeds is often considered the finest, especially for moulded and relief decoration. The clear glaze varied from very fine to rather thick and gluey at the poorer quality factories. In America creamware and a type of queenware were manufactured and used extensively. But the shapes remained generally simple. England remained the home of really fine creamware.

Creamware, English, Wedgwood, c.1764.

Early form, lead-glazed creamware pot with Wedgwood-type handle.

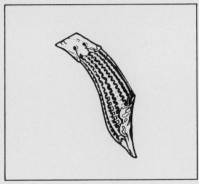

Spout, Whieldon-Wedgwood partnership, c.1755.

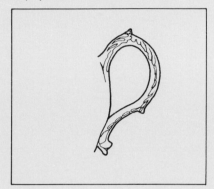

Form of early scroll handle, later imitated elsewhere, Wedgwood.

Form of creamware, Cockpit Hill, English, Derby, c.1765.

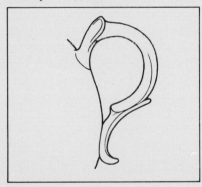

Detail of creamware handle, English, Cockpit Hill, c.1765.

Creamware, print by Radford, English, Cockpit Hill, c.1765.

Creamware, relief decorated, faceted spout, English, Cockpit Hill.

Creamware, 'crabstock' handle and spout, English, Cockpit Hill, c.1765.

Creamware, English, Cockpit Hill, c.1770.

Teapots

Creamware, English, attributed to Leeds, c.1770–79.

Creamware, red and black decoration, English, Leeds, c.1775.

Creamware, enamel decoration, attributed to Leeds, c.1770–79.

Detail of spout, English, Leeds 'Original Drawing Book No. 1'.

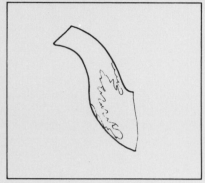

Form of creamware spout, English, Leeds, c.1800.

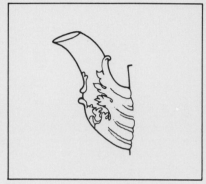

Form of creamware spout, English, Whitehead, Hanley, late 18th c.

Notice the similar shapes of these four Yorkshire teapots, with 'crab-stock' handles and spouts. At one time these two (bottom, centre and right) were thought to have been made at Leeds but it is now known that they are too early in date. Heather Lawrence (*see* bib.) has proved that Leeds did not begin until 1770. Look for the small details which can help to distinguish one factory's work, as it has with Melbourne ware—the attachment of a handle, the idiosyncratic modelling of a flower knob, the curve of a

spout. Decoration is a little more tricky—often simple pieces were sold 'in the white' to decorating shops or well-known artists. The German *Hausmalerei* (home-painting) provide good examples, and the work is identified by the painting, regardless of the factory which made the ware itself.

Early creamware teapot, previously attributed to Leeds, English, c.1765.

Type of teapot now known to be too early for Leeds, c.1765.

Creamware, decorated by Robinson & Rhodes, English, Yorks c.1765.

Creamware, decorated by Robinson & Rhodes, English, Yorks. c.1765.

Creamware, Rothwell print, English, Cockpit Hill, c.1767.

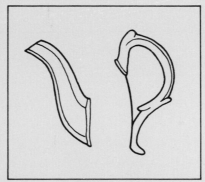

Detail of creamware spout and handle, English, Cockpit Hill, c.1765.

Creamware teapots like the ones on this page were being produced from 1751 at Cockpit Hill, Derby, England. Most of the recent research has been contributed by Donald Towner (*see* bib.). A distinctive feature of Cockpit Hill is the use of elaborate moulded decoration especially on the spout. The round globular shape seems to have been the favourite (*see* page 205).

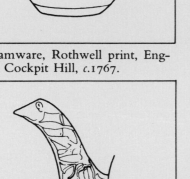

Detail of creamware spout, English, Cockpit Hill, c.1770.

Creamware, English Cockpit Hill, c.1770. Spout shown alongside.

Late form of creamware, English, Cockpit Hill, c.1770–79.

Fine creamware teapot, English, Cockpit Hill, 1770–79.

Creamware with floral moulded spout, English, Cockpit Hill, c.1770.

Creamware, distinctive handle, English, Cockpit Hill, c.1770–79.

Many Leeds wares have been traced through their published pattern book (1783) and later designs were added in new editions which were published up to 1814. Very early shapes were not included, so it seems to have been more of a sample chart for orders rather than a record of production. Painted decoration was often added, even to elaborate shapes, and there were special prints of American scenes which were obvious candidates for export.

Creamware, decoration by outside decorators, English, Leeds, c.1770.

Creamware, moulded decoration, English, Leeds, c.1770–79.

Teapots

Selection of English earthenware teapots. Notice the unusual shape of the Rockingham (Swinton) teapot (top right) in the form of a peach, which must have been a little difficult to handle. The pleasantly uneven Rockingham glaze was obtained from manganese and iron and is still very popular for teapots today in England and America, although not very fashionable perhaps.

Earthenware, brown glaze, English, Rockingham, c.1825–30.

'Cadogan' pot, formed as a peach. English, Rockingham.

Detail of earthenware handle. English, Staffs. Enoch Wood.

Earthenware, lid missing, English, documented to Enoch Wood.

Ironstone China (Patented 1813), English, Masons, c.1813–20.

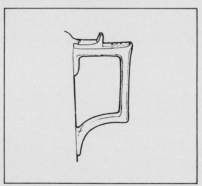

Earthenware handle, English, Minton, c.1805.

These teapots were made by John Davenport who produced many wares of white earthenware decorated with good quality blue prints (boat-shape and octagonal). The early teapots were mostly decorated with blue prints but later painted scenes, often in monochrome on a blue or coloured ground. 'Stone china' was made to compete with Masons, with their own version of imari patterns. Compare the general shape of this example (bottom, right) with the American New England pot (p. 198).

Earthenware, underglaze-blue decoration, English, Davenport, c.1830.

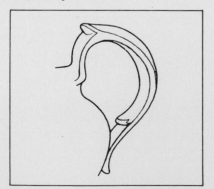

Handle of adjacent boat-shaped pot.

Earthenware, solid salmon colour, English, Davenport, c.1805–15.

Hexagonal earthenware pot, English, Davenport, c.1850–60.

German potters generally adopted distinctive marks from an early period, although the best known have been 're-interpreted' by imitators until the present day. However, in Vienna during the du Paquier period wares were mostly unmarked, helping to identify them, as does the use of moulded spouts and handles (*see* main text) and the lovely comfortable silver shapes. The Wallendorf 'riveted' handle should be compared with Pinxton (*see* p. 196) but the sharp right angle on the latter is unique.

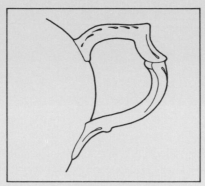

Hard-paste porcelain handle, German, Berlin, 1770–80.

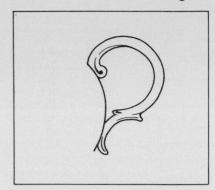

Typical porcelain handle, German, Fürstenberg, late 18th century.

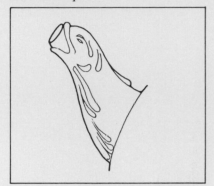

Porcelain spout, German, Würzburg, (Lower Franconia), 1775–80.

Outline of porcelain teapot, German, Würzburg, 1775–80.

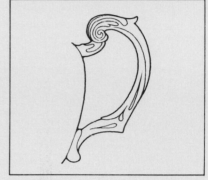

Detail of porcelain handle, German, Würzburg, pot impressed 'W'.

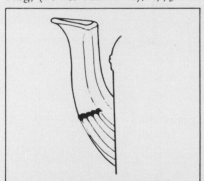

Porcelain spout, German, Wallendorf, (Thuringia), late 18th century.

Typical teapot, classical form, German, Wallendorf, late 18th century.

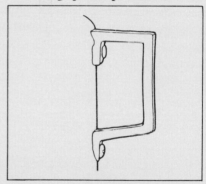

Porcelain, simulated rivets classical shape, German, Wallendorf.

Porcelain spout, Du Paquier period, Austrian, Vienna, 1719–44.

Silver-shaped porcelain teapot, Austrian, Vienna.

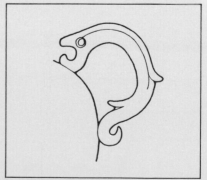

Handle of teapot shown alongside, *c.*1730–35.

Teapots

Böttger's red stoneware could be cut, engraved and polished like a precious stone. Even after discovering true porcelain, he still used the baroque forms which influenced other German factories: globular, lobed, conical or pear-shaped, with simple loop or double-curved handles and bird-beak spouts. Later pots, made at Nymphenburg often used the baroque snake-head spout. Early rococo Höchst wares were obviously based on Meissen and Frankenthal, with moulded spouts and 'J'-shaped handles.

Detail of red stoneware spout, German made by Böttger. *c.*1715.

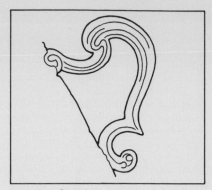

Detail of red stoneware handle, German made by Böttger, *c.*1715.

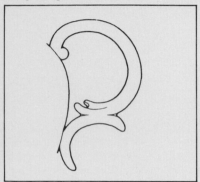

Hard-paste porcelain handle, German, Nymphenburg, 1755–65.

Combination of baroque and rococo styles, German, Nymphenburg.

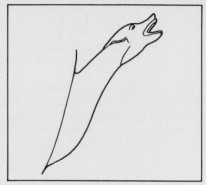

Late use of baroque-type spout, German, Nymphenburg, *c.*1760.

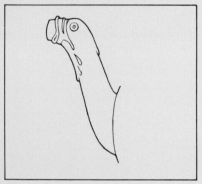

Teapot spout, German, Nymphenburg, 1755–65.

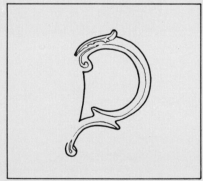

Teapot handle, German, Höchst, *c.*1770.

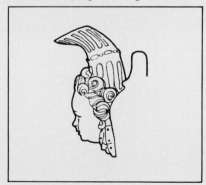

Teapot spout, classical form, German, Höchst, *c.*1780.

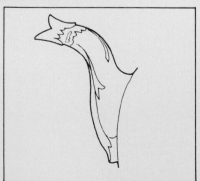

Teapot spout, decoration added at the Hague, German, Höchst.

Popular 'J' type handle, Dutch decoration, German, Höchst.

Stoneware, black glaze and gilt decoration, made by Böttger, *c.*1715.

Soft -paste porcelain teapots of St Cloud in France often show the influence of contemporary silver shapes but they were rather heavily potted because of the nature of the paste. At Mennecy they were usually of 'egg-shape' with low foot rings and double curved handles. Notice on this page the nicely proportioned Sèvres teapot (third row, centre) and the similar handle on the Tournai example (bottom, centre). The 'ear' handle (third row, right) is quite like a model used at Plymouth and Bristol (p. 198).

Spout of adjacent teapot.

Heavily potted, soft-paste porcelain, St. Cloud, 1725-30.

Handle of same teapot. Typical square section.

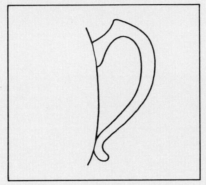

Porcelain, typical enamel flower-painting, French, Mennecy, *c.*1750.

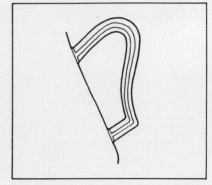

Porcelain handle of conical form teapot. French, Vincennes, *c.*1750.

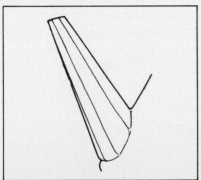

Matching porcelain faceted spout, French, Vincennes, *c.*1750.

Popular form of soft-paste porcelain teapot. French, Sèvres.

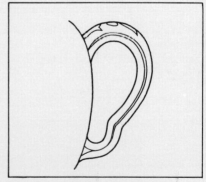

Detail of soft-paste handle, French, Sèvres, *c.*1780.

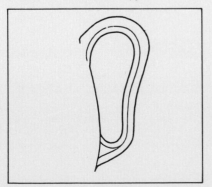

Handle of rare soft-paste porcelain teapot, French, Sceaux, *c.*1775.

Soft-paste porcelain, Belgian, Tournai, late 18th century.

Acorn knob of same teapot.

Teapots

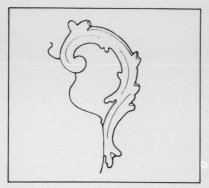

Ornate teapot handle, Italian, Le Nove, c.1765.

Unusual form of teapot, Italian, Le Nove, c.1765.

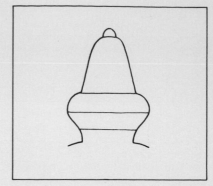

Teapot knob, Italian, Doccia, c. 1740–50.

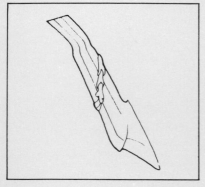

Teapot spout, Italian, (Vezzi), Venice, c.1725.

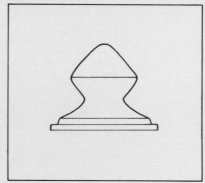

Typical knob of teapot lid, Italian, (Vezzi), Venice.

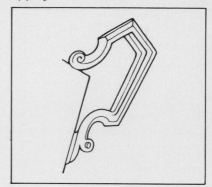

Unusual teapot handle, angular form, Italian, (Vezzi), Venice.

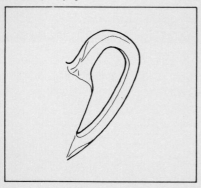

Typical handle on octagonal teapots, Italian, (Vezzi), Venice.

Outline of teapot, Italian, (Cozzi), Venice, c.1770.

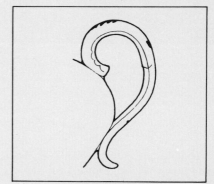

Detail of handle typical of hard-paste porcelain teapots, Italian.

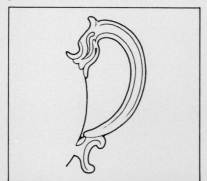

Teapot handle, Italian, Doccia, 1860–70.

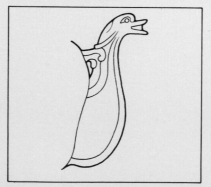

Teapot spout of rare example, printed decoration, Italian, Doccia.

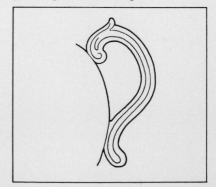

Teapot handle, Italian, Doccia, 1740–45.

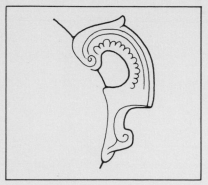

Ornate handle, Italian, Capodimonte, 1745–50.

Teapot handle, Italian, attributed to Buen Retiro, *c*.1775.

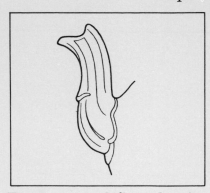

Teapot spout, Italian, Capodimonte, 1745–50.

These last two pages show examples of Italian, Dutch and Belgian teapots with their individual features. One interesting example is the Tournai teapot which for a long time was thought to be from Derby because of its 'crabstock' handle and spout.

The Hague factory only began to manufacture its own porcelain in about 1776 and made some fine teapots. Up to then, the Hague had acted as a decorating establishment for ware imported from Germany and elsewhere in Europe. Their shapes seem to fulfil the same need as Delftware, capacious, solid and, above all, practical.

Teapot, type made at The Hague, Holland, *c*.1780.

Teapot of French form. Dutch, Oude Loosdrecht, *c*.1775.

Detail of teapot knob, Dutch, Oude Loosdrecht, 1775–80.

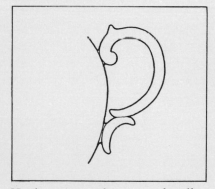

Hard-paste porcelain teapot handle, Dutch, Oude Loosdrecht, *c*.1780.

Teapot, enamel flower-painting, Belgian, Tournai, 1765–70.

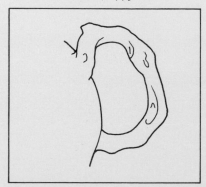

Unusual use of 'crabstock' handle, Belgian, Tournai.

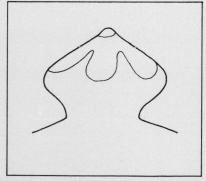

Knob of same teapot, unusually large for this period.

Coffee-pots

Porcelain coffee-pot, Geyger, German, Würzburg, c.1775.

Unusual snake-like porcelain coffee-pot handle, German, Würzburg.

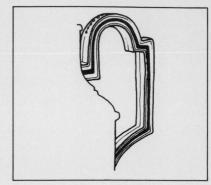

Classically shaped porcelain coffee-pot handle, German, Höchst, c.1780.

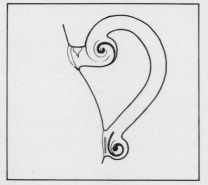

Simple robust porcelain coffee-pot handle, Austrian, Vienna, 1725.

Hard-paste porcelain coffee-pot, Austrian, Vienna, c.1725.

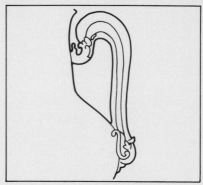

Porcelain coffee-pot handle, Italian, Doccia, c.1775.

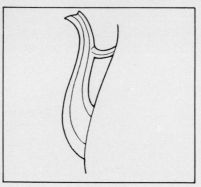

Porcelain coffee-pot spout, Italian, Doccia, late 18th century.

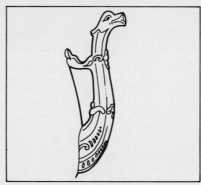

Typical baroque porcelain coffee-pot spout, Italian, Doccia, c.1760.

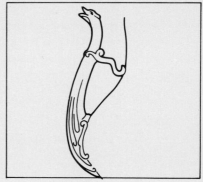

Porcelain spout, Italian, Doccia, c.1775. Note strengthening tie.

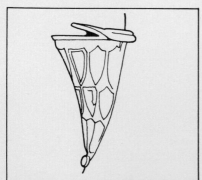

Porcelain, inserted pouring lip, Italian, (Cozzi), Venice, c.1770.

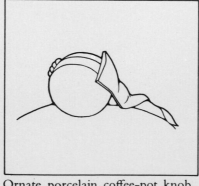

Ornate porcelain coffee-pot knob, Italian, (Cozzi), Venice, c.1770.

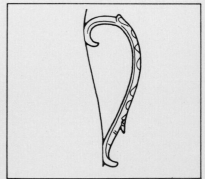

Many Cozzi coffee-pot handles c.1770 appear too light.

Coffee-pots are in some ways very different from tewares, less responsive to passing whims and ornamental fripperies, and fairly simple in shape throughout their history. Seldom made cheaply, fine creamware and porcelain followed typical silver shapes, sometimes with gilded and painted alleviation. In contrast, early American coffee-pots had to be made for heavy use; pottery was too fragile and everyday pots were usually enamelled iron or tin.

Porcelain, 'crabstock' handle, English, Longton Hall, *c*.1757.

Soapstone porcelain, English, Worcester, *c*.1775.

Bone porcelain coffee-pot, flower knob, English, Lowestoft, *c*.1770.

Porcelain, English, attributed to Chaffers, Liverpool, *c*.1760.

Porcelain, English, attributed to Chaffers, Liverpool, 1760–65.

Porcelain, chamferred base, English, (Chaffers), Liverpool, *c*.1760.

Porcelain coffee-pot, English, attributed to Chaffers, Liverpool, *c*.1760,

Typical form of soapstone coffee-pot, English, Caughley, 1785–95.

Porcelain, underglaze-blue decoration, English, Plymouth, *c*.1770.

Porcelain, note angular handle, English, Pinxton, *c*.1800.

Hard-paste porcelain, American, Tucker, Philadelphia, *c*.1835.

Bone-china coffee-pot, English, New Hall, 1814–20.

Hard-paste porcelain coffee-pot, English, Champion, Bristol.

Hard-paste porcelain, typical 'clip' handle, English, New Hall.

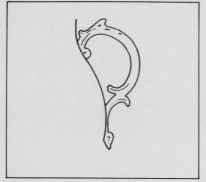

Coffee-pot handle, German, Fürstenberg, c.1760.

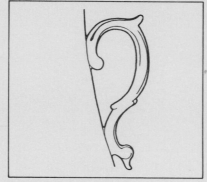

Typical handle, English, (Chaffers), Liverpool.

Earthenware, transfer-printed decoration, Welsh, Swansea, c.1795.

Pottery coffee-pot, reddish-brown lead glaze, English, Rockingham.

Earthenware, brown glaze, English, impressed 'ROCKINGHAM'.

Black basaltes coffee-pot, Welsh, Swansea, c.1790–1800.

Fine creamware, English, painted by Robinson, Leeds, c.1770–79.

Creamware, moulded spout, English, attributed to Leeds, c.1770–79.

Flint enamel coffee-pot, American, Bennington, Vermont, 1849–58.

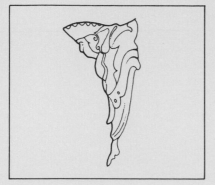

Soft-paste coffee-pot, ornate lip, Italian, Capodimonte, 1745-50.

These examples of Melbourne coffee-pots show clearly the moulded terminals used to join the handles to the body in both teapots and coffee-pots. These have provided the necessary clues to the Melbourne production and are always points to be noticed. Broken pieces and wasters on the factory site have also established the kind of painting used there—purple was the favourite colour, usually including a long, feather-like leaf.

Creamware, high temperature colours, Welsh, Swansea, c.1790.

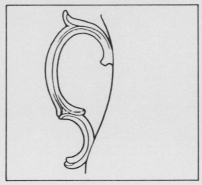

Detail of shape of creamware handle, English, Melbourne.

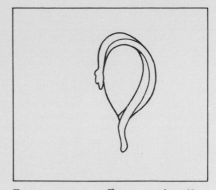

Creamware coffee-pot handle, English, Wedgwood, c.1775.

Creamware with convolvulus knob, English, Melbourne, c.1770.

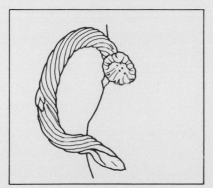

Distinctive creamware handle, English, Melbourne, c.1770.

Creamware with convolvulus knob. English, Melbourne, c.1770.

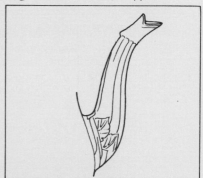

Unusual form of creamware spout, English, Melbourne, c.1770.

Flint enamel coffee-pot, sunken lid, American, Bennington, Vermont.

Coffee-pot from 'Donatello' service, German, Rosenthal, 1907.

Coffee-pots styles are usually conservative and 19th century American styles often followed silver shapes. The ever-popular sturdy shape (bottom, left) and opposite (bottom, right) was made in England too, but American potters used it for Rockingham, porcelain, stoneware and 'flint enamel' a special Bennington finish. Modern shapes became even simpler and the adjacent German Pot shows how pared down the 'new' continental pots could be.

Sauce-boats

Sauceboats were one of the most common wares produced in England in the 18th century, and from the numbers produced, it would seem that every household had several on the table at once. Since there are so many shapes and patterns, sauceboats make a good collector's field and English examples in particular turn up all over the world. Lowestoft, for instance, sold them in matching pairs. In the 1770s this factory produced a range of sauceboats in imitation of Worcester.

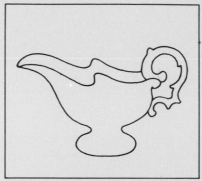

Early form of soft-paste porcelain sauce-boat, English, Bow, c.1752.

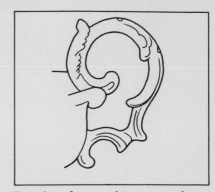

Detail of porcelain sauce-boat handle, English, Bow.

'Queen's Sauce Boat', Leeds Pattern Book No. 14, 1814.

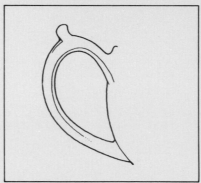

Handle of adjacent sauce-boat which is in style of Worcester.

Moulded porcelain sauce-boat, English, Lowestoft, c.1763–65.

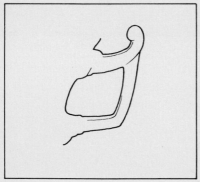

Handle used on sauce- and cream-boats, English, Worcester, c.1755.

Porcelain, painted in enamel colours, Dutch Weesp, 1764-71.

Tin-glazed earthenware, painted in colours, French, Meillonas, 18th c.

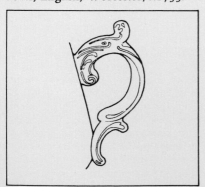

Handle used on porcelain sauce boats, English, Worcester, c.1775.

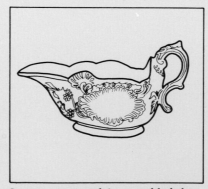

Soapstone porcelain, moulded decoration, English, Worcester, c.1775.

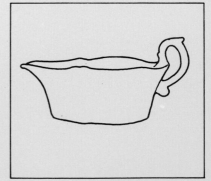

Early form of porcelain sauce-boat, blue decoration, English, Bow.

Porcelain, moulded as leaf and 'pendant fig', English, Longton Hall.

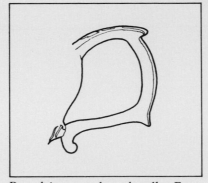

Porcelain sauce boat handle, English, Longton Hall, *c*.1755.

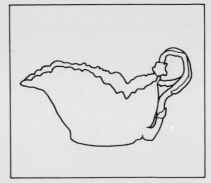

Porcelain, crudely moulded, blue decoration, English, Longton Hall.

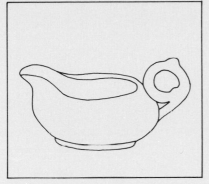

Parianware, American, Bennington, Vermont *c*.1850.

Liverpool often produced a rather small range of sauceboats using four major forms in different sizes. They were usually decorated in underglaze-blue transfer-prints, and the so-called 'pleasure boat' or Fisherman design was the one most frequently used. In America, sauceboats tended to be rather plain by comparison, often made in Parianware or replaced by the more popular small pitcher. There are some European examples but the majority are English.

Early bone-porcelain, English, (Chaffers), Liverpool, *c*.1755.

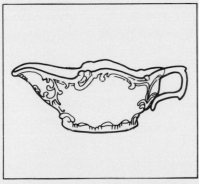

Soapstone porcelain, English, (Chaffers), Liverpool, *c*.1758.

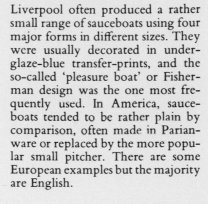

Moulded porcelain, English, (Chaffers), Liverpool, *c*.1758.

Porcelain, underglaze-blue painting, English, (Chaffers), Liverpool.

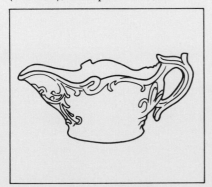

Porcelain, English, (Chaffers), Liverpool, *c*.1758.

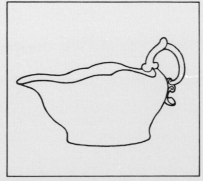

Porcelain, English, (Gilbody), Liverpool, *c*.1754-60.

Porcelain, underglaze-blue decoration, English, probably Ball, 1755.

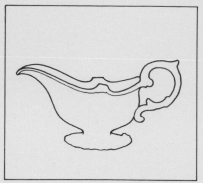

Porcelain, underglaze-blue decoration, English, probably Ball. *c*.1755.

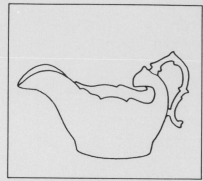

Porcelain, English, attributed to Ball of Liverpool, *c*.1755–69.

Porcelain, English, attributed to Ball of Liverpool, *c*.1755–69.

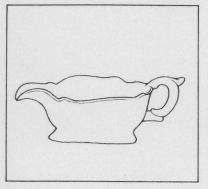

Porcelain, made by W. Reid at Shelton or Liverpool, *c*.1760.

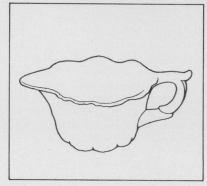

Porcelain, made by W. Reid at Shelton, or Liverpool.

Porcelain, made by W. Reid at Shelton, or Liverpool, 1755–61.

Poor quality porcelain sauce-boat, English, Pennington, 1755–80.

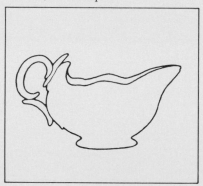

Earthenware, American, (Bethabara pottery), North Carolina, 1773-89.

Documentary sauce-boat, English, Plymouth, 1770.

Hard-paste porcelain, moulded decoration, English, Plymouth, *c*.1770.

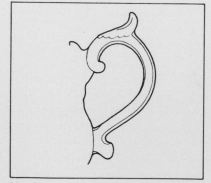

Hard-paste porcelain · sauce-boat handle, English, Plymouth, *c*.1770.

Hard-paste porcelain, English, Plymouth. Marked with sign for tin.

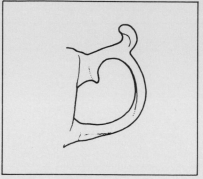

Handle used on sauce-boat, English, (Lund & Miller), Bristol.

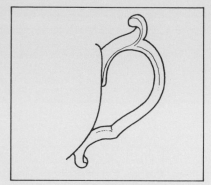

Porcelain handle, underglaze-blue decoration, English, Caughley.

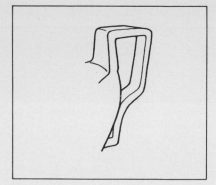

Sauce-boat handle, English, Leeds, early 19th century.

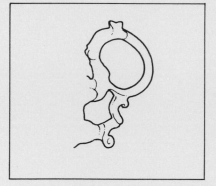

Type of handle used on early soft-paste sauce-boats, English, Bristol.

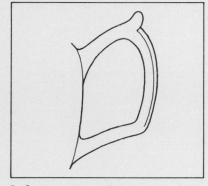

Soft-paste porcelain sauce-boat handle, English, Derby, c.1760.

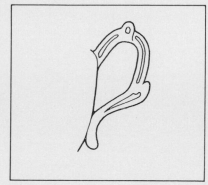

Porcelain sauce- or butter-boat handle, English, Derby, c.1770.

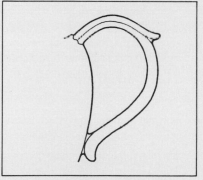

Porcelain blue-and-white sauce-boat handle, English, Derby, c.1765.

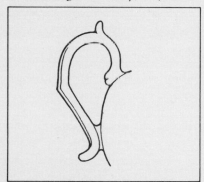

Sauce-boat handle, underglaze decoration, English, Derby, c.1765.

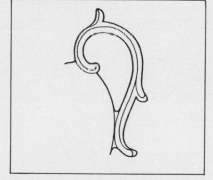

Porcelain sauce-boat handle, English, Derby, c.1760-65.

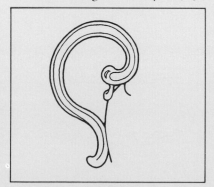

Porcelain sauce-boat handle, English, Derby, c.1760-65.

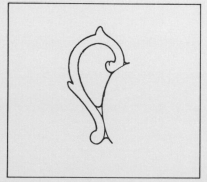

Porcelain blue-and-white butter-boat handle, English, Derby, c.1765.

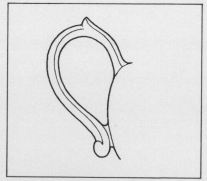

Porcelain blue-and-white sauce-boat handle, English, Derby, 1760.

Tureens

Tureens are a special kind of table-ware. Made for a single helping of peas, or large enough to hold soup for 24 hungry diners. Styles follow current fashions fairly closely and once more, characteristic knobs and handles are a good guide. They were also made extravagantly in the form of animals, fruit, vegetables and especially birds of all kinds. Such pieces were considered important and most are marked.

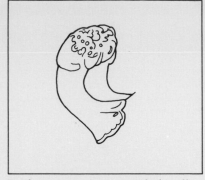

Earthenware tureen side-handle, English, Spode, c.1830.

Knob to tureen cover, 'Pearlware', English, Wedgwood, c.1785.

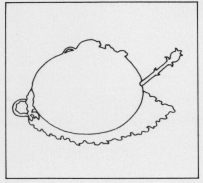

'Melon Terrine & Spoon', English, Leeds Pattern Book, c.1790.

Handle of 'Oval Royal Terrine', creamware, English, Leeds, c.1790.

Creamware 'Oval Royal Terrine', English, Leeds.

Creamware bowl and cover, Josiah Wedgwood II, c.1810.

English creamware tureen from Wedgwood Shape Book, 1810.

Cream- or pearl-ware tureen from Wedgwood Shape Book.

English tureen and stand, from Wedgwood Shape Book c.1810.

English tureen and stand, from Wedgwood Shape Book 1810.

Queen's ware tureen and stand, English, Wedgwood c.1810.

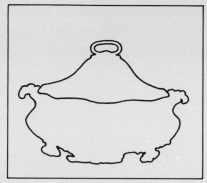

Soft-paste porcelain tureen and cover, blue painted, English, Bow.

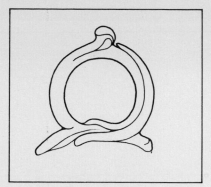

Porcelain tureen handle, English, Derby, 1770–84.

Tureen and cover, English, (W. Reid), Liverpool or Shelton, *c.*1758.

Porcelain tureen and cover, English, (W. Reid), Liverpool or Shelton.

Unique form of tureen knob, English, (Christian), Liverpool, *c.*1770.

Bone-china sauce tureen, relief decoration, English, New Hall, *c.*1820.

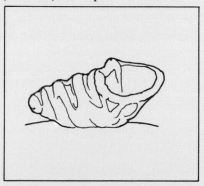

Porcelain tureen knob, English, Caughley or Coalport, *c.*1800–10.

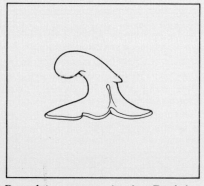

Porcelain tureen knob, English, Caughley or Coalport, *c.*1790–1800.

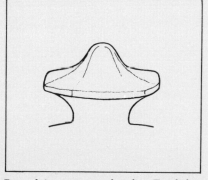

Porcelain tureen knob, English, Minton, 1800–10.

Porcelain tureen knob. English, J. & W. Ridgway, *c.*1815.

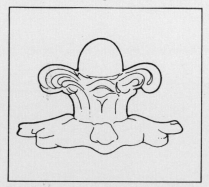

Small porcelain tureen knob, English, J. & W. Ridgway, *c.*1810.

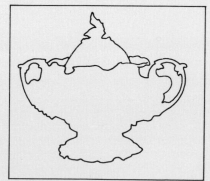

Porcelain, typical of revived rococo, Bohemian, 1856.

223

Earthenware tureen cover handle, English, Rockingham, c.1820–30.

Earthenware tureen, English, (J. Meir & Son), Tunstall, 1841–50.

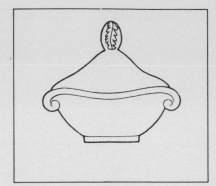

English oval creamware *soupière* from Castleford Pattern Book.

English oval creamware *soupière* knob from Castleford Pattern Book.

Tureen knob from Castleford Pattern Book No. 138, c.1796.

Knob of creamware *soupière* from Castleford Pattern Book.

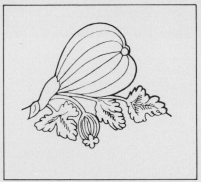

Knob of creamware tureen from Castleford Pattern Book.

Knob of creamware tureen, Whitehead Pattern Book 1798.

Knob of tureen, Royal Pattern, English, (Whitehead), Hanley, Staffs.

Creamware tureen handle, Royal pattern, English, Whitehead, c.1798.

Creamware tureen, after Wedgwood. Welsh, Swansea, c.1790.

Creamware cream cooler handle, English, Wedgwood, c.1800.

Tea-caddies, sucriers & castors

From here, the subjects become too widespread to cover individually. Potteries from the late 18th century through the whole of the 19th century made hundreds of small dishes, containers and accessories for the dining table.

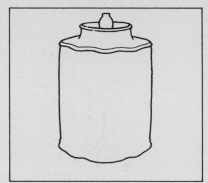

Porcelain tea caddy, silver-shape, English, New Hall.

Porcelain tea caddy, decorated with landscape, English, Pinxton.

Porcelain tea caddy, faceted sides, English, New Hall, c.1785.

Tea caddy, blue and gold decoration, English, New Hall, c.1785.

Tea caddies served an obvious purpose as did sugar bowls (or sucriers). The majority of tea-services would have matching tea-caddies, often made with a lock to prevent pilfering of this expensive commodity.

Porcelain Sucrier, note 'twin' lines on flutes, English, Chamberlain.

Finely potted, highly translucent porcelain sucrier, English, Pinxton.

Porcelain sucrier and cover, ring handles, English, Pinxton.

Porcelain sucrier, usually decorated with landscapes, English, Pinxton.

Bone-china sucrier, English, J. & W. Ridgway, c.1815–20.

Porcelain sucrier, English, (Chamberlain), Worcester, c.1800.

Hard-paste porcelain sucrier, English, New Hall, 1795–1810.

Sucrier, painted landscape, typical yellow ground, English, Pinxton.

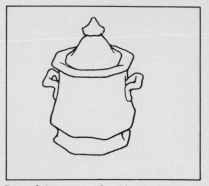

Porcelain sugar bowl, American, Bennington, Vermont, 1850–58.

Creamware Castors did their best to imitate silver openwork and sometimes very effectively. Patterns were used by specific factories and we are gradually beginning to distinguish one from another.

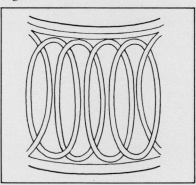

Pierced work on 'Bottle Stand', English, Leeds.

'Oil and Vinegar Stand', English, Leeds Pattern Book 1814.

Creamware 'Small Furnish'd Castor' English, Leeds Pattern Book.

Section of oil and vinegar stand or castor, English, Castleford, c.1796.

'Oval Single Waiter for Oil and Vinegar', English, Whitehead, c.1800.

Section of 'Round Waiter' five condiment bottles, English, Whitehead.

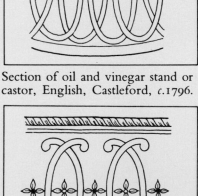

Stand of 'Large Furnish'd Castor', English, Leeds Pattern Book, 1814.

Stand of 'Large Furnish'd Castor' five bottles, English, Castleford.

Bowls were decorated in characteristic ways, red and black enamel transfer-prints, underglaze-blue and modelled knobs and handles, and printed decoration to match the plates and dishes. Early Italian porcelain is very rare and seldom consistently marked, so it is hard to recognize. One point is the simple knob often used at Doccia. With careful study, modelling techniques can be evaluated and catalogued.

Rare form of bone-china bowl and cover, English, New Hall, 1814–31.

Knob of soft-paste porcelain covered bowl, Italian, Naples, c.1800.

Knob of covered bowl. English, Chelsea 'Girl in a swing', c.1750.

Knob of porcelain covered bowl, Italian, Doccia, 1755–58.

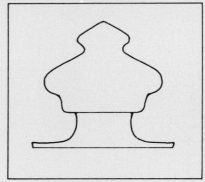

Knob of covered bowl, Austrian, (Du Paquier), Vienna, c.1740.

Knob of covered bowl, Austrian, (Du Paquier), Vienna, c.1730.

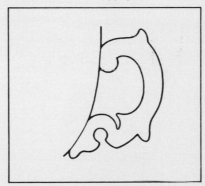

Handle of porcelain covered bowl, Italian, Doccia, 1755–8.

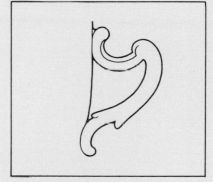

Handle of porcelain covered bowl, Italian, Doccia, 1770–80.

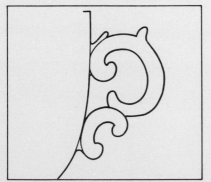

Side handle of porcelain bowl, Italian, Le Nove, 1781–1802.

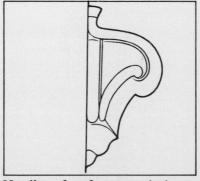

Handle of soft paste *chachepot*, Italian, Capodimonte, 1743–59.

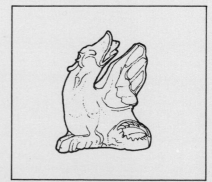

Knob of covered jar, Spode, 1804–06.

Veilleuses

The word *veilleuse* derives from the French *veiller*, to keep a night vigil and it was originally used for the pottery or porcelain utensil used to warm food (a réchaud) or drink, usually tea, (a théière) in the sickroom or nursery. These utensils usually consist of a hollow stand with a circular opening in the top in which the covered bowl or teapot rests. They were made in many European countries in the 18th and 19th centuries—the later ones were usually teawarmers.

Food-warmer *(Réchaud)* made at Nymphenburg, Bavaria, c.1765.

Food-warmer, hard-paste porcelain, German, Höchst, c.1770.

Food-warmer, hard-paste porcelain, Austrian, Vienna, c.1785.

Food-warmer, hard-paste porcelain, French, Niderviller, 1770–84.

Food-warmer, soft-paste porcelain, French, Sèvres, c.1770.

Food-warmer, tin-glazed earthenware, English, Lambeth, c.1775.

Food-warmer, lead-glazed earthenware of 'Whieldon' type, English.

Cream-coloured earthenware, English, Wedgwood, early 19th century.

Food-warmer, tin-glazed earthenware, French, Marseilles, c.1775.

Food-warmer, cream-coloured earthenware, French, Creil, c.1770–90.

Tin-glazed earthenware *(fayence)*, German, Durlach, c.1760-65.

Food-warmer with candle-holder, English, Chelsea, c.1758.

Food-warmer with candle-holder, English, Lowestoft, c.1770.

Food-warmer with candle-holder, English, Leeds, c.1775.

Food-warmer hard-paste porcelain, Swiss, Zurich, c.1775.

Tea-warmer, hard-paste porcelain, Austrian, Vienna, 1828.

Tea-warmer, hard-paste porcelain, Jacob Petit, French, Fontainebleu.

Tea-warmer, hard-paste porcelain, French, Vierzon, c.1880.

Tea-warmer, ·porcelain, Russian, Gorbunovo (nr. Moscow), c.1835.

Tea-warmer, porcelain, American, (Tucker & Hemphill), c.1835.

Tea-warmer, tin-glazed earthenware, Italian, Nove, c.1770.

Tea-warmer, German, Zell Baden, early 19th century.

Tea-warmer, porcelain, Bohemian, Elbogen, mid-19th century.

Miscellaneous

Miscellaneous has to cover everything from chestnut baskets to fish pitchers: but it cannot be said too often that the details will provide the necessary clues. The two Melbourne openwork patterns use the same forms and the American dolphin was a form used in American glass for everything from oil lamps and candlesticks to toothpick holders. The Bonnin and Morris sweetmeat stand is a rare example of early American porcelain. There were asparagus shells, butter dishes, posset pots, salad or side dishes, compotes; the list, as a glance at any Victorian catalogue will show, is endless. Many of these items are available today and can make an attractive addition to any collection.

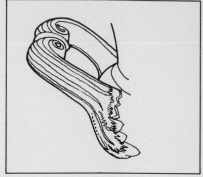
Side handle, popular antique-shaped ice pail, English, Spode, c.1800–10.

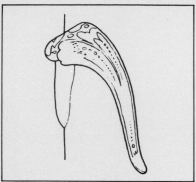
Side handle, traditionally shaped ice pail, English, Caughley, c.1785.

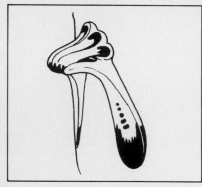
Side handle, ice pail or jardinière, English, Caughley, c.1780.

'Glass Tray for Ten or Twelve Glasses', Leeds Pattern Book.

3 in. creamware salt, typical pierced cover, English, Leeds, c.1800.

Conventional form of 'Round Plain Salt with Feet', English, Leeds.

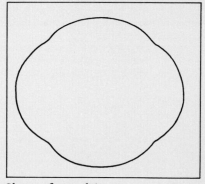
Shape of porcelain spoon tray, English, New Hall.

Bone porcelain teapot stand, English, Bow, c.1756.

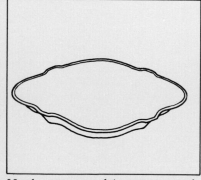
Hard paste porcelain teapot stand, English, New Hall, c.1790–1805.

Moulded porcelain rosette foot used on teapots, English, New Hall.

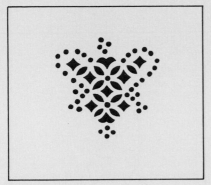

Pierced work, stand of chestnut basket, English, Melbourne, *c.*1770.

Creamware chestnut basket and stand, English, Melbourne, *c.*1770.

Detail of pierced decoration on adjacent chestnut basket, Melbourne.

Majolica pitcher, American, East Liverpool, Ohio, late 18th c.

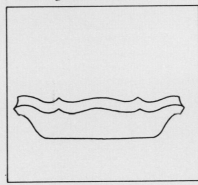

'Oval Radish Dish', English, Leeds Pattern Book No. 175, *c.*1785.

Creamware custard or dessert cup, English, Wedgewood, *c.*1810.

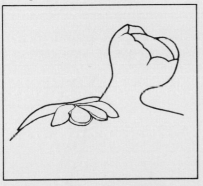

Detail of porcelain mustard pot knob, English, Caughley, *c.*1780–85.

Sweetmeat stand, (Bonnin & Morris), Philadelphia, *c.*1770.

In addition to the pattern books issued by the Leeds pottery 'for the use of Pottery agents and traders in England and abroad', drawing books still exist consisting of well-drawn designs intended for the guidance of the factory workers involved in shaping and decorating the wares.

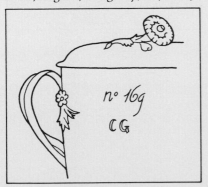

Creamware knob, common style, English, Leeds Drawing Book.

Type of creamware knob, Leeds Drawing Book No. 1.

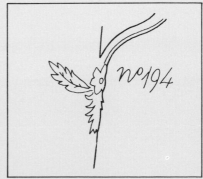

Design for terminal, Leeds Drawing Book No. 1, late 18th century.

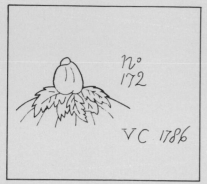

Design for creamware knob, Leeds Drawing Book No. 4.

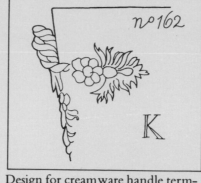

Design for creamware handle terminal, Leeds Drawing Book No. 4.

Creamware knob, 'lap-dog', Leeds Drawing Book No. 1.

Creamware knob formed as 'Rose Tops', Leeds Drawing Book No. 4.

Creamware knob formed as acorn, Leeds Drawing Book No. 4.

Ring handle, creamware cover, Leeds Drawing Book No. 4.

Creamware knob formed as pine cone, Leeds Drawing Book No. 4.

Creamware knob formed as a globe, Leeds Drawing Book No. 4.

Creamware knob formed as daisy, Leeds Drawing Book No. 4.

Creamware knob formed as fruit, Leeds Drawing Book No. 4.

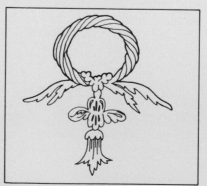

Ring handle used on creamware 'Oval Royal Terrines', Leeds.

Knob formed as a cauliflower used on creamware, Leeds.

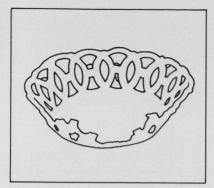

Incomplete earthenware fruit dish,
American, New England, 19th c.

Salt-glazed stoneware basket, English, Cockpit Hill, Derby, c.1760.

Small porcelain cream pot, French,
St. Cloud, c.1730.

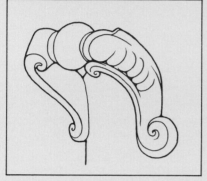

Handle of porcelain wine cooler,
Austrian, (Du Paquier), Vienna.

Outline of chocolate pot, German,
Ludwigsburg, 1765-75.

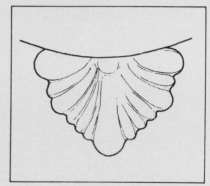

Detail of handle, porcelain drainer,
English, Caughley, c.1785–99.

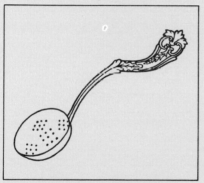

Creamware 'Pierced Sugar Spoon',
English, Leeds Pattern Book.

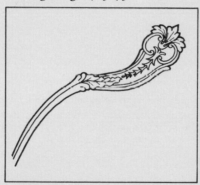

Detail of handle, pierced sugar
spoon, English, Leeds, c.1800.

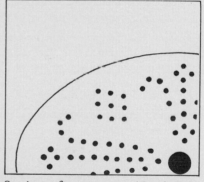

Section of creamware 'Oval Fish
Drainer for Dishes'.

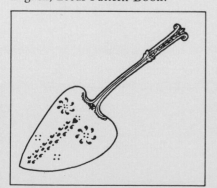

Creamware 'Pierced Fish Trowell',
English, Leeds Pattern Book.

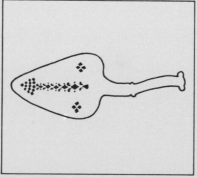

Pierced fish trowel, similar type to
Leeds, English, Castleford, c.1800.

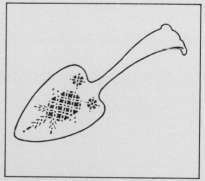

Creamware fish trowel, English,
Whitehead, Hanley, c.1800.

Miscellaneous

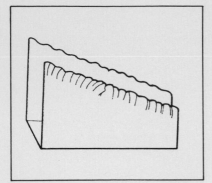

Creamware 'Asparagus Stand', English, Castleford Pattern Book.

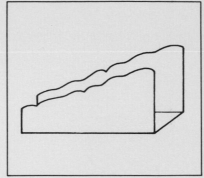

Similar 'Asparagus Tray' in the same Castleford Pattern Book.

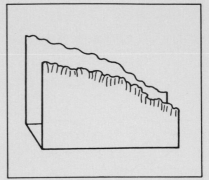

Creamware 'Asparagus Shell', English, Leeds Pattern Book c.1790.

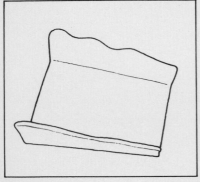

Porcelain asparagus server, English, New Hall, c.1782.

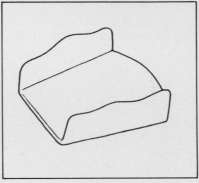

Soapstone porcelain asparagus server, English, Caughley, c.1785–95.

Shell-edge ragou dish, Leeds Pattern Book.

Oval ragou dish, Leeds Pattern Book.

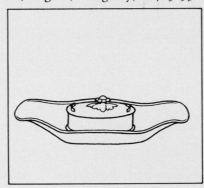

Queen's ware butter tub and stand, English, Wedgwood, c.1810.

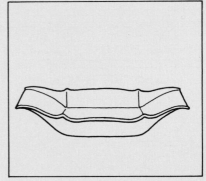

Queen's ware radish stand, English, Wedgwood, c.1810.

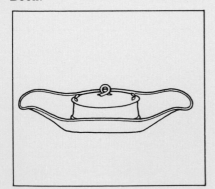

Queen's ware asparagus and melted butter dish, English, Wedgwood.

'Oval Plain Butter Tub and Stand', English, Leeds Pattern Book.

'Oval Feather Butter Tub and Stand', English, Leeds Pattern Book.

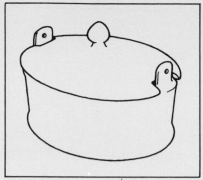

Porcelain butter dish or cooler, English, Lowestoft, *c.*1770.

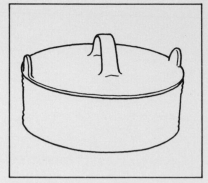

Porcelain butter dish or cooler, English, Bow, *c.*1753.

Salt-glazed stoneware posset pot, English, *c.*1700.

Creamware 'Oval Queen's Sallad', English, Leeds Pattern Book No. 30.

'Triangular Feather Compotier', English, Leeds Pattern Book, No. 39.

Creamware 'Oval Shell Edge Sallad', English, Leeds Pattern Book.

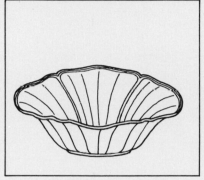

Porringer, enamel decoration, English, Lowestoft, *c.*1775.

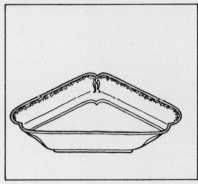

Porcelain porringer handle, moulded decoration, English, Worcester.

Creamware pierced egg cup, English, Leeds Pattern Book No. 57.

Creamware egg cup, English, Leeds Pattern Book No. 56.

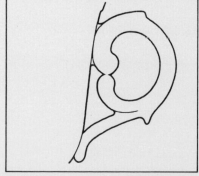

Porcelain egg cup handle, English, Caughley, *c.*1790-99.

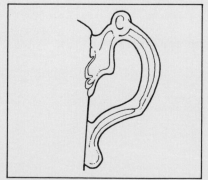

Porcelain mustard pot handle, English, Caughley, *c.*1780-85.

Index

Opposite: TEA-WARMER *of hard-paste porcelain, decorated in enamel colours and gilt. United States of America (Philadelphia, factory of Tucker & Hemphill), c.1836.*